Robert Seidel
LUX AETERNA

Robert Seidel
LUX AETERNA
—
Videoinstallationen, Filme und Zeichnungen

Inhalts-verzeichnis/ Table of Contents

Intro
—
07–31

Vorwort/Foreword
—
Volker Regel
34–35

Grußwort/Preface
—
Holger Peter Saupe
36–37

LUX AETERNA
—
Claudia Tittel
38–51

Betrachter im Orbit/ Viewer in Orbit
—
Joost Rekveld
52–59

Im Universum digitaler Bilder/
In the Universe of Digital Images
—
Interview
60–73

Geraffte Zeit/
Nested time
—
Peter Forster
74–77

Filme und Installationen/
Movies and Installations
—
81–165

Fotografien und Zeichnungen/
Photographies and Drawings
—
167–183

Biografische Auswahl/
Selected Biography
—
184–187

Arbeiten/
Body of work
—
188–189

Autoren/
Authors
—
190

Colophon
—
191

Intro
—
07–31

magnitude
Laser-Performance
Epicenter Projects
Coachella Valley
USA 2015
08–09

grapheme
Projektionsskulptur
Museum Wiesbaden
DE 2013
10-11

advection
Wasserfontänenprojektion
CAFKA Biennial
Kitchener/Waterloo
CA 2014
12–13

erratic
Video-Performance
Vienna Independent
Shorts Festival
AT 2012
14–15

tearing shadows
Projektionsskulptur
Museum für
Angewandte Kunst Gera
DE 2015
16–17

suturae #2
Laserinstallation
Museum für
Angewandte Kunst Gera
DE 2015
18–19

scrape
LED-Fassade
GanaArt Center
Seoul
KR 2011
20–21

glimmer
Laser-Performance
Tschechische Nationalgalerie
Prag
CZ 2015
22–23

sputter #5
Rasterelektronen-
mikroskop-Aufnahme
DE 2014
24–25

ligature
Fassadenprojektion
Manhattan Bridge
New York
USA 2014
26-27

chiral
Projektionsskulptur
Museum für
Angewandte Kunst Gera
DE 2015
28-29

vitreous
Kinetische Projektion
Kunstverein Gera
DE 2015
30-31

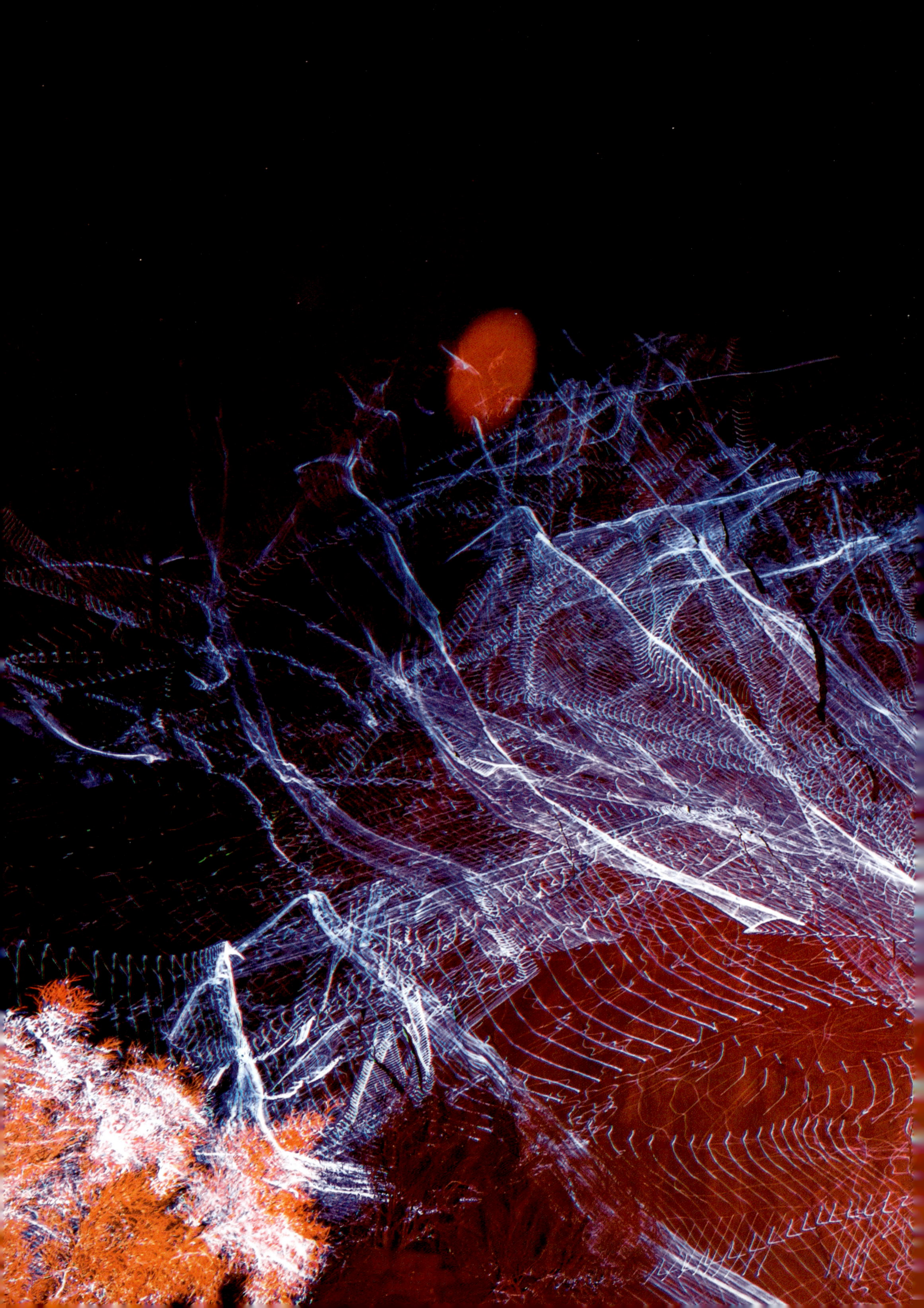

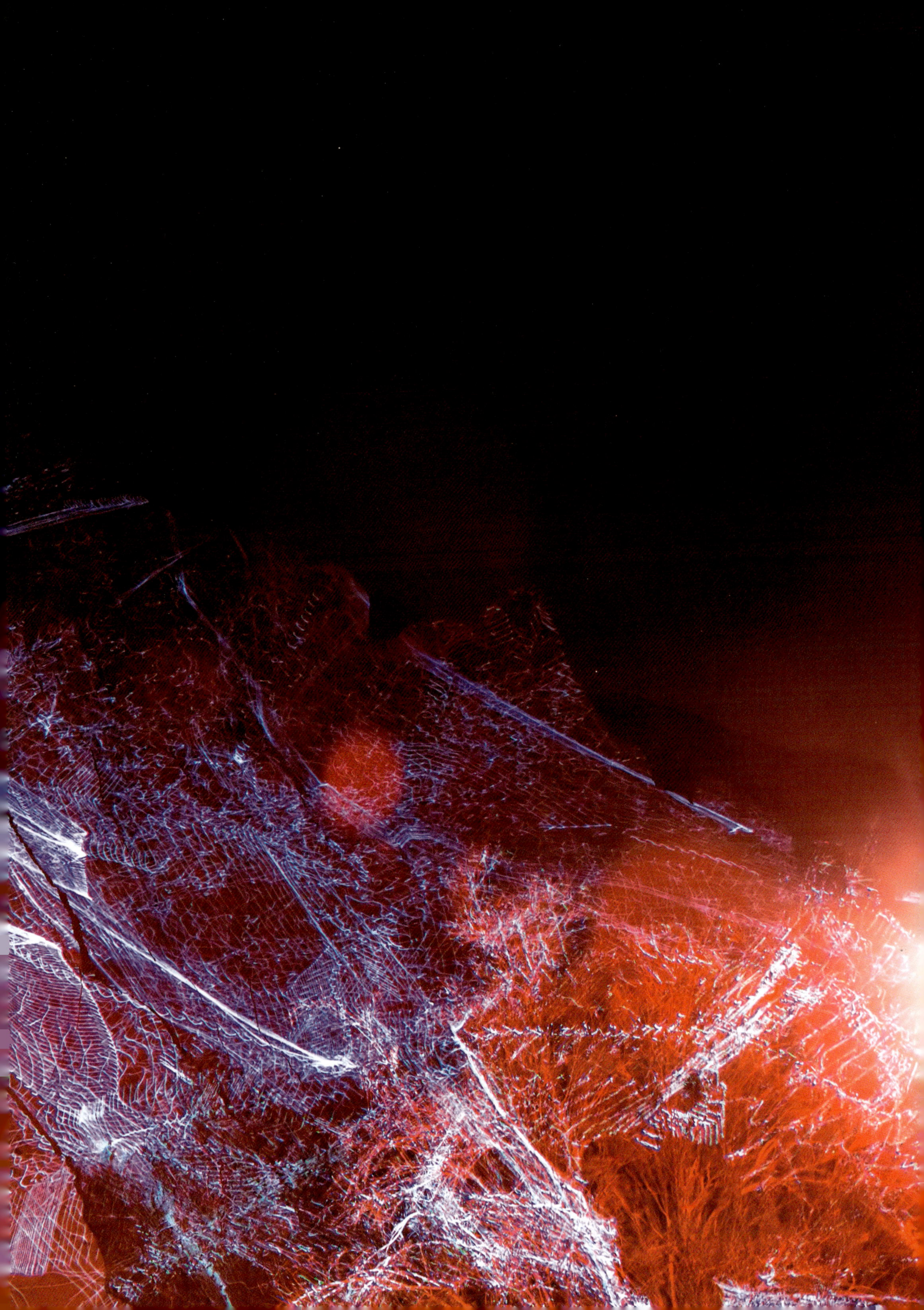

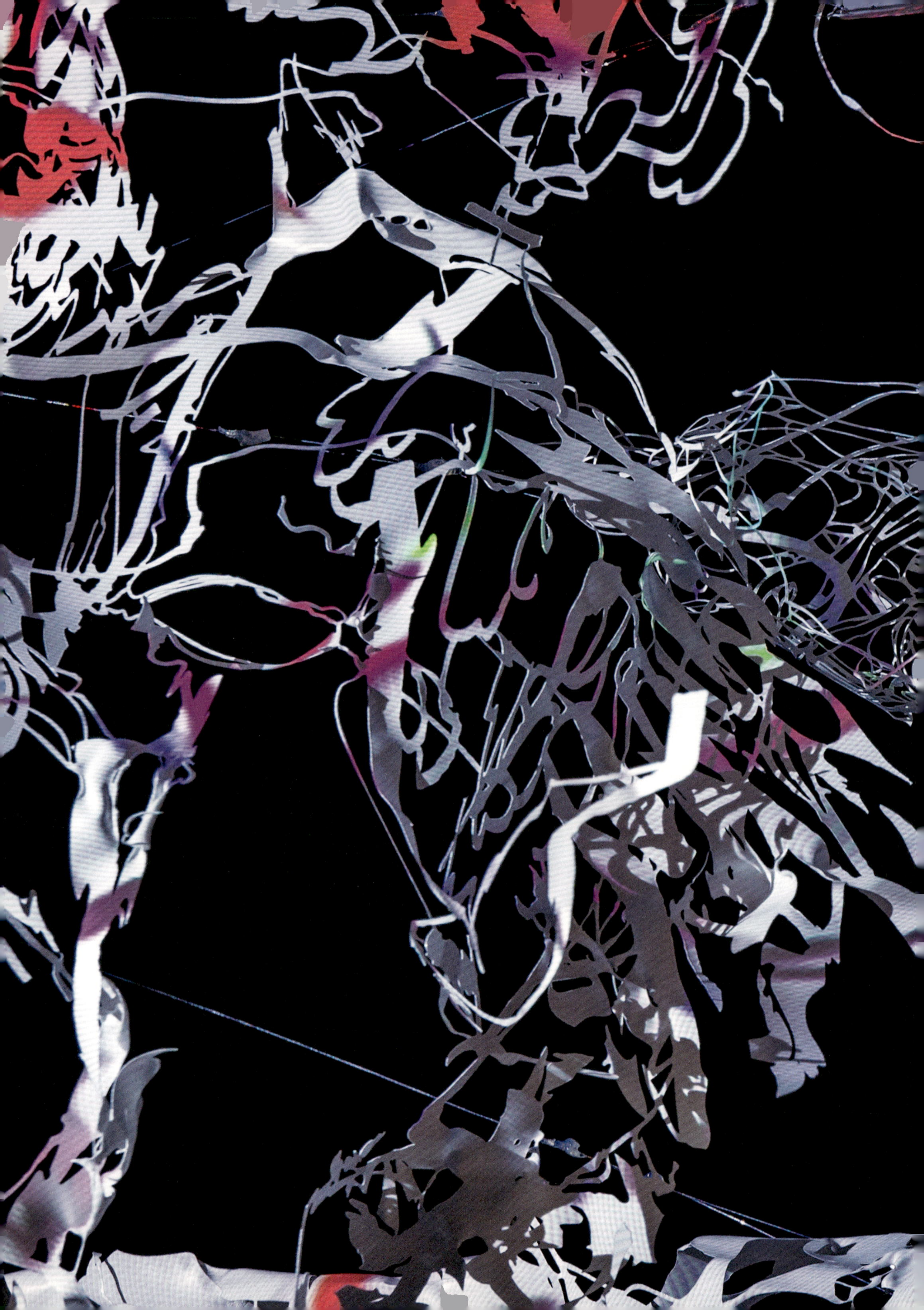

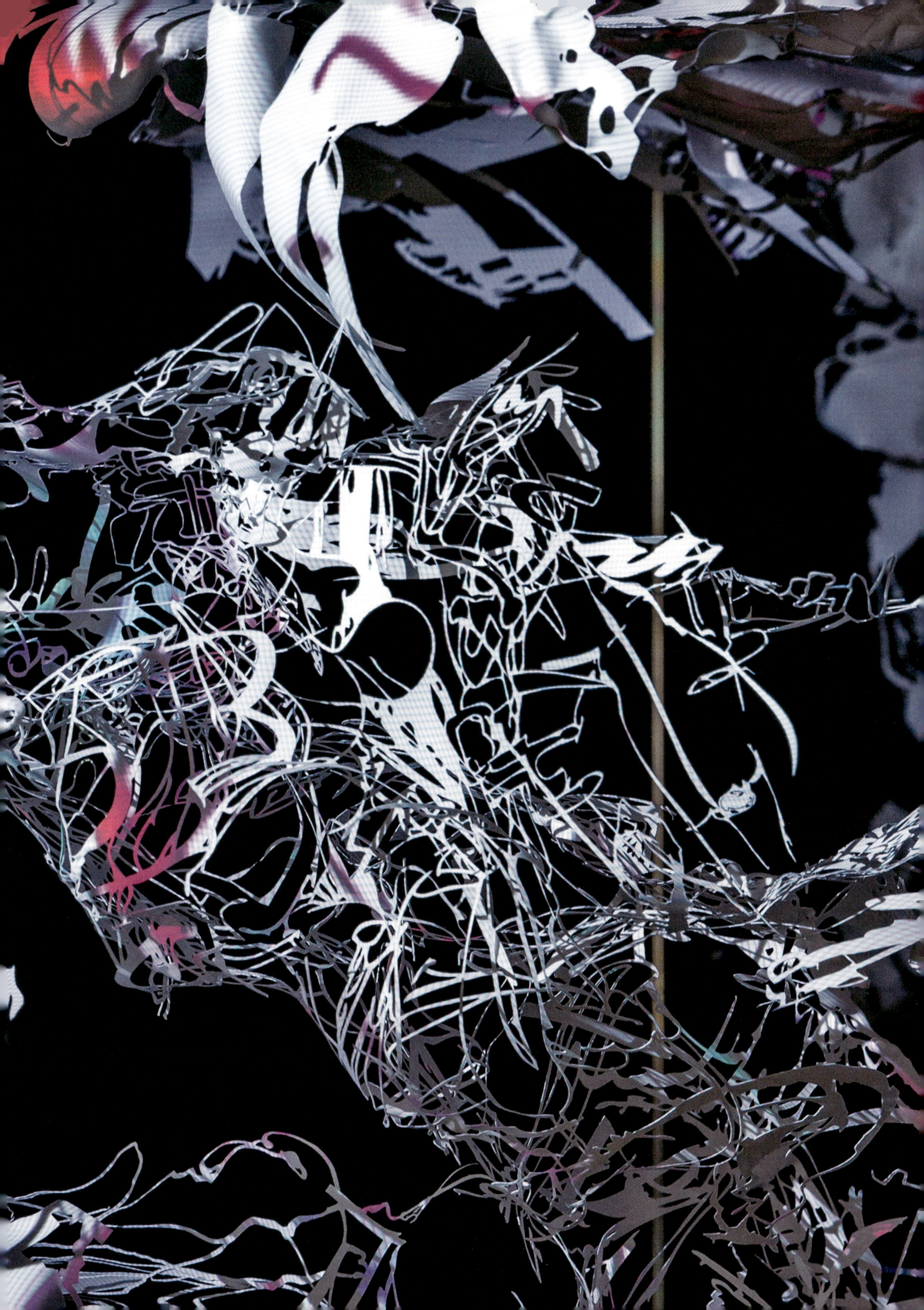

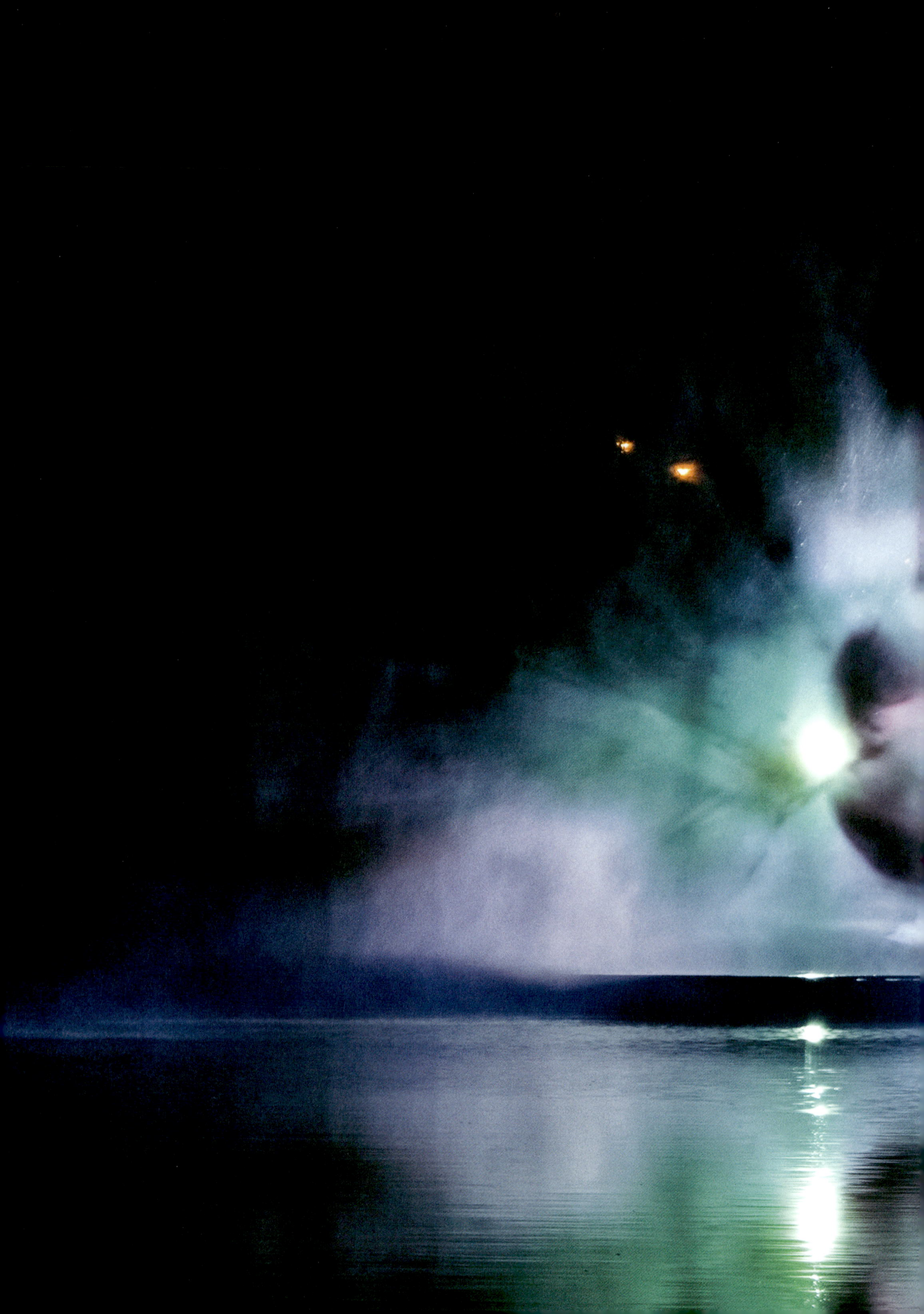

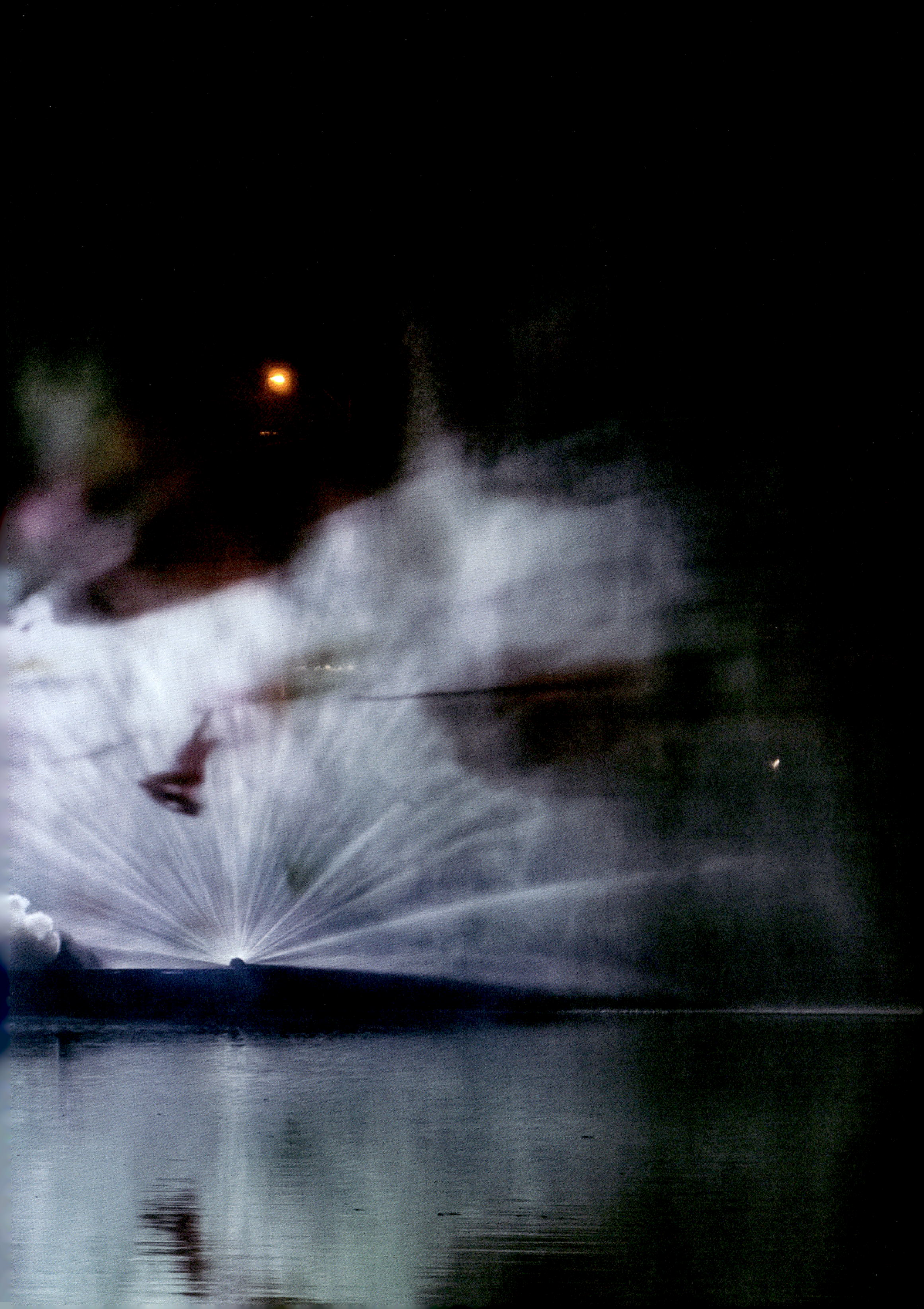

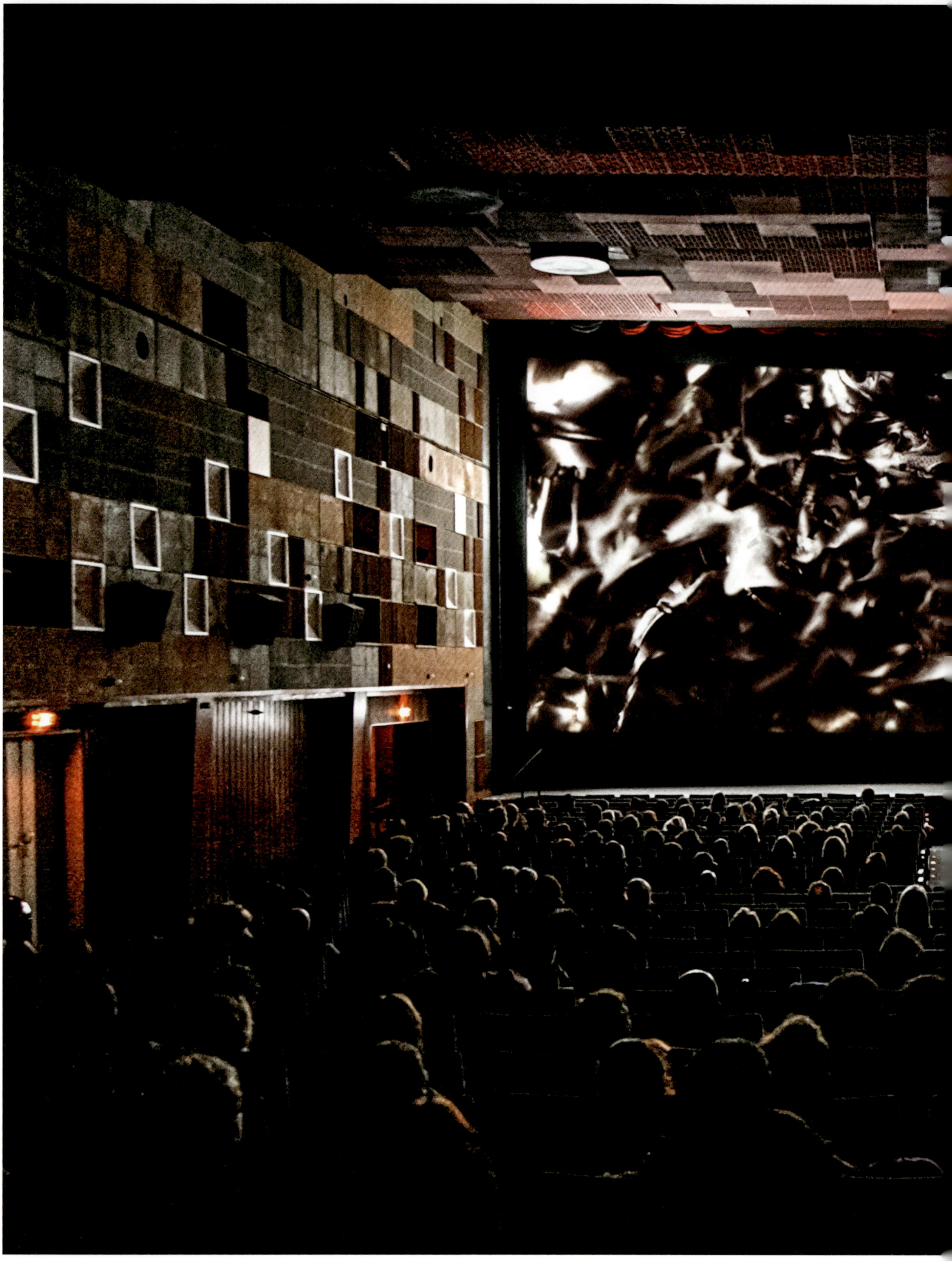

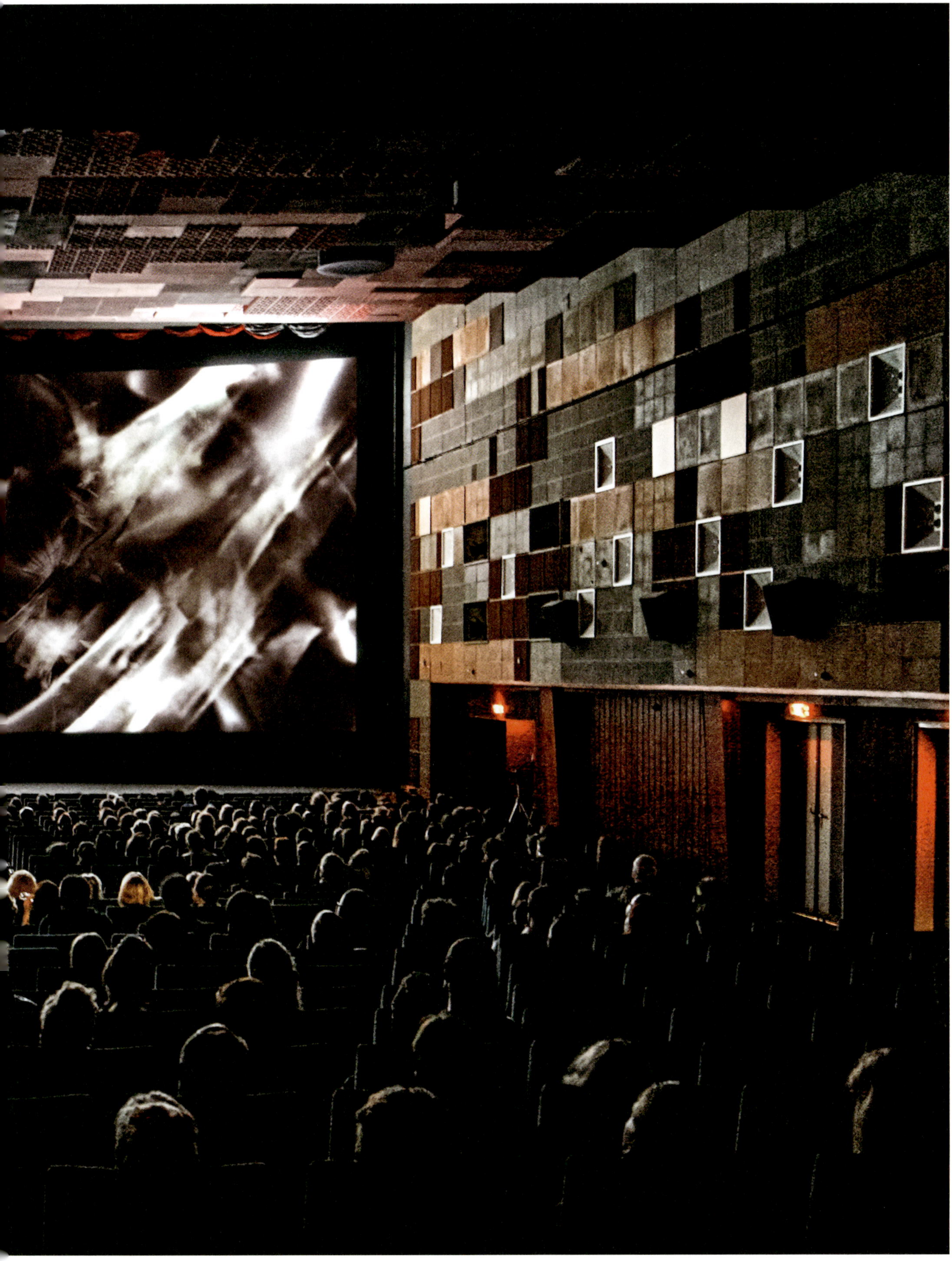

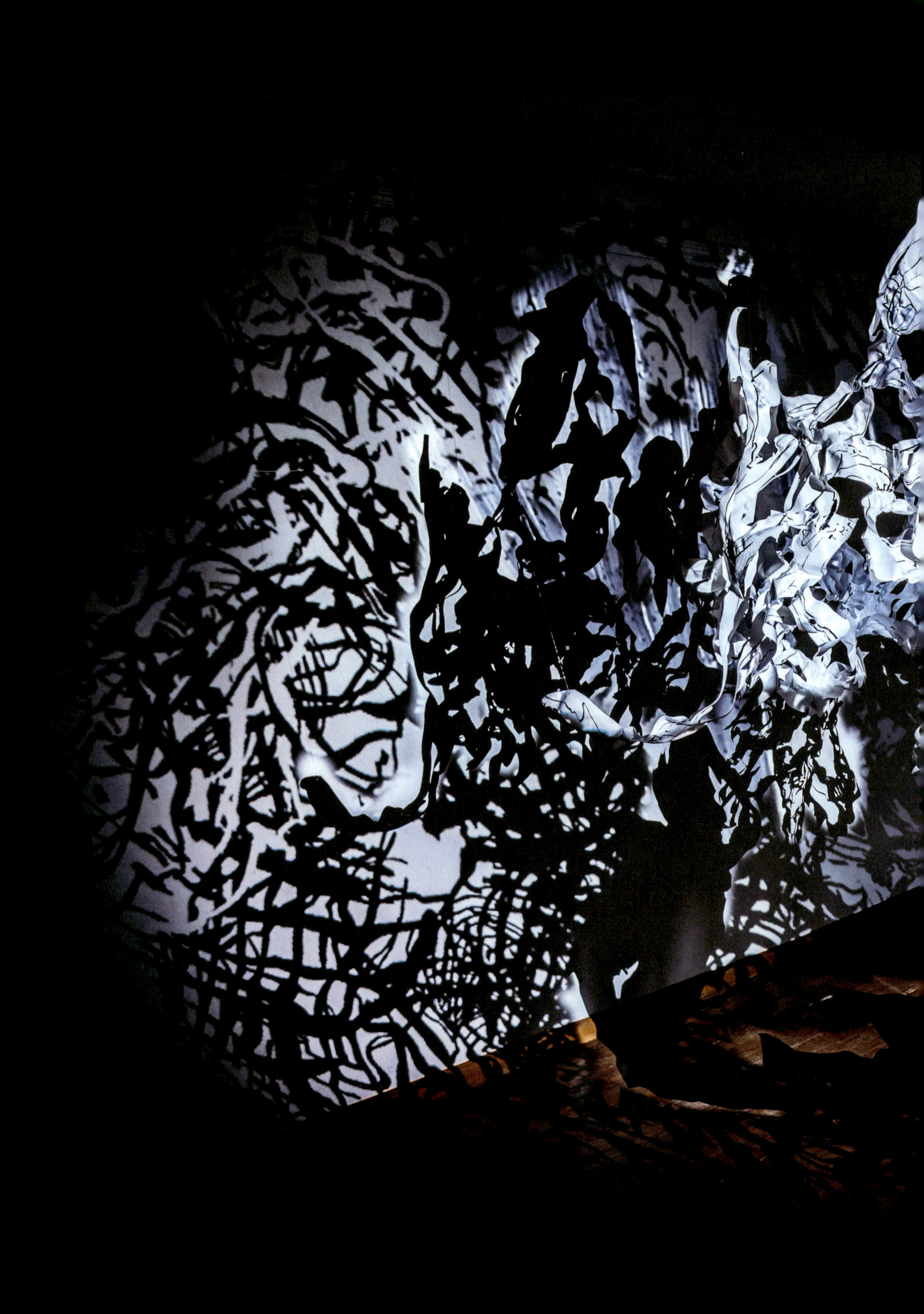

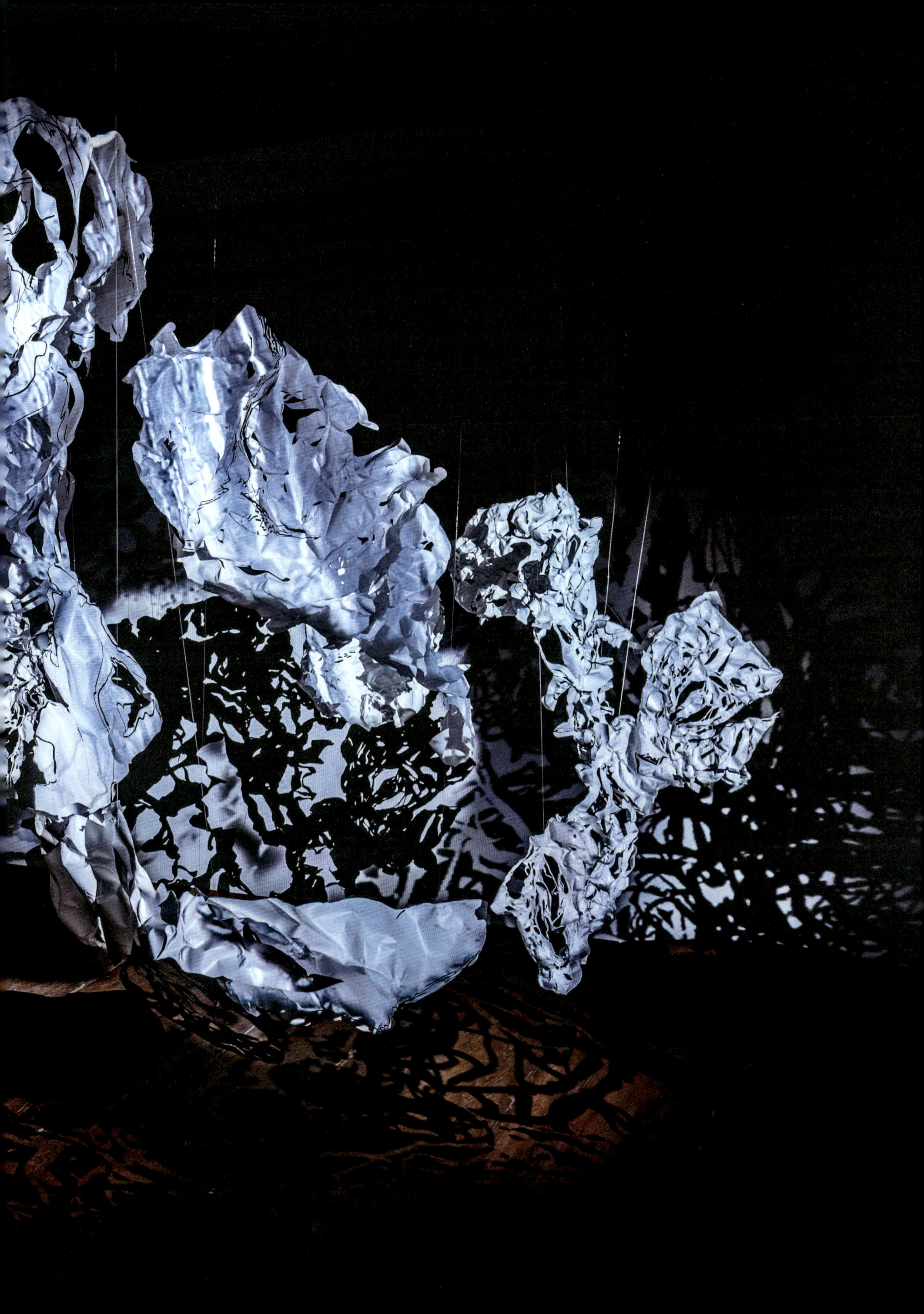

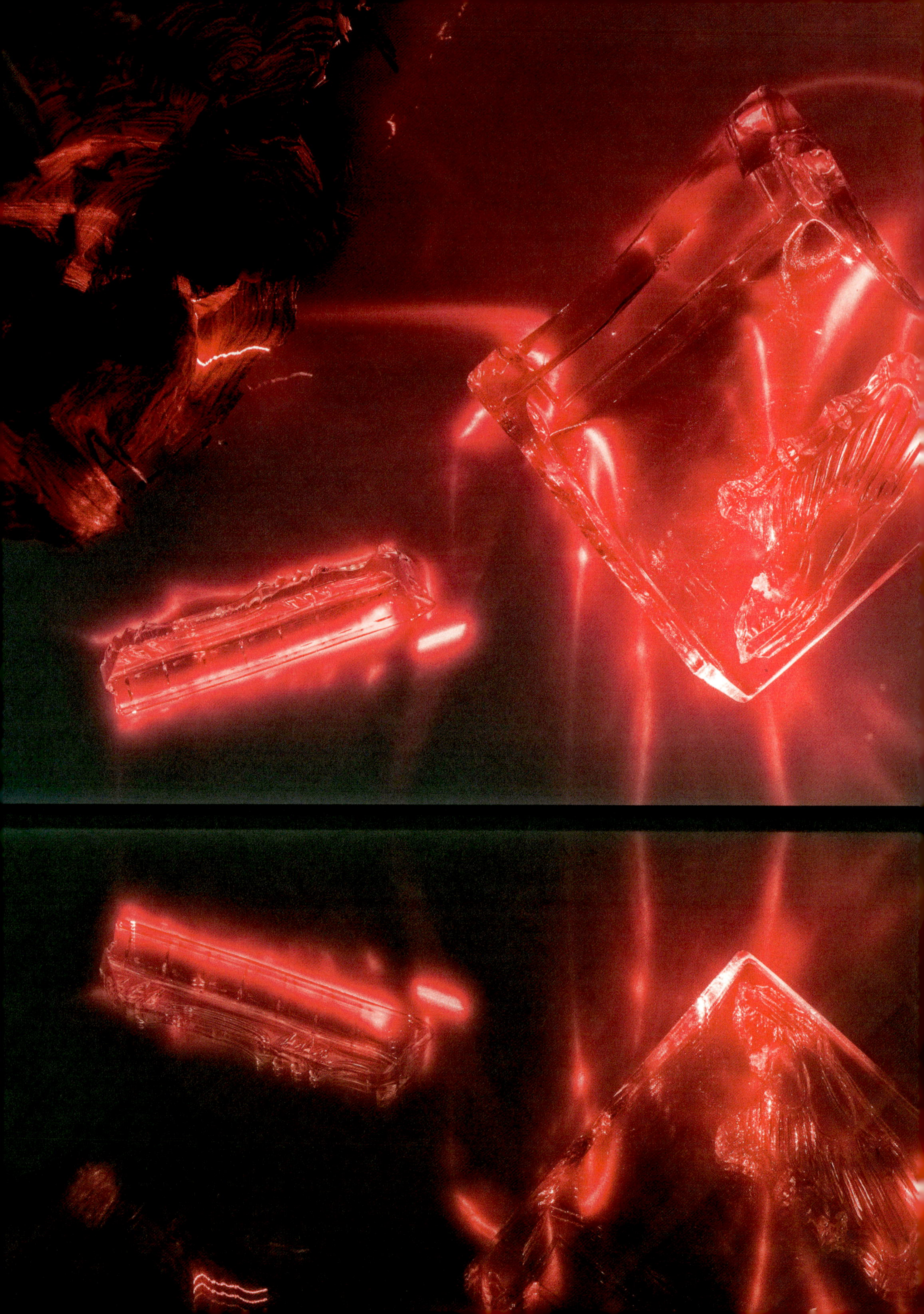

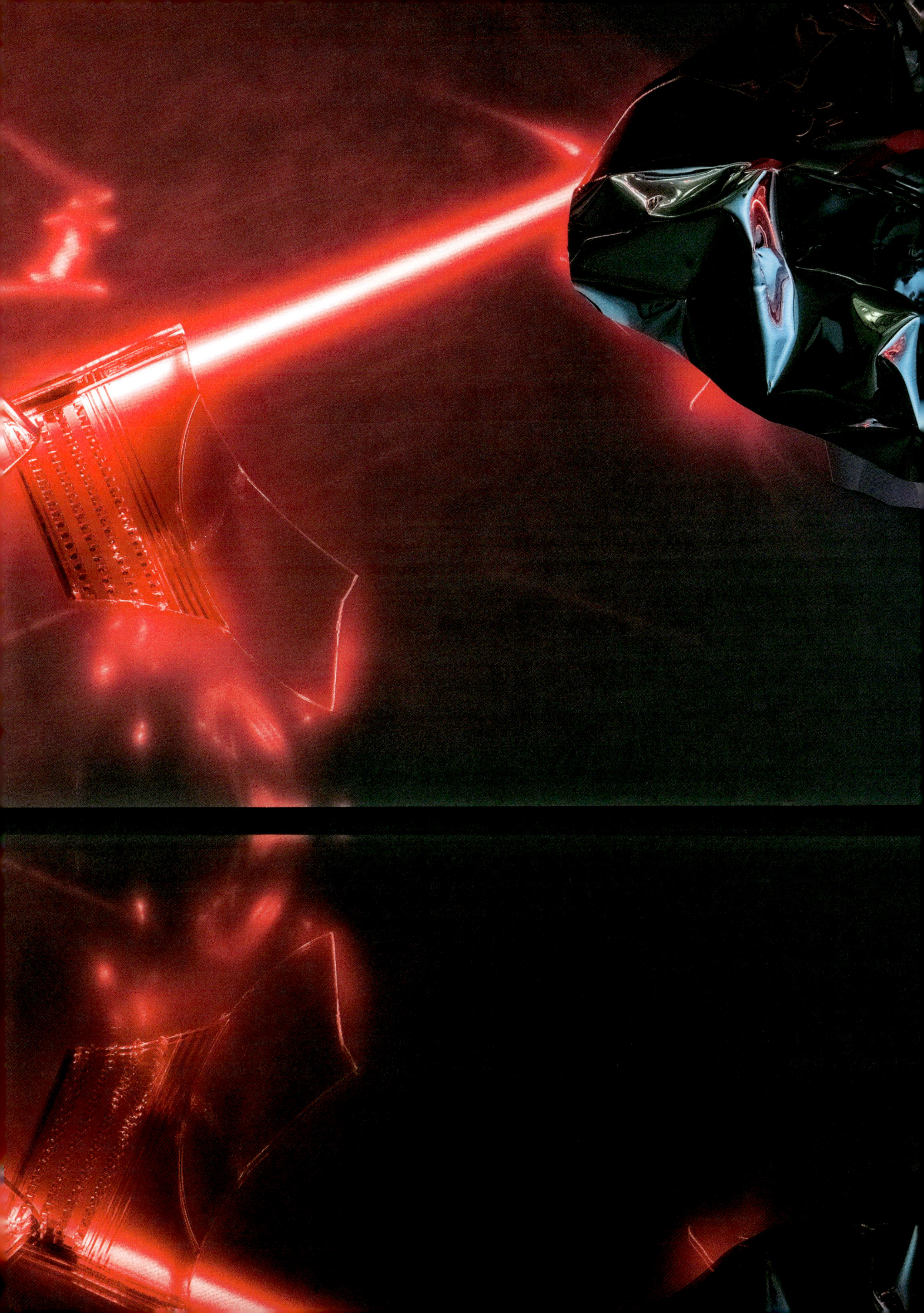

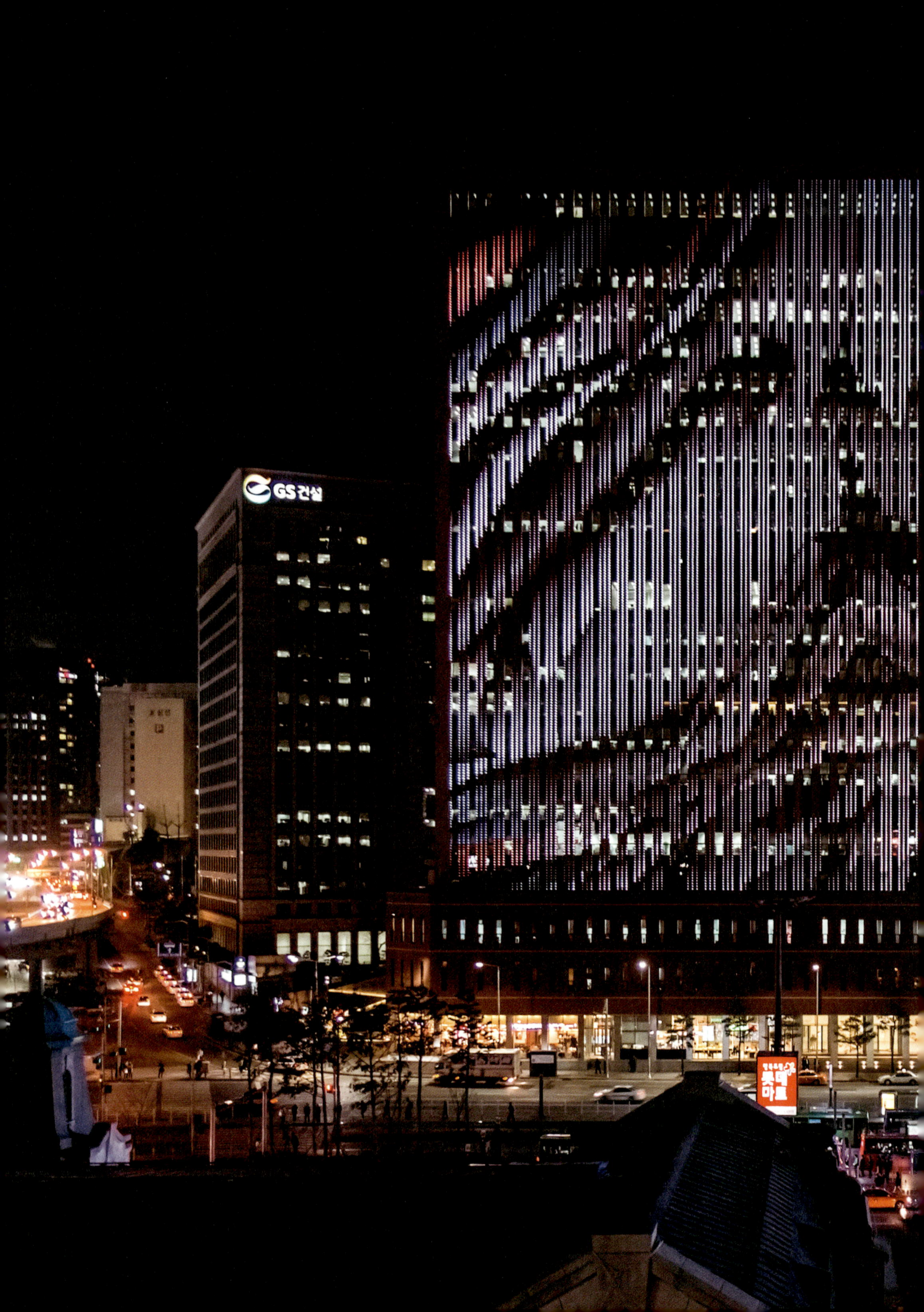
GS건설

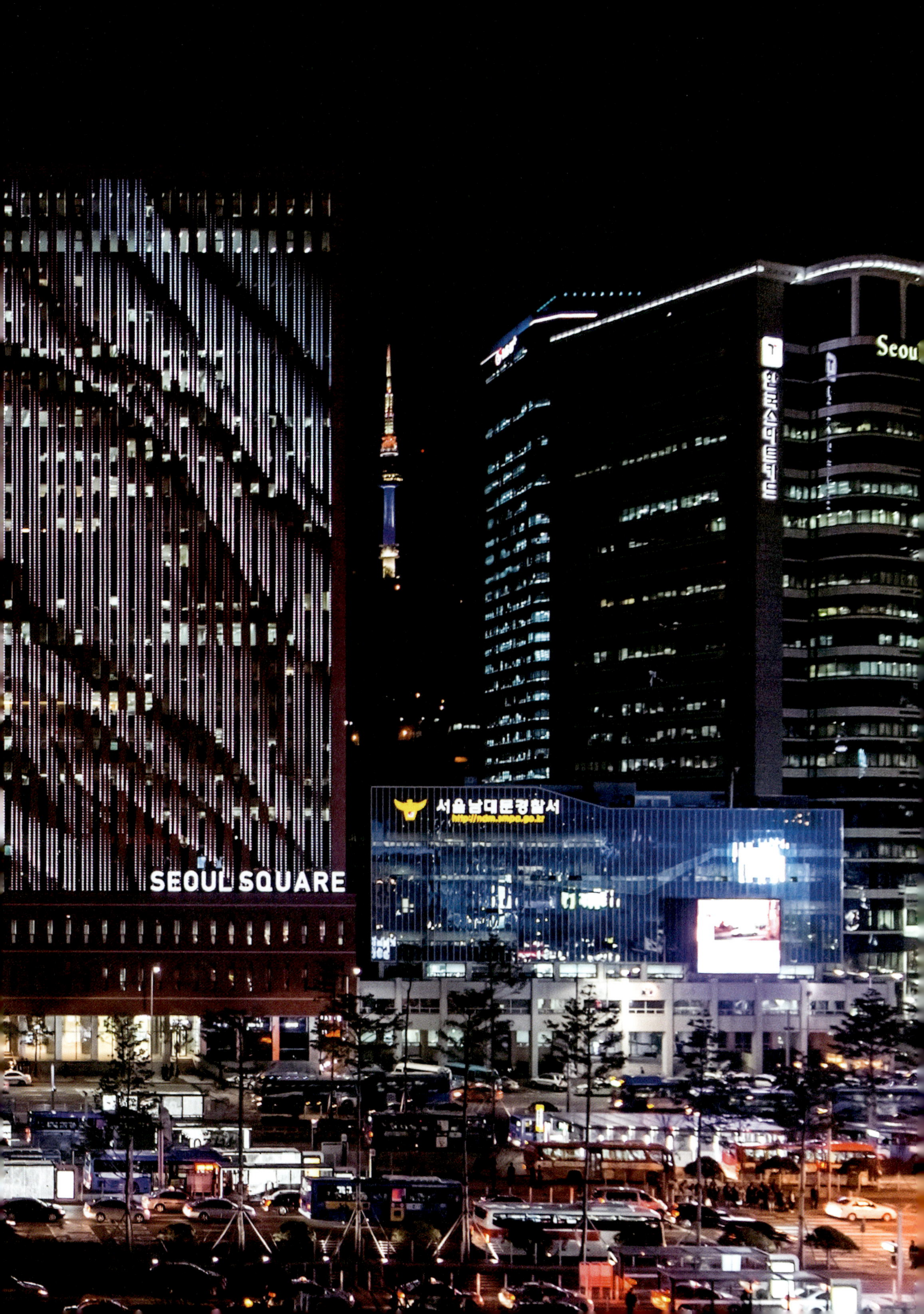
SEOUL SQUARE
서울남대문경찰서

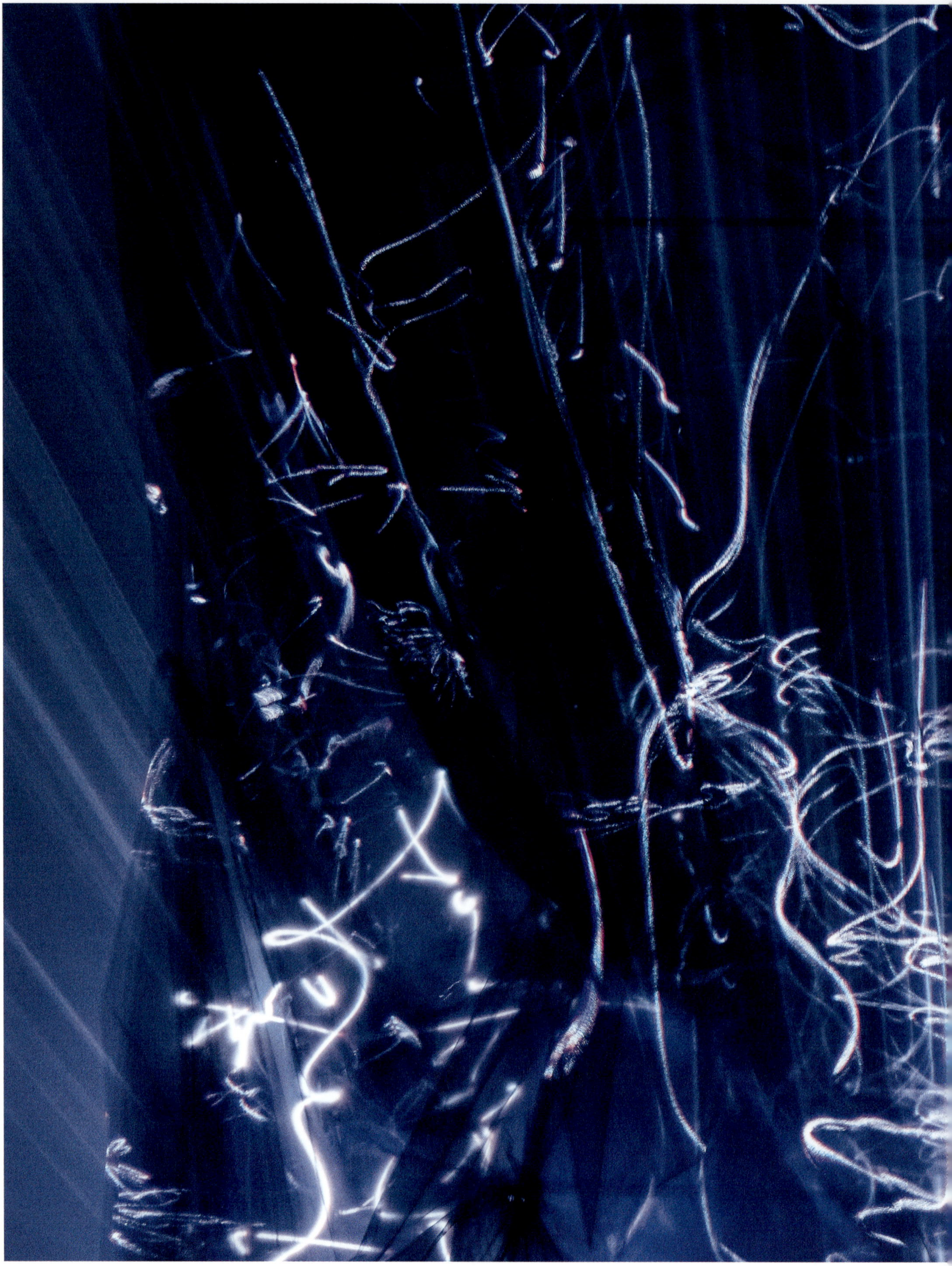

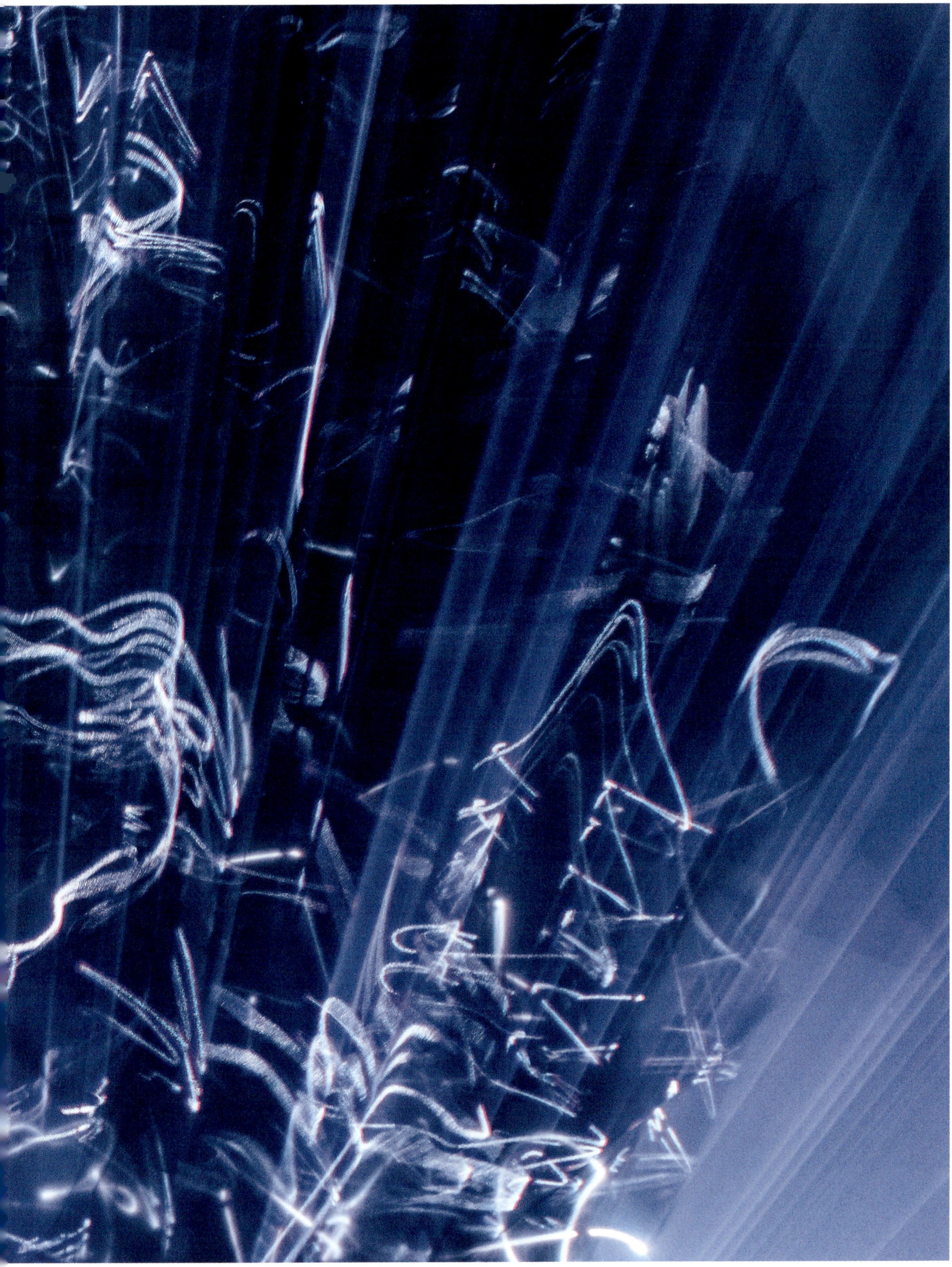

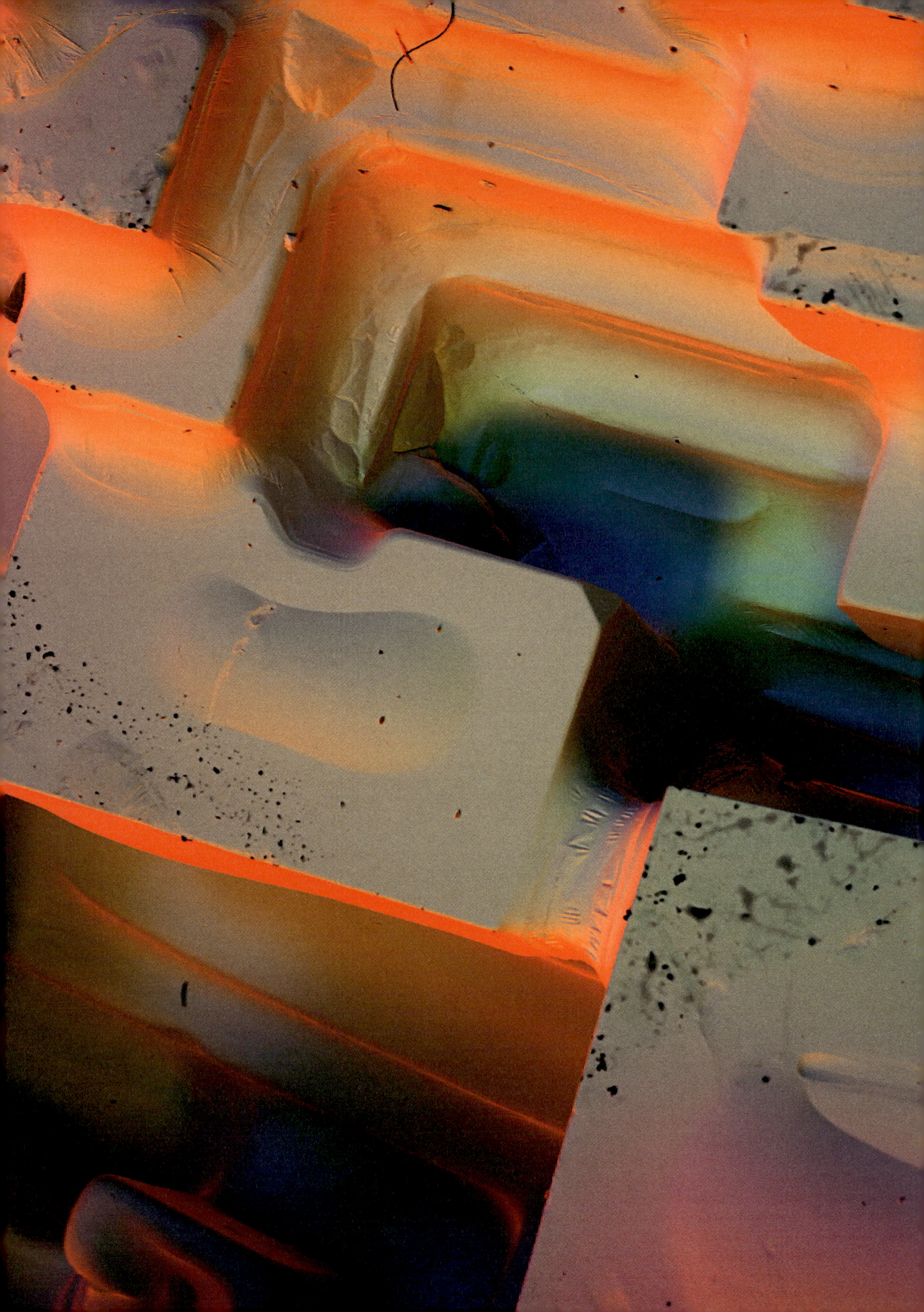

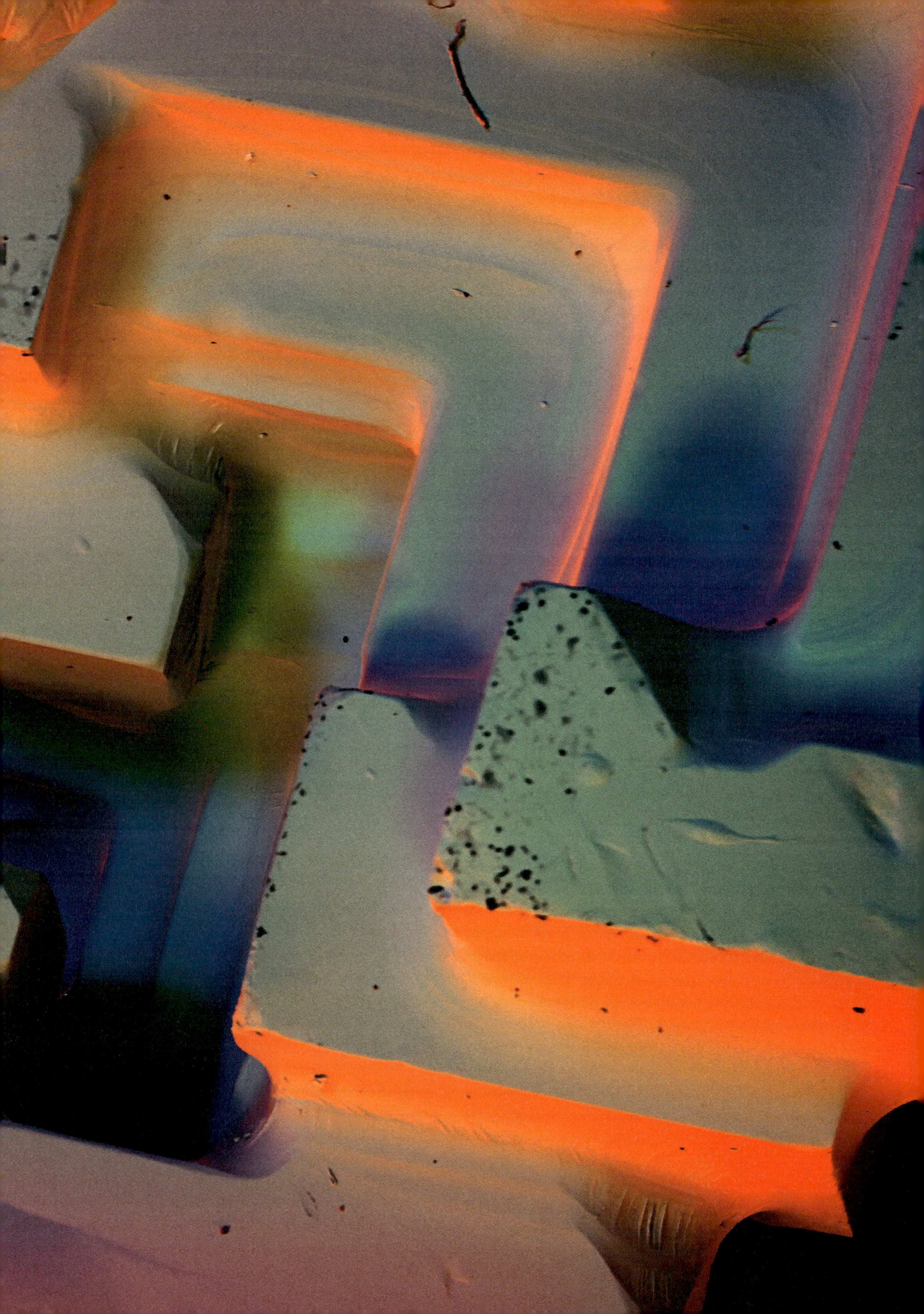

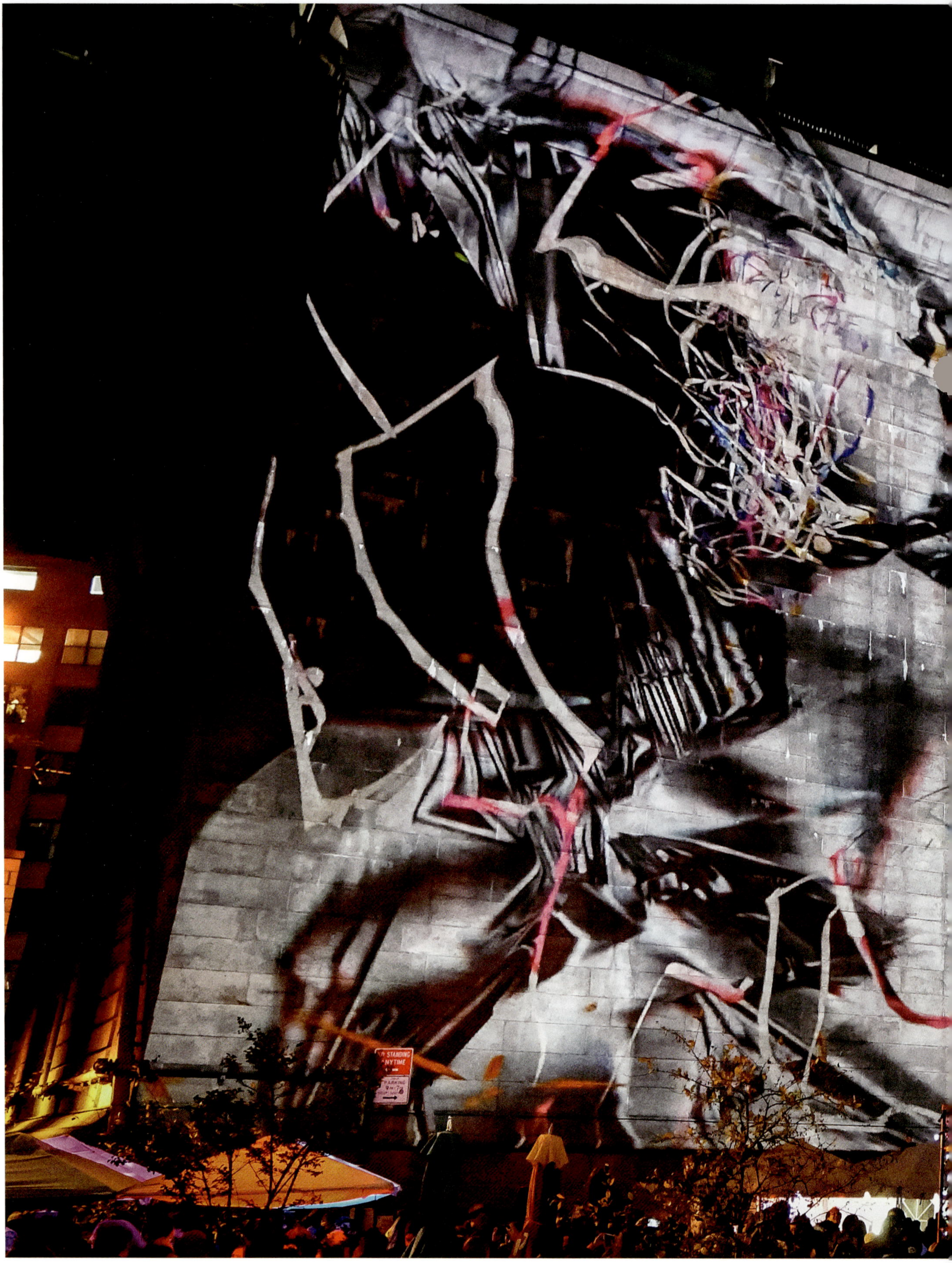

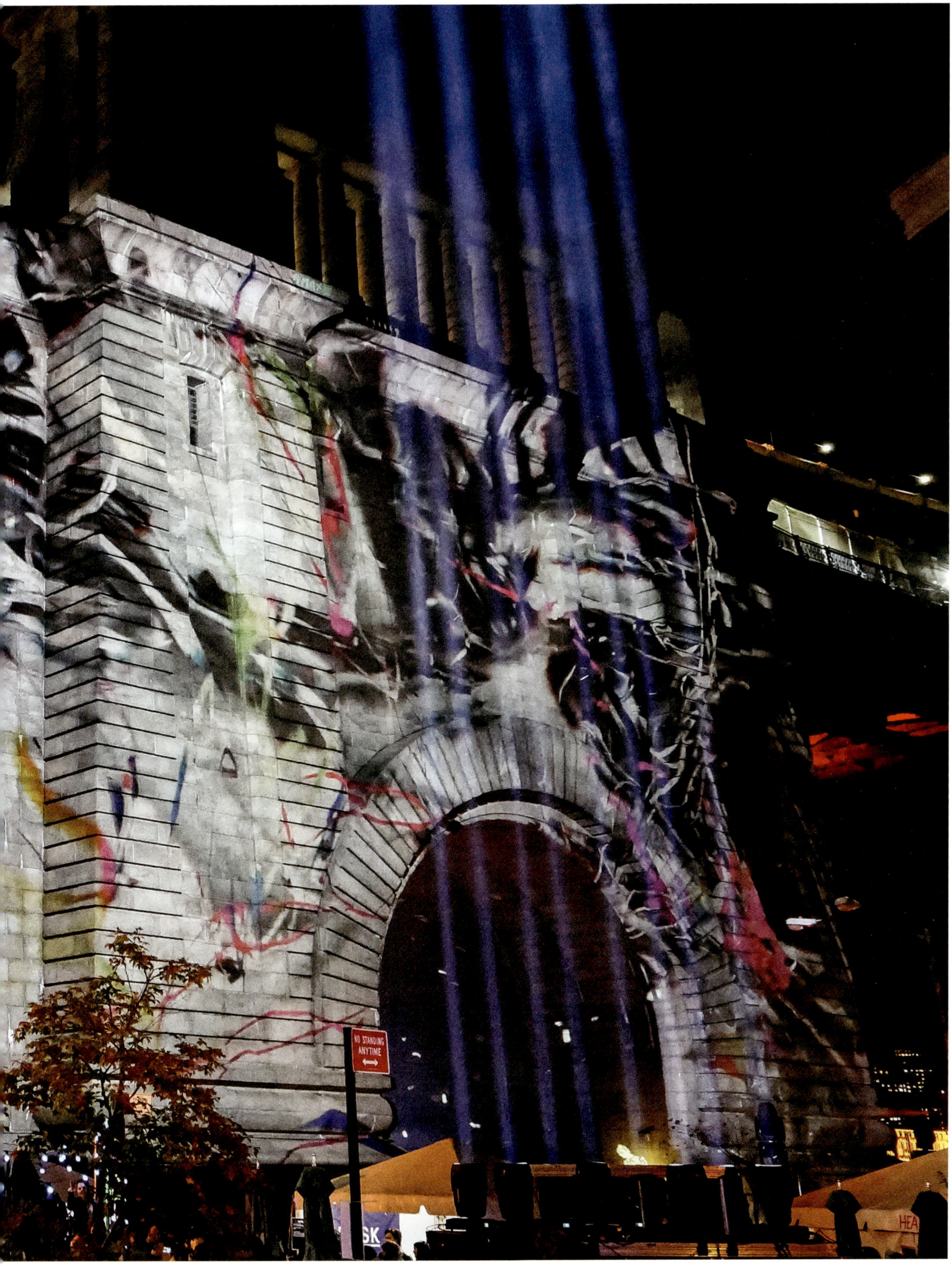
NO STANDING
ANYTIME

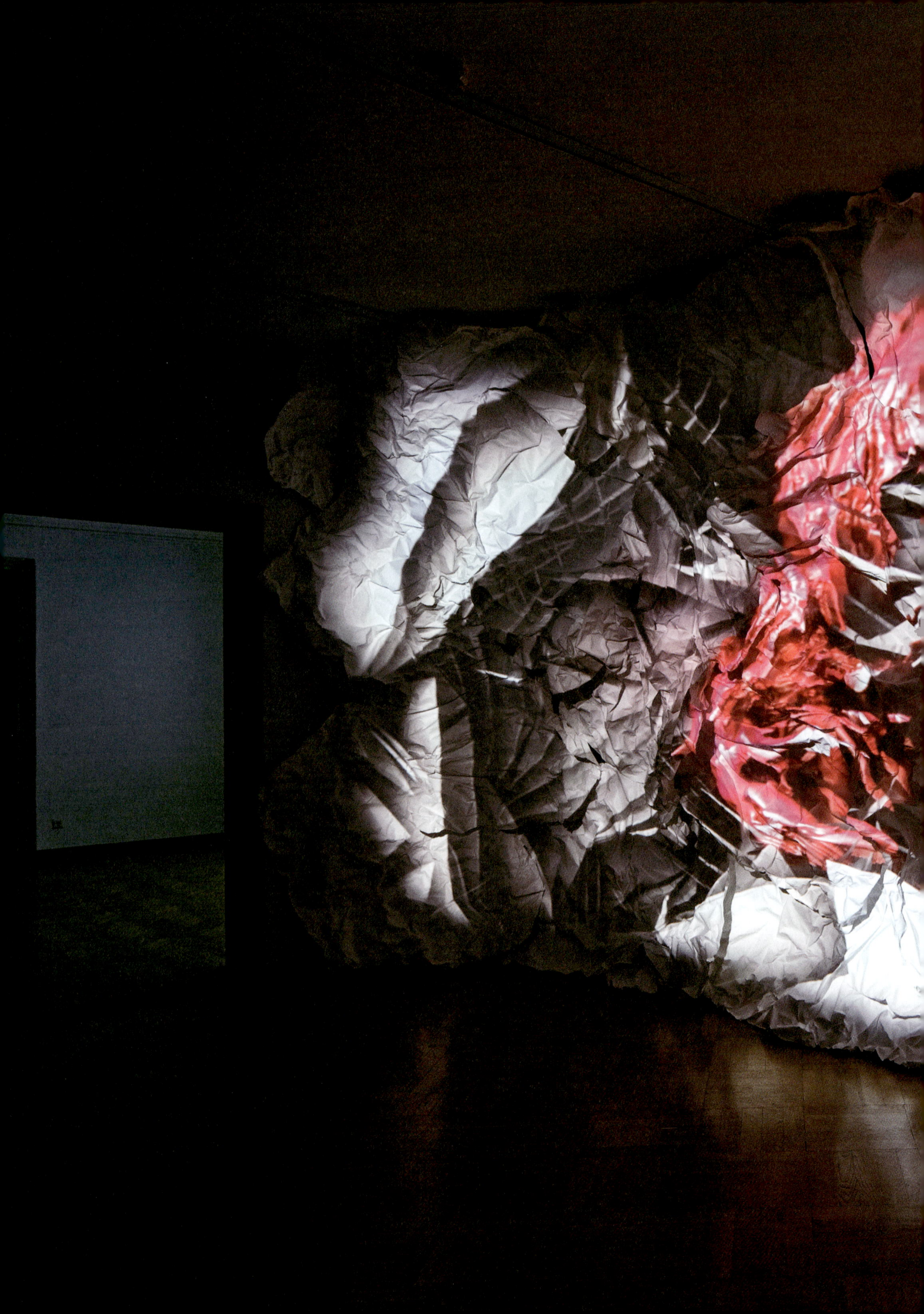

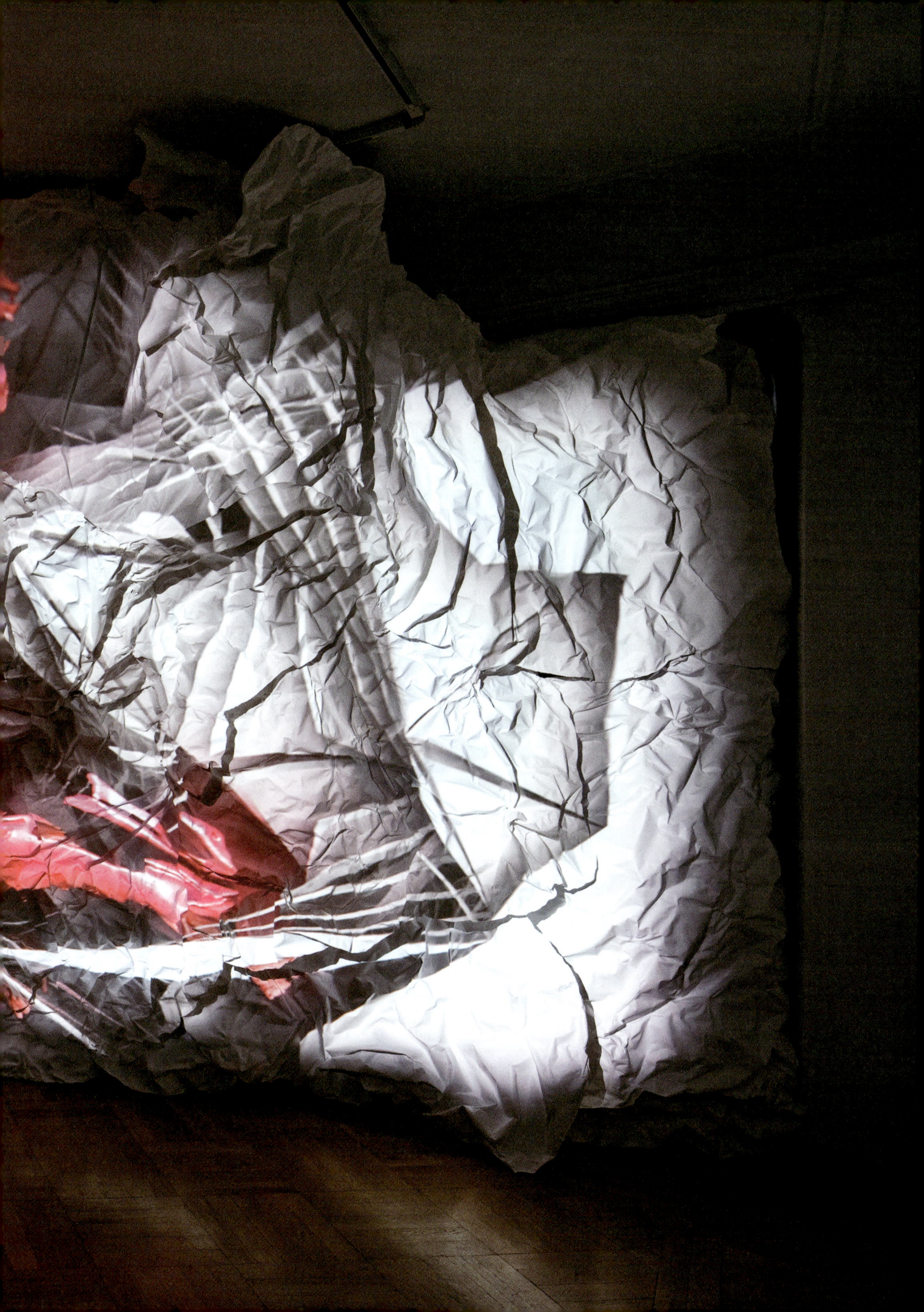

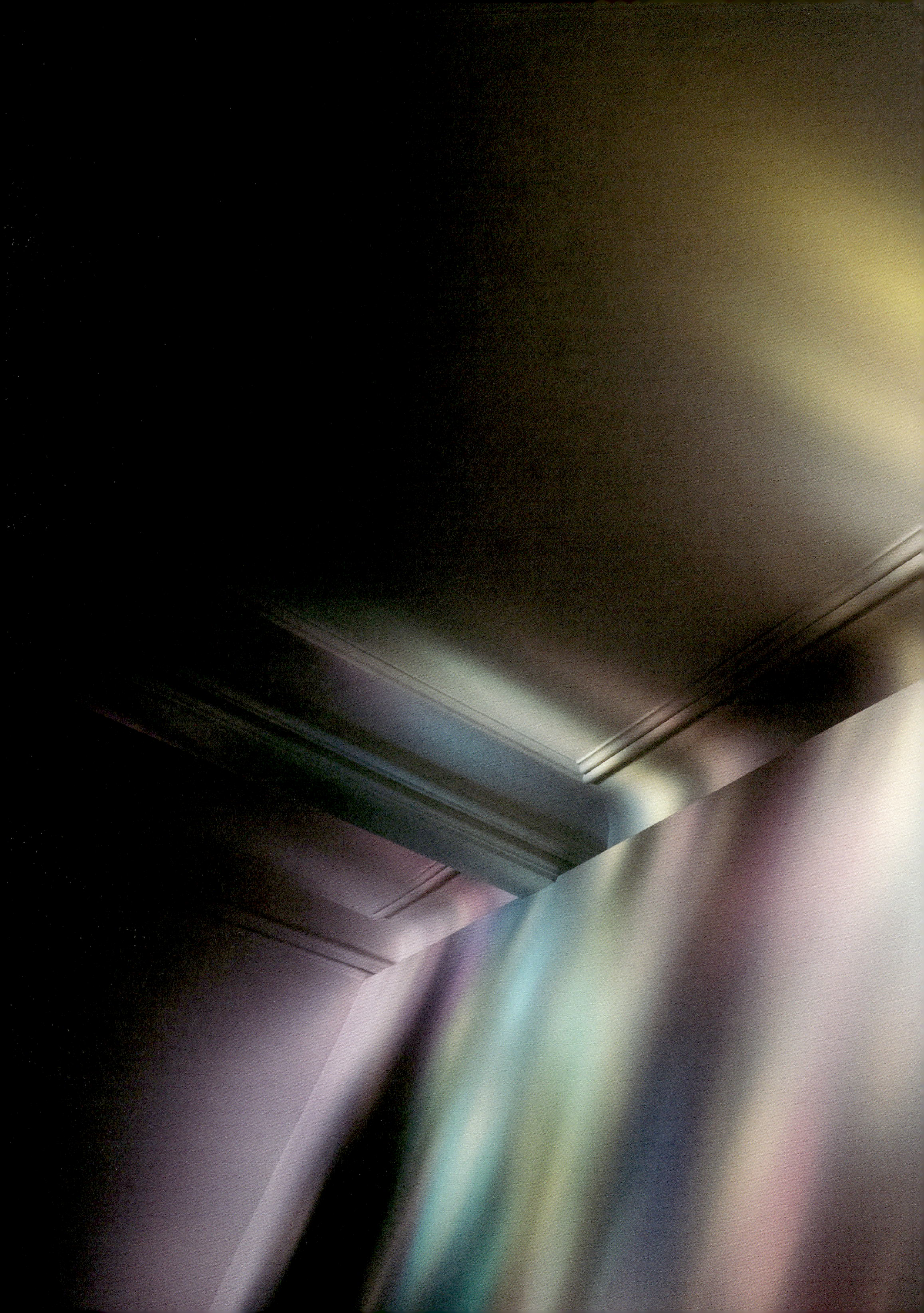

Vorwort

—

Volker Regel

Der Kunstverein Gera als Mittler und Förderer der zeitgenössischen Kunst möchte mit dieser Exposition seinen Fokus weiterhin auf innovative künstlerische Strömungen in der aktuellen Kunstentwicklung richten. Mit der Ausstellung LUX AETERNA, eine Kooperation des Kunstvereins mit der Städtischen Kunstsammlung Gera, wird medial erweiterte Kunst gezeigt, die im aktuellen Kunstbetrieb ihren festen Platz hat, aber im klassischen Galeriebetrieb immer noch eher unterrepräsentiert ist.

Ich freue mich, dass es gelungen ist, eine Werkschau des Videokünstlers und Filmemachers Robert Seidel zu präsentieren. Neben ortsspezifischen Arbeiten, Zeichnungen, Projektionen, Videoinstallationen sowie Fotografien vermittelt sie Einblicke in seinen Schaffensprozess. Die anspruchsvolle Konzeption von Dr. Claudia Tittel, die diese Ausstellung kuratierte, hat den räumlichen Rahmen des Kunstvereins gesprengt. Für die Umsetzung unseres Vorhabens wurde deshalb die Kooperation mit der Städtischen Kunstsammlung gewagt. So konnte die Ausstellungsfläche des Kunstvereins um die Raumfolge des Museums für Angewandte Kunst erweitert werden.

Im Mittelpunkt der Ausstellung steht das Licht als künstlerisches Medium, aber auch das Licht in seiner vieldeutigen Begrifflichkeit, worauf der Titel der Ausstellung verweisen will: LUX AETERNA – „Ewiges Licht", das der Künstler mit unterschiedlichsten Mitteln und Methoden zum Schwingen bringt sowie zur abstrakten Form in Raum und Zeit werden lässt. Ein wesentliches bildnerisches Mittel ist der Computer, mit dem Seidel in vielfacher prozessualer Überlagerung digitalisierter Daten ganz neuartige Formwelten gewinnt. Er generiert „virtuelle Biotope", in denen er aus einem digitalen Quellgrund ungesehene abstrakte Bilder zu schöpfen scheint. Damit modelliert er über gewisse Entscheidungs- und Formulierungsprozesse gleichnishaft Vorgänge in Natur und Gesellschaft. Die digitale Bildebene wird so zum Medium selbst.

Im Interview, das in dieser Publikation enthalten ist, postuliert Robert Seidel: „Meine Arbeiten sind keine digitalen Ready-Mades". Mit dieser Aussage grenzt er sich von konzeptuellen Strategien ab und setzt eher auf Kontingenz in seinem Schaffen. Ergebnisoffene Werkprozesse, auftretende Fehler, Zufälle und Eigendynamiken leiten ihn zu abstrakten Formgebungen. Funktionalisierung und scheinbare Klarheiten sind ihm suspekt.

Ich freue mich, dass in Verbindung mit dieser Ausstellung ein umfangreicher Katalog erscheint, der nicht nur die ausgestellten Arbeiten dokumentiert, sondern der auch das bisherige Schaffen und Werk des Künstlers mit kunstwissenschaftlichen Beiträgen und Abbildungen würdigt.

Mein Dank geht an den Künstler Robert Seidel, an die Kuratorin Dr. Claudia Tittel, an die Mitglieder des Vorstands des Kunstvereins und seine Helfer, an die Mitarbeiter des Museums für Angewandte Kunst, den Verein der Freunde des Ferberschen Hauses e.V. und die Kunstschule, die für die praktische Umsetzung der kuratorischen Idee sorgten. Insbesondere danke ich der Kulturstiftung des Bundes und deren Fonds Neue Länder, die die kontinuierliche anspruchsvolle Arbeit des Geraer Kunstvereins im überregionalen Kontext erkannt und mit ihrer großzügigen Förderung Vertrauen in unsere Arbeit gesetzt hat. Nicht zuletzt gilt mein besonderer Dank allen im Katalog aufgeführten Förderern, die die Ausstellung materiell unterstützt und uns erst in die Lage versetzt haben, die Konzeption mit den besonderen Anforderungen einer technisch komplexen Ausstellung umzusetzen.

Kataloge und Dokumentationen ersetzen nie die direkte Begegnung mit einem Kunstwerk. Daher wünsche ich mir, dass viele Besucher an diesem vielschichtigen Parcours mit Neugier und Vergnügen teilhaben.

Volker Regel
Vorsitzender des Kunstvereins Gera e.V.

Foreword
—
Volker Regel

As a facilitator and patron of contemporary art, the Kunstverein Gera (Art Association of Gera) would like to continue its focus on innovative artistic trends in contemporary art. The exhibition LUX AETERNA, a collaboration between the Kunstverein and Gera's Municipal Art Collection (Städtische Kunstsammlung), displays medially-enhanced art which has a firmly-established place in the current art scene, but is still underrepresented in the classic gallery sector.

It is a pleasure to successfully present a retrospective of the video artist and filmmaker Robert Seidel. Along with site-specific works, drawings, projections, and video installations, as well as photographs, the exhibition offers insights into the creative process of this Thuringian artist. Curator Dr. Claudia Tittel's sophisticated conceptualization exceeded the spatial scope of the Kunstverein. Because of this, we ventured a cooperative undertaking with the Municipal Art Collection in order to bring our project to fruition. It was due to this collaborative effort that the exhibition area of the Kunstverein was able to be expanded to utilize the exhibition space of the Museum of Applied Arts.

Light – not only as an artistic medium, but also in its conceptual multivalence – is the focus of the exhibition, and is the also the reference for its title: LUX AETERNA – "Eternal Light." The artist employs the most diverse of means and methods to bring light's medial and conceptual resonance into play, thereby allowing light to become an abstract form in time and space. An essential artistic instrument in this process is the computer, which Seidel uses to create completely novel worlds of forms via a multiplicative processual superimposition of digitized data. He generates "virtual biotopes," in which he appears to create unseen abstract images from a digital source, thereby allegorically modeling processes in nature and society via "certain procedures of decision-making and formulation." In this way, the digital image-plane becomes the medium itself.

In the interview included in this publication, Robert Seidel states: "My works are not digital readymades." With this declaration he distances himself from conceptual strategies, focusing instead on contingence in his creative work. Open-ended working processes, occurring errors, coincidences, and internal dynamics which all lead him to abstract forms. Seidel is suspicious of functionalization and apparent clarities.

I am pleased that a comprehensive catalogue has been published in conjunction with this exhibition. The catalogue not only documents the exhibited works, but also accompanies the artist's earlier works with art-historical articles and images.

My gratitude goes to the artist Robert Seidel, to the curator Dr. Claudia Tittel, to the members of the executive board of the Kunstverein and to its supporters, to the employees of the Museum of Applied Arts, the Association of the Friends of the Ferber House (Verein der Freunde des Ferberschen Hauses) and the art school, all of whom have made the curatorial concept's practical implementation possible. I would like to acknowledge in particular the German Federal Cultural Foundation (Kulturstiftung des Bundes) and its New Länder Fund, which have recognized the consistently ambitious work of the Gera Kunstverein within a supra-regional context, and have, with their generous support, placed their trust in our work. Last but not least, our appreciation is extended to the sponsors listed in the catalogue, all of whom have provided material support for the exhibition and first put us in the position to implement the concept within the requirements of a technologically complex exhibition.

Catalogues and documentation can never replace the experience of a direct encounter with a work of art. With this in mind, it is my hope that many will enjoy the experience of exploring this multifaceted exhibition with great curiosity.

Volker Regel
Chairman of the Kunstverein Gera e.V.

Grußwort

—

Holger Peter Saupe

Zunächst möchte ich die Gelegenheit nutzen, dem Geraer Kunstverein zu dem Wagnis und der Realisierung dieser Ausstellung zu gratulieren, denn Medienkunst verlässt meist schon im Ansatz den traditionellen Präsentationsrahmen und ist im Hinblick auf die technische Umsetzung für Institutionen eine besondere Herausforderung. LUX AETERNA ist eine Ausstellung mit Arbeiten des Künstlers Robert Seidel, die als Kooperationsprojekt zwischen dem Geraer Kunstverein e.V. sowie dem Museum für Angewandte Kunst in Gera entstand und zeitgleich in den Räumlichkeiten beider Institutionen präsentiert wird. Zu sehen ist eine umfangreiche Werkschau Robert Seidels, in der neue und erstmals auch wesentliche Arbeiten aus den letzten Jahren vereint und dokumentiert sind. Das Zustandekommen der Ausstellung ist der engagierten und in Gera lebenden Kunstwissenschaftlerin Dr. Claudia Tittel zu verdanken, die nicht nur die Idee für die Ausstellung entwickelte, sondern darüber hinaus für die finanzielle Untersetzung und Realisierung sorgte.

Die Ausstellung schlägt mit ihrem Titel LUX AETERNA – „Ewiges Licht" – den Bogen zu zahlreichen aktuellen Jubiläen auf physikalisch-wissenschaftlichem Terrain wie beispielsweise dem 100. Jahrestag der Veröffentlichung der Allgemeinen Relativitätstheorie durch Albert Einstein im Jahre 1915 – ein fundamentales Ereignis, welches die UNESCO veranlasst hat, das Jahr 2015 als „Internationales Jahr des Lichts" auszurufen. Auf der ganzen Welt finden ganzjährig Veranstaltungen statt, die sich mit der Bedeutung des Lichts für Wissenschaft und Gesellschaft beschäftigen.

Die menschliche Vorstellung von Licht hat sich in den letzten 200 Jahren grundsätzlich erweitert, und Einstein hat mit seiner Theorie die Grundlagen für ein wissenschaftliches Beschreibungsmodell zum modernen Verständnis des Seins geschaffen. Dem gegenüber steht jedoch, dass sich die rein physikalischen Vorgänge der Lichtentstehung oder von Reflexion, Streuung, Absorption und Lichtbrechung nicht verändert haben. Diese verschiedenen Ebenen reflektiert auch diese Ausstellung.

Ausgangspunkt für die künstlerische Arbeit von Robert Seidel ist die Natur. Nur ist es nicht die Natur der sichtbaren, an der Oberfläche stattfindenden Erscheinung, sondern der Künstler zielt meist auf inhärente Strukturen natürlicher Prozesse ab. Die Basis sind seine computergenerierten Bilder und abstrakten Filmsequenzen, die er für raumgreifende Lichtprojektionen verwendet, in denen er malerische, grafische und mitunter mehrdeutige skulpturale Elemente zu eigenwilligen, sinnlich-poetischen Videoinstallationen verdichtet. Die Kunst von Robert Seidel erfasst keine anekdotischen Alltagsprozesse, sondern seine bildnerischen Mittel und virtuellen Bildwelten bringen uns vielmehr Bewegung, Veränderung, Transformation sowie Überlagerung vor Augen und vermitteln uns ein Bild des Urtümlichen und Zeitlosen. Er berührt einen Wahrnehmungsbereich, der zwischen äußerer Welt und einem inneren Schwebezustand zu pendeln scheint und den Eindruck hinterlassen kann, dass sich alles in einer Art Übergangsstadium befindet.

Insbesondere Kunst kann dazu beitragen, dass unser Denken, unsere Auffassung und Vorstellung von Natur, vom Menschen und vom Sinn des Daseins beweglich bleibt und erweitert wird. Die Kunst von Robert Seidel birgt in dieser Hinsicht vielfältiges Potential, das im individuellen Rezeptionsprozess erschlossen werden kann und beim Betrachter neue Gedanken, Emotionen und Perspektiven zu evozieren vermag. In diesem Sinne wünsche ich allen Besuchern viel Freude und der Ausstellung nachhaltigen Erfolg.

Holger Peter Saupe
Leiter Kunstsammlung Gera

Preface

—
Holger Peter Saupe

Firstly, I would like to use this opportunity to congratulate the Kunstverein Gera for its successful realization of this exhibition. Media art to some extent abandons traditional exhibition frameworks and, in view of its implementation, presents a particular challenge for institutions. LUX AETERNA is an exhibition featuring works by the artist Robert Seidel which arose as a collaborative project of the Kunstverein Gera and the Museum for Applied Arts in Gera, and which is simultaneously presented in both institutions. The exhibition is a comprehensive retrospective for Robert Seidel's works, in which new as well as important earlier works are united and documented. The realization of the exhibition is the result of the dedication of art historian and Gera based Dr. Claudia Tittel, who not only developed the idea for the exhibition, but also provided for its financial support and implementation.

With its title LUX AETERNA – "Eternal Light" – the exhibition provides a link to numerous current scientific anniversaries, such as the centenary of the 1915 publication of Albert Einstein's general theory of relativity; a fundamental occasion that has led UNESCO to declare 2015 "the year of light." Year-round events engaging with light's scientific and societal importance are taking place throughout the world. Over the last 200 years, humanity's conception of light has fundamentally broadened, and Einstein laid the foundations for a scientific model describing the modern understanding of being. In contrast to this monumental shift in understanding, however, the purely physical processes of the formation of light, or reflection, diffusion, absorption, and refraction have not changed. The exhibition reflects these different levels as well.

The point of origin for Robert Seidel's artworks is nature. However, rather than focusing on nature's visible surface phenomena, Seidel most frequently aims at the inherent structures of natural processes. The foundations for his work are computer-generated images and abstract film sequences that he uses for expansive light projections, in which he condenses painterly, graphical, and sometimes polysemic sculptural elements into idiosyncratic, sensual-poetic video installations. Robert Seidel's art does not capture anecdotal daily processes. Rather, his visual means and virtual image worlds show us movement, mutation and transformation, as well as superposition. They also impart a picture of the primal and the timeless. He touches a realm of perception that appears to oscillate between the outer world and an inner state of limbo, giving the perception that everything is in a transitional stage.

Art, in particular, can contribute to the expansion and the flexibility of our thinking, perceptions, and conceptions of nature and the meaning of existence. In this respect, the art of Robert Seidel harbors diverse potential that can be unfolded in the viewer's individual processes of reception, evoking new thoughts, emotions, and perspectives. With this in mind, I hope that visitors will enjoy what I am sure will be a resoundingly successful exhibition.

Holger Peter Saupe
Director of the Kunstsammlung Gera

LUX AETERNA.
Robert Seidels digitale Bildwelten zwischen Lichtmetaphorik, Abstraktion und Naturerfindung
—
Claudia Tittel

Aus dem Dunkel heraus durchdringt ein Nebel aus farbigem Licht die rechteckige Bildfläche. Körperlose und doch deutlich sichtbare Flächen und Linien aus grünen, rosa, blauen und gelben Lichtstrahlen durchmessen einen diffusen, im Schwarz sich beinahe auflösenden Raum. Ihre Immaterialität nicht verbergend, fächern sich die diaphanen Strukturen im gesamten Spektrum des Lichts auf, so als würden sie sich an einer geborstenen Glasscheibe brechen. Dabei zeigen sie nichts, lassen nichts sichtbar werden – außer sich selbst. Die Lichter bilden virtuelle, nicht greifbare Texturen, Schichtungen, Strukturgefüge. Sie spannen sich wie abstrakte Netze im Raum, ändern unvorhersehbar die Richtung, um schließlich vom grellen Sonnenlicht geschluckt zu werden. Wie eine traumhafte Sequenz zerrinnt das Gesehene und lässt die mystische Seite des Lichts in den Vordergrund treten.

Um die Wucht und den Schock eines nicht darstellbaren Ereignisses sichtbar werden zu lassen, greift Seidel in seinem Film _grau (2004) auf die metaphorische Bedeutung des Lichts als er- und durchscheinendes Medium zurück, in dem sich fiktive sowie reale Vorstellungswelten treffen. Seidels Eingangssequenz erinnert an das durch bemalte Kirchenfenster gotischer Kathedralen fallende Licht, das den Kirchenraum in die herrlichsten Farben taucht und ihn gleichzeitig von Innen erleuchtet. Licht als transzendentes Medium – ephemer, fließend und durchscheinend, von augenblicksbezogener Schönheit und immerwährendem Wandel bestimmt, – wurde nicht nur im Mittelalter mit dem Übernatürlichen und Göttlichen gleichgesetzt, sondern war Inbegriff des Absoluten.[1] Als solches, als absolutes Licht, wird es auch in der finsteren Szenerie am Anfang von _grau eingesetzt, um die „Unbegreifbarkeit archaischer Gefühle eines Schockzustandes" darzustellen.[2] Sowohl Erscheinendes als auch Erlöschendes, Sicht- und zugleich Unsichtbares, Greif- und gleichermaßen Ungreifbares werden auf einer ästhetisch abstrakten Ebene verhandelt, die keine konkreten, aber umso stärker emotionale Bilder erzeugt. Seidel versucht hier einen Zustand zu beschreiben, der zwischen Erinnerung und Zukünftigem pendelt und dabei individuelle Gedankensplitter eines fiktiven Autounfalls finalisiert.[3]

In jener lichterfüllten Szene, die sich im dunklen Ur-Raum des Äthers abzuspielen scheint, erscheint in der Bildmitte kurz flackernd „_grau". Danach weitet sich der Screen und wird vom Breitwandkino zum weniger dramatischen 16:9-Format.[4] Die farbdurchwebte ätherische Schönheit des sich von der Finsternis abhebenden immateriellen Lichts wird im nun folgenden Teil abgelöst von einem hellweißen Bildraum, durch den grauschwarze amorphe Gewebemassen zum oberen Bildrand fliehen. Diese gerinnen zu knochenähnlichen, scheinbar von Stacheldrähten gehaltenen Gebilden, an denen, abgeschnittenen Nervenbahnen gleich, dünne Fäden wuchern. Die Knochenformationen wachsen weiter zu kristallinen Strukturen, verästeln sich und lösen sich später im weißen Nichts auf. Als formlose malerische Texturen – die ebenso vage sind, wie sie im nächsten Moment konkrete Assoziationen an biologische Mikrostrukturen, etwa Chromosomen, Knochen, Wurzeln oder gar deformierte Metallteile gestatten – kehren sie zurück. Sich in dauerhafter Transformation befindend, schweben die amorphen Objekte durch den Bildraum und scheinen den Titel der Arbeit zu visualisieren: Als indifferente und sich jeden Moment verändernde graue Rhizome verweisen sie nicht nur farblich auf Grau als jene Farbe, die das Geheimnisvolle und Verborgene andeutet, sondern auch auf das sich zwischen den beiden Polen des Lebens bewegende Pendel zwischen Schwarz und Weiß, zwischen dem Sein und Nichts, zwischen An und Aus, zwischen 1 und 0.[5] In dramatischen, rhythmisch pulsierenden Bildern und Klängen entfaltet Seidel ein abstraktes Endzeitszenario. _grau wird dabei zur Projektionsfläche einer imaginären Wirklichkeit, welche die äußere Welt in die innere Vorstellungskraft der Betrachter holt und dort sinnlich ästhetisch resonieren lässt. Mithilfe der digitalen Technik erfindet Robert Seidel immer wieder ungesehene Formen und aufwühlende

---

1   Hartmut Böhme, *Das Licht als Medium der Kunst. Über Erfahrungsarmut und ästhetisches Gegenlicht in der technischen Zivilisation*, Manuskript der Antrittsvorlesung von Hartmut Böhme an der Humboldt-Universität zu Berlin am 2. November 1994, in: Schriften der HU Berlin, Heft 66, 1996, S. 3, abgerufen unter http://edoc.hu-berlin.de/humboldt-vl/boehme-hartmut/PDF/Boehme.pdf, S. 12 (Letzter Zugriff 27.11.2015).
2   Ulrike Pennewitz, *Hinter dem Vorhang der Dinge*, in: Robert Seidel. Folds, Ausstellungskatalog Lindenau-Museum Altenburg, Altenburg 2011, S. 11.
3   Insbesondere diese Sequenz lässt an die Heckscheibenkameraeinstellungen der amerikanischen Autofilme der 1970er Jahre denken, die diese Analogie zwischen dem Blick durch die Heckscheibe eines Autos und dem Kinoscreen gern herstellten und sich auf eine lange Kinotradition des *Phantom Rides* stützen. Bei jener „geisterhaften Fahrt" wurde die Kamera an einem bewegten Objekt, etwa einem Auto oder eine Lokomotive befestigt und so eine für den Betrachter ungewohnte Perspektive als filmisches Mittel etabliert.
4   Ich verdanke diesen Hinweis Verena Krieger.
5   Pennewitz 2011, S. 11.

Bilder. Die abstrakten Filme folgen dabei ihren eigenen Gesetzen und weisen Bezüge zur Realität auf, gleichwohl sie einem schöpferischen Geist, einer ästhetischen Welt der Imagination entspringen.

_grau (2004), S. 84–89

I.

Seidels Bilder sind allesamt am Computer konstruiert. Sein Ausgangsmaterial entstammt zwar häufig der Natur und ist seinem Interesse für ihre Komplexität, Formenvielfalt, prozessualen Verläufe, Ordnungen und physikalischen Gesetze geschuldet, dennoch sind seine Bilder rein erfunden: modelliert, errechnet, abstrakt. Seidel gehört zu einer Künstlergeneration, die nicht nur seit dem Kindesalter mit technischen Medien und deren mannigfaltigen Möglichkeiten aufgewachsen ist, sondern diese auch nutzt, um der Natur entliehene Strukturen in digitale Formen zu verwandeln und zu einem eigenen Bildkosmos zu verdichten. Dabei wird die innere, meist unsichtbare Schönheit der Gegenstände dargestellt, sodass die Naturerfahrung in eine digital-abstrakte Bildlichkeit transformiert wird und somit in einer neuen ästhetischen Dimension hervortritt. In der Überlagerung und Verschachtelung amorpher Bild-Ton-Gefüge lässt Seidel dabei neuartige Wahrnehmungsräume entstehen. Er stützt sich auf naturwissenschaftliche Verfahren, die für das Auge normalerweise unsichtbare Strukturen freilegen, und offenbart den Betrachtern damit einen artifiziellen Blick auf die Schönheit der Methoden und die Erhabenheit der Natur.

Seine Begeisterung für organische Formen, natürliche Phänomene und zeitliche Entwicklungen resultiert aus seiner langen Beschäftigung mit der Biologie.[6] Bevor Robert Seidel Mediengestaltung an der Bauhaus-Universität in Weimar studierte, widmete er sich zeitweise einem Biologiestudium. Dort vertiefte er sich in die abstrahierenden, das heißt errechneten Bilder der Wissenschaft, die abseits der Kunst eine eigene Bildästhetik und Semiotik besitzen. Diese Wissenschaftsbilder dienten ihm als Ausgangspunkt für Computeranimationen, in denen er Forschungsergebnisse visualisierte und teilweise in Bewegung versetzte. Dabei stellte er fest, dass seine Faszination weniger der exakten Visualisierung der Daten, sondern vielmehr ihren Brüchen und Fehlern galt. In Folge adaptierte er die bildgebenden Programme aus Medizin und Biologie für seine Kunst, welche ihm ein unermessliches Konfigurations- und Möglichkeitsfeld neuartiger Bilder zur Verfügung stellen. Gleichzeitig verdeutlicht Seidel die abstrakte Logik der Rechenmaschinen und macht damit abstraktes logisches Denken im Allgemeinen sichtbar: Jedes digitale Bild ist letztlich die mehrfache Übersetzung eines Programmiercodes.

Seidel kreiert somit Arbeiten an der Schnittstelle von Experimentalfilm, Computeranimation, Wissenschaft und Technik. Im Gegensatz zu vielen Werken der Videokunst folgt er keiner Narration und ist trotzdem einer kohärenten Bildlogik verpflichtet. Seine Bilder sind keine Abbilder der Wirklichkeit, sondern „digitale Manifestationen"[7], die der Imaginationskraft des Künstlers entspringen. Während man in ihnen Spuren der Natur und des Gegenständlichen zu erkennen meint, bleiben sie trotzdem abstrakt. Doch gleichwohl sie keine Geschichten erzählen, sie weder naturalistisch, noch realistisch sind, negieren sie das Figurative nicht. Vielmehr sind sie Erweiterungen der Realität, in der die Möglichkeiten einer digitalen Welt und damit anders gewichtete Wahrscheinlichkeiten des Jetzt formuliert werden. Seidels Bilder und Formen überwinden somit gleichzeitig die Abstraktion, denn sie lassen Assoziationen an Erlebtes und Gesehenes zu. Seine Arbeiten schwanken grundsätzlich zwischen emotionaler Erfahrbarkeit und mehrdeutiger Abstraktion.

Seidel nutzt den Computer als kreatives Werkzeug, das in der Lage ist, über die physikalischen Gesetze und Grenzen der Materie hinweg, artifizielle

6 Siehe dazu das Interview mit Robert Seidel in diesem Band: Claudia Tittel, *Im Universum digitaler Bilder. Interview mit Robert Seidel,* in: Robert Seidel. LUX AETERNA. Videoinstallationen, Filme und Zeichnungen, Ausstellungskatalog Kunstverein Gera e.V. und Museum für Angewandte Kunst Gera, Jena 2016, S. 60.

7 Robert Seidel, *Falten,* in: Robert Seidel. Folds, Ausstellungskatalog Lindenau-Museum Altenburg, Altenburg 2011, S. 48.

Gewebe, virtuelle Skulpturen sowie immersive Landschaften zu entwerfen und damit die künstlerischen Ausdrucksmöglichkeiten fundamental zu erweitern.[8] Ebene für Ebene schichtet Seidel mithilfe des Digital Compositing [Digitales Zusammensetzen] verschiedene, einzeln hergestellte computergenerierte Bildelemente zu abstrakten Vorstellungswelten.[9] Der Computer bietet ihm ein weites Spektrum an Möglichkeiten, in denen ein neuer Abstraktionsgrad des Realen erst denkbar wird. Seidel hat somit nicht nur die unabdingbare Vergegenständlichung und Repräsentation der Welt hinter sich gelassen, sondern gleichsam die Abstraktion selbst. In seinen Filmen verliert sich unser Blick in Strukturen, die zwischen Fläche und Tiefe, Gegenstand und Idee, der Zukunft und Vergangenheit changieren. Sie können als Materialausschüttungen der digitalen Welt verstanden werden, die Zuschreibungen infrage stellen und neue Denkweisen formen. Es entstehen illusionistische Licht- und Schattenräume sowie imaginäre Wirklichkeiten, die vielfältige Assoziationsräume bieten und im Geist der Betrachter vollendet werden sollen.[10] Seidels synthetische Arbeiten entwerfen luzide Welten und erweitern damit das Feld der Kunst, aber auch der Maschine. Wie in anderen Werken abstrakter Kunst gehorchen seine Bilder eigenen Gesetzen und überwinden dabei die materielle Formensprache.[11]

In diesem Sinne steht Robert Seidel auch einem der Urväter der abstrakten Malerei Wassily Kandinsky nahe, der in seinen Bildern geistige Prozesse darzustellen versuchte. In seinem als Manifest verfassten Buch *Über das Geistige in der Kunst* von 1911 rechtfertigte er eine abstrakte Bildsprache als genuine Form des Denkens.[12] Doch während Kandinsky und die frühen modernen Abstrakten den Gegenstand überwinden und sich dabei von jedem Materialismus lösen wollten, sind Seidels Bilder von vornherein immateriell, aus Codes und Daten bestehend und somit „reine Illusionen".[13] Erst als Projektionen auf einer Oberfläche oder als Lichtschein auf einem Bildschirm werden Seidels Arbeiten sicht- und greifbar – materiell sind sie damit jedoch noch nicht.[14] Das, was dem Licht als vielleicht abstraktesten aller Bildmedien zugeschrieben wird, kann hier erfahren werden: Das Eintauchen in eine Welt, die nicht der Funktionalität oder dem Mimetischen, sondern der ästhetischen Erfahrung verpflichtet ist.[15]

II.

Wenn noch vor dem Beginn der Abstraktion in der Kunst Wilhelm Worringer 1907 in *Abstraktion und Einfühlung*[16] die Verbindung von Abstrakten und Imaginierten in der emotionalen Vorstellungswelt der Künstler, das heißt in der reinen Imagination verortete, dann sind diese Beobachtungen nicht nur auf die abstrakte Malerei der Moderne – auch Kasimir Malewitsch verstand die Abstraktion 1927 als „Gestaltwerdung der Empfindung"[17] – sondern rund hundert Jahre später auch auf Seidels Arbeiten übertragbar. Ausgangspunkt vieler Arbeiten Seidels sind häufig Assoziationen und Emotionen, die er in Skizzen erstmals materialisiert und später zu synthetischen Bildern verdichtet.[18] In *E3* (2002) hat er Gouachen, die als Tagebucheintragungen während seines dreimonatigen Aufenthalts in England entstanden sind, in einen digitalen Fluss gebracht. In chromatischen Fortschreitungen und Auflösungen werden die malerischen Sequenzen zu pulsierenden Mutationen in Rot und Schwarz.[19] Die fließenden Bilder sind nicht nur Ausdruck des Innenlebens des Künstlers, sondern visualisieren in abstrakter Form sein Leben in einer fremden Umgebung: Von den ersten Erkundungen, der Neugier auf andere Menschen, den schönen Tagen bis zu den traurigen Stunden kann der Betrachter

---

8 Robert Seidel, *Aftershock into Today,* in: Cindy Keefer und Jaap Guldemond (Hg.), Oskar Fischinger 1900-1967. Experiments in Cinematic Abstraction, Ausstellungskatalog EYE Filmmuseum, Amsterdam / Center for Visual Music, Los Angeles 2013, S. 224.
9 Zsuzsanna Kiràly und Daniel Ebner, *Interview mit David OReilly und Robert Seidel,* in: Revolver. Zeitschrift für Film, Heft 29/2013, S. 46-71, S. 48.
10 Pennewitz 2011, S. 10.
11 Brigitte Oetker, *Vorwort,* in: Friedrich Meschede (Hg.), Etwas von Etwas. Abstrakte Kunst, Jahresring 52, Jahrbuch für moderne Kunst, Köln 2005, S. 5.
12 Wassily Kandinsky, *Über das Geistige in der Kunst* (1911), Bern 1980.
13 Pennewitz 2011, S. 10.
14 Während Licht die Basis aller Bildmedien bildet, doch üblicherweise Licht und Medien getrennten Systematiken angehören, wird durch die Video- und Filmkunst selbst Licht in Form von Helligkeit erzeugt. Videokunst ist somit immer auch Lichtkunst. Insbesondere in Seidels ortsspezifischen Videoinstallationen, in denen ein neues Bild-Raum-Gefüge hergestellt wird, tritt dieser Aspekt deutlich hervor – hier wird Raum sowohl direkt als auch indirekt durch Licht geformt. Vergleiche dazu auch den Aufsatz von Joost Rekveld, *Betrachter im Orbit,* S. 52
15 Böhme 1996, S. 4.
16 Wilhelm Worringer, *Abstraktion und Einfühlung. Ein Beitrag zur Stilpsychologie* (1907), Amsterdam 1996.
17 Kasimir Malewitsch, *Die gegenstandslose Welt* (1927), Mainz 1980.
18 Siehe hierzu auch das Interview mit Robert Seidel im Katalog: Tittel 2016, S. 60.
19 Leah Ollmann, *A fluid stream of consciousness,* in: Los Angeles Times, 29. April 2011, S. 16.

diese nun zeitlich komprimiert nachempfinden. Ereignisse fließen ineinander, verschmelzen, teilen sich und lösen sich wieder auf. Man könnte meinen, Seidels Filme seien animierte, abstrakt-ephemere Gemälde, ohne endgültige bildnerische Manifestationen zu sein.[20] *E3* entwickelt sich fortwährend weiter – einem gedrehten Unendlichzeichen gleich: ∞.

Seidels Arbeiten erinnern stärker an Malerei als an computergenerierte Bilder. Während die Malerei jedoch statisch ist, versucht der Künstler „nicht deren Endzustand, sondern die verschiedenen Stadien ihrer Manifestationen festzuhalten: das Ringen mit jedem Strich, das Auffasern und Verästeln in komplexe Gespinste oder das Absterben ganzer Verzweigungen."[21] Seine computeranimierten Malereien, Figurationen und Modellierungen füllen dabei nicht nur eine Bildebene, sondern können aneinandergereiht, kontinuierlich verändert, in einen Fluss versetzt und in seinen Installationen sogar von allen Seiten betrachtet werden. So verschmelzen in ihnen die auf Flüchtigkeit und Immaterialität beruhenden digitalen Medien mit der Authentizität der Malerei. In seinen Filmen lässt Seidel komplexe Formen und zarte Gebilde entstehen, fragmentierte Körper, Organe, Gewebe, die sich durch den Raum bewegen. Er vermischt sowohl Farben als auch Formen, digitalen Flüssigkeiten gleich, jedoch ohne an die Welt der Physik gebunden zu sein. So erscheinen viele seiner Werke als malerische Impressionen.[22]

chiral (2010/2011), S. 100–105

Mit *chiral* (2010), einer Arbeit, die er erstmals im Museum of Contemporary Art in Taipeh zeigte, hat Seidel die Zweidimensionalität der Bildfläche verlassen und seine Arbeit in Zeit und Raum überführt. Ausgangspunkt dieser Arbeit war seine Beschäftigung mit der asiatischen Kunst der Kalligrafie. Aus handgeschöpftem Papier formte er fragile Papiergeflechte und ließ sie von der Decke herabhängend mit den fließenden Lichtbildern verschmelzen. Dadurch verlieh er den zwischen dem Moment- und Dauerhaften oszillierenden Eigenschaften jener Schriftkunst eine adäquate Form. Für die Adaption von *chiral* in Gera hat er die ursprüngliche Papierskulptur durch eine Wand aus aufgeworfenem Kunststoffoberflächen ersetzt, die wie eine monumentale weiße Wolke in den Raum ragt. Wenn nun die ersten feinen Linien auf die Projektionsfläche treffen und sich ihre Strukturen immer weiter verdichten, scheint der gesamte Raum zu vibrieren. Die zuvorderst an Malerei erinnernden Projektionsbilder werden dabei nicht nur von der Oberfläche reflektiert, sodass das Weiß der „Wolke" noch leuchtender erscheint, sondern mit jedem Bild verändert sich auch die Materialität der Projektionsskulptur selbst. Wenn rotes Licht auf die Bildfläche trifft, sich auf sie ergießt, werden Assoziationen an Blutkreisläufe aber auch an Kriegsbilder oder Schlachtenpanoramen geweckt – die „Wolke" wird zum blutdurchtränkten Textil. Wenn Seidel hingegen zarte Liniencluster über die Oberfläche gleiten lässt, wird sie zu einem Strukturfeld, auf dem sich asiatische Kalligrafiekunst mit Einflüssen der europäischen Malerei des Informel mischen.[23] Insbesondere Künstler des Informel haben das „Prinzip der Formlosigkeit im Spannungsfeld von Formauflösung und Formwerdung"[24], das auch die Arbeiten Seidels auszeichnet, zu ihrer Methode erklärt.

III.
Seidels abstrakte Bildwelten oszillieren zwischen dem Materiellen und Immateriellen und sind dabei getragen von der Faszination für luzide Lichtbilder. Diese bringen in ihrer flüchtigen Form nicht nur in jedem Moment etwas Neues hervor, sondern ermöglichen auch die Verwandlung von Räumen in abstrakte Illusionsgefüge. War vor allem mit der

20 Ollmann 2011, S. 16.
21 Seidel 2011, S. 48.
22 Ollmann 2011, S. 16.
23 Seidel selbst hat diese Verwandtschaft angedeutet, etwa im Künstlerstatement auf seiner Homepage: http://www.robertseidel.com (Letzter Zugriff 20.12.2015).
24 Rolf Wedewer, *Die Malerei des Informel. Weltverlust und Ich-Behauptung,* München/Berlin 2007, S. 15 f.
25 Zu Beginn des Films standen deshalb auch weniger narrative Strukturen, denn „Schauwerte" des Kinos im Zentrum. Den Künstlern ging es um die Eigenschaften und künstlerischen Formen, das heißt die Lichtspiele auf der Oberfläche und damit die neuen technischen Möglichkeiten des Films selbst. Tom Gunning hat deshalb auch den frühen Film als „Cinema of Attraction" und ihn im Gegensatz zu anderen Kritikern nicht als primitiv, sondern als Spektakel mit hohem Schauwert bezeichnet. Siehe Tom Gunning, *The Cinema of Attractions. Early Film, Its Spectator and the Avant-Garde,* in: Thomas Elsaesser (Hg.), Early Cinema. Space, Frame, Narrative, Amsterdam 1990, S. 56-62.

Erfindung des Kinematografen durch die Brüder Lumière der Film zu einem wichtigen (Licht)Medium geworden, mit dem die Wirklichkeit neuartig abgebildet werden konnte, so begeisterte vor allem die mit dem neuen Medium Film verbundene Lichttechnik die Künstler und regte sie zum Experimentieren an.[25] Licht und Bewegung entwickelten sich zu entscheidenden Kategorien einer neuen ästhetischen Erfahrung der Moderne, die die Künstler verwendeten, um die neue Welt und das moderne Leben zu kommentieren. So gelang es dem Bauhauskünstler László Moholy-Nagy mit seinem *Licht-Raum-Modulator* den Raum mithilfe von Lichteffekten zu erweitern und visuell zu verwandeln, indem er verschiedene Formen, Farben, Schatten und Bewegungen an die Wände projizierte. Auch in Seidels neueren Arbeiten durchqueren die digitalen Lichtbilder den Raum. Seit einigen Jahren werden seine Werke nicht mehr nur als Einkanal-Projektion gezeigt und somit nicht mehr durch einen Bildschirm oder eine Leinwand begrenzt, sondern er verschränkt sie mit skulpturalen Elementen im Raum. Im Ausstellungsraum und an den verschiedenen Oberflächen wandern die Bilder entlang. Sie brechen sich an der Decke, am Boden und den Wänden oder an den zu einer großen Skulptur aufgebäumten Kunststoffflächen. Sie schweben durch den Bildraum, drehen und neigen sich vermeintlich und verbinden sich zu neuen Strukturen, um sich erneut zu vermischen und im nächsten Moment wieder aufzulösen. Wie zuvor in seinen Filmen wird nun der Raum zu einer abstrakt-digitalen Landschaft, zu einem Bild- und Illusionsraum, in dem immer wieder neue formale Ordnungen und Ansichten des Digitalen hervorgebracht werden und sich mit der Realität reiben. Wie die frühen Experimente der kinematografischen Abstraktion, zum Beispiel von Oskar Fischinger, Hans Richter oder Viking Eggeling, die die abstrakte Malerei um eine zeitliche Ebene erweitern wollten, changieren auch Seidels Filme zwischen Imagination und Realität. In seiner Projektionsskulptur *tearing shadows* [zerreißende Schatten] werden die Lichtbilder zu einem verschachtelten Schattenbild, das sich mit verschiedenen Wirklichkeitsebenen verschränkt. Bestehend aus handgeschnittenen Kunststofffolien wirkt die Skulptur wie ein aus Seidels Filmen in der Realität manifestiertes Geflecht.

Diesem raumzeichnerischen Gespinst wohnt bereits aufgrund seiner fragilen Gestalt Bewegung inne. Wie die Mobiles Alexander Calders kann sie ein leichter Luftzug zum Schwingen bringen. Doch diese aus der Fragilität geborene Anspannung der Installationen wird noch weiter gesteigert: Schattenbilder gleiten über die Oberfläche, in schnellen Rhythmen werden Lichtblitze gesetzt, sodass es scheint, als würden sich die Strukturen tatsächlich bewegen. Gleichzeitig werfen die fragilen Gestalten selbst Schatten an die Wände und den Boden und zeichnen somit zweidimensionale Schattenbilder im Raum. So werden diese Schattengeflechte von anderen künstlich erzeugten Projektionsschatten überlagert und es entsteht ein Wechselspiel aus Wirklichkeit und Imagination, aus Wahrnehmungs- und Realitätsebenen, das den Prozess der „Entstehung, Veränderung und Aneignung nicht nur zu einer rein gedanklichen Erfahrung [...], sondern zu einem visuellen Erleben" werden lässt.[26]

tearing shadows (2013/2015), S. 124–127

IV.
Trotz der technischen Entwicklung und der wissenschaftlichen Erkenntnisse hat sich die Faszination für das Licht über Jahrhunderte erhalten, auch wenn sich sein Wesen änderte: Durch die Nutzbarmachung der Elektrizität und vor allem die Erfindung der Glühbirne, die man Thomas Alva Edison zuschreibt, war Licht nicht mehr nur ein Naturphänomen, sondern wurde zu einem eigenem Medium und veränderte die Lebenswelt der Menschheit. Die Nacht wurde nun zum Tag, die Stadt verwandelte sich bei zunehmender Dunkelheit in ein großes Lichtermeer und die Straßen und Häuser strahlten in neuem Glanz.[27] Während die einen die Aura des künstlichen Lichts bejubelten, reagierten andere, wie zum Beispiel der Soziologe und Filmtheoretiker Siegfried Kracauer kritisch auf diesen Lichterregen:

---

26 Robert Seidel, *grapheme – Raumzeichnungen und Projektion im Museum Wiesbaden,* Konzepttext zur Installation (2013), Archiv Museum Wiesbaden, unveröffentlicht.

27 Siehe Wolfgang Schivelbusch, *Lichtblicke. Zur Geschichte der künstlichen Helligkeit,* Frankfurt am Main 1986.

„Das Licht blendet eher, als daß [sic!] es erhellte, und vielleicht dient die Fülle des Lichts, die sich neuerdings über unsere Großstädte ergießt, nicht zuletzt einer Vermehrung der Dunkelheit."[28] Angesichts der Ubiquität der vielfältigen Lichtspektakel in den Städten durch architektonische Inszenierungen, riesenhafte Leuchtreklamen und Medienfassaden scheint diese Kritik vor allem auf heutige urbane Szenarien zuzutreffen. Mit der fortschreitenden Technisierung und digitalen Revolution hat dabei auch die Lichtmetaphorik einen neuen Höhepunkt erreicht: Aufgrund seiner Immaterialität und Ephemerität ist Licht zum sichtbaren Kennzeichen der digitalen Welt geworden.

scrape (2011), S. 110–113

Doch obwohl Seidel mit denselben technischen Lichtmitteln arbeitet, schafft er in den pulsierenden Städten Räume der Entschleunigung und Kontemplation.[29] Indem er die digitale Technik umkodiert und sie als Möglichkeitsfeld zur Generierung neuer (Licht)Bilder und Erfahrungen einsetzt, werden seine Arbeiten zu Reflexionen des Heute. Er untersucht dabei grundverschiedene Arten von Licht und reflektiert gleichsam die Möglichkeiten der technischen Bildmedien.[30] Dabei sind seine temporären Bilder ebenso aufsehenerregend wie faszinierend. Doch sie arbeiten weder mit schnellen Bild- oder Szenenwechseln, noch sind sie narrativ oder aufdringlich, sondern sie zeigen eine Abstraktion, die die Betrachter sinnlich überwältigt. Beim Betrachten der Bilder ist man in den fragilen Konstellationen, den virtuellen Skulpturen und den sich in endloser Metamorphose befindlichen Strukturen gefangen. Die Bilder entfalten einen Sog, dem wir uns als Betrachter nur schwer entziehen können. Die fließenden Formen entwickeln eine intensive Schönheit und sind in ihrer Referenzlosigkeit Inbegriff des Erhabenen. Sie brechen sich auf den unterschiedlichsten Oberflächen und überformen sie mit Licht. Mithilfe der digitalen Technik hat Seidel Räume der reinen Wahrnehmung geschaffen, in denen Licht, Farbe, Klang und Bewegung alle Sinne des Betrachters ansprechen sollen. Trotz ihrer Wandelbarkeit hat der Künstler Bilder für die Ewigkeit geschaffen. Bilder, deren Wirkmacht und Bedeutung auch in hundert Jahren ihre Geltung nicht verloren haben werden. Es sind Bilder, Resonanzen des ewigen Lichts – LUX AETERNA.

28 Siegfried Kracauer, *Asyl für Obdachlose* (1929), in: ders., Die Angestellten, Frankfurt am Main 1971, S. 91-101, hier S. 93.
29 Seidel realisiert seit 2007 Projection Mappings im öffentlichen Raum oder bespielt Medienfassaden mit seinen Filmen. Er versucht dabei dem kommerzialisierten Stadtraum andere Bilder gegenüberzustellen. Siehe wiederum sein Interview in diesem Band, S. 60.
30 Robert Seidel, *Penetrating Surfaces,* in: filmmuseum, Mai/Juni 2014, Broschüre des Filmmuseums Wien 2014, S. 32-35, hier S. 32.

LUX AETERNA.
Robert Seidel's Digital Image Worlds between Light Metaphors, Abstraction and the Invention of Nature
—
Claudia Tittel

Emerging from the darkness, a fog of colored light permeates the rectangular screen. Incorporeal, yet clearly visible areas and lines made up of green, pink, blue, and yellow rays of light make their way across a diffuse space, which almost dissolves into blackness. Not concealing their immateriality, the diaphanous structures unfold across the whole spectrum of light, as if refracted through a shattered pane of glass. They show nothing and let nothing become visible – except for themselves. The lights form virtual, intangible textures, layers, structural components. They span the room like abstract webs, unpredictably change directions, and are finally swallowed by harsh sunlight. What has just been seen dissolves like a dream sequence, letting the iconographic side of light come to the fore.

_grau (2004), p. 84–89

In order to let the impact and the shock of an unrepresentable event become visible, Seidel, in his film _grau (2004), draws on the metaphorical meaning of light as a medium which luminously appears and penetrates, in which fictive as well as real worlds meet. Seidel's starting sequence is evocative of light falling through the painted glass windows of a Gothic cathedral, immersing the church's interior in glorious colors and simultaneously illuminating it from within. In the Middle Ages, light as a transcendent medium – ephemeral, flowing, and translucent, defined by momentary beauty and everlasting change – was not merely equated with the supernatural and the divine, but was rather the epitome of the Absolute.[1] As such, absolute light is also deployed in the dark scenery at the beginning of _grau in order to portray the "incomprehensibility of the archaic feelings of a state of shock."[2] What appears, as well as what disappears; the visible and simultaneously invisible; the tangible and, equally, the intangible, are always dealt with on an aesthetically abstract level, which produces no concrete imagery, but creates images that are all the stronger for their emotional impact. Here, Seidel attempts to describe a condition oscillating between recollection and the future. In this process, he finalizes the individual shards of thought arising from the memories of a car accident.[3]

In this light-filled scene, which appears to take place in the dark primeval space of the ether, the word "_grau" quickly flickers in the center of the screen. Afterwards, the screen expands, changing from a cinemascope format to the less dramatic 16:9 ratio.[4] The ethereal, color-woven beauty of the immaterial light withdraws from the darkness and is subsequently replaced by a bright white pictorial space, through which gray-black amorphous masses of tissue flee towards the upper edge of the screen. These congeal into bonelike entities, seemingly bound by barbed wire, on which thin threads, like stripped nerves, proliferate. The bone formations continue to grow, becoming crystalline structures, ramifying and later dissolving into white nothingness. They return as formless painterly textures, which are just as vague at one moment as the associations they next give rise to are concrete, conjuring up images of biological microstructures such as chromosomes, bones, roots, or even deformed metal parts. Continually transforming, the amorphous objects float across the screen and appear to visualize the title of the work: as indifferent, gray, constantly-mutating rhizomes, they not only refer to gray as the color that implies the mysterious and the hidden, they also point towards the pendulum swinging between both poles of life, between black and white, between being and nothingness, between on and off, between 1 and 0.[5] In dramatic, rhythmically-pulsing images and sounds, Seidel develops an abstract doomsday scenario. In the process, _grau becomes the projection device of an imaginary reality

1 Hartmut Böhme, *Das Licht als Medium der Kunst. Über Erfahrungsarmut und ästhetisches Gegenlicht in der technischen Zivilisation,* manuscript of Hartmut Böhme's inaugural lecture at the Humboldt-University Berlin on November, 2nd, 1994, in: Schriften der HU Berlin, issue 66, 1996, p. 3, http://edoc.hu-berlin.de/humboldt-vl/boehme-hartmut/PDF/Boehme.pdf, p. 12 (last accessed 27.11.2015).
2 Ulrike Pennewitz, *Behind the curtain of things,* in: Robert Seidel. Folds, Exhibition Catalogue Lindenau-Museum Altenburg, Altenburg 2011, p. 15.
3 This sequence in particular is evocative of 1970s American car movies and rear-window camera placement, which built on the analogy – based on a long cinematic tradition of phantom rides – between looking at a movie screen and looking through a car's rear window. For each "phantom ride," the camera would be attached to a moving object such as an automobile or locomotive, thus establishing a novel perspective as a filmic device.
4 My gratitude goes to Verena Krieger for this reference.
5 Pennewitz 2011, p. 15.

which summons the outer world into the inner imagination of the viewer, letting it resonate both sensually and aesthetically. Aided by digital technology, Robert Seidel continually creates unseen forms and stirring images. The abstract films follow their own logic, exhibiting relations to reality, as well as springing from a creative spirit and aesthetic world of the imagination.

I.

All of Seidel's images are constructed on the computer. His source material, however, often originates in nature; this is due to his interest in natural complexity, its diversity of forms, its processual development, hierarchies, and physical laws. His images, however, are nonetheless clearly imaginary: modeled, calculated, abstract. Seidel belongs to a generation of artists who not only grew up from an early age with technological media and their manifold possibilities, but who also use them in order to transform structures borrowed from nature into digital forms, condensing them into their individual visual cosmos. In doing so, the inner and often unseen beauty of the object is depicted, with the result that the experience of nature is transformed into digital abstract imagery and consequently emerges in a new aesthetic dimension. By superimposing and interlacing amorphous images and sounds, Seidel gives form to new spaces of perception. He adopts scientific procedures that expose structures that are normally invisible to the naked eye, thereby revealing an artificial glimpse of the beauty of these procedures and nature's sublimity.

His enthusiasm for organic forms, natural phenomena and temporal developments is the result of his long engagement with biology.[6] Before Robert Seidel studied media design at the Bauhaus University in Weimar, he temporarily devoted himself to the study of biology. He became immersed in the abstract – that is to say calculated – images of science, which possess their own visual aesthetics and semiotics which are independent of art. For him, these scientific images served as a starting-point for computer animations in which he visualized the results of research, partially translating them into motion. In the process, he discovered that his fascination was less focused on the exact visualization of the data than it was on its fractures and errors. He subsequently adapted imaging software from the fields of medicine and biology for his art, which placed an immeasurable range of possibilities and configurations of novel images at his disposal. At the same time, Seidel illustrates the abstract logic of computing devices, visualizing abstract logical thought: Every digital image is ultimately the multiple translation of a programming code.

Seidel creates works on the cutting edge of experimental film, computer animation, science and technology. In contrast to many works of video art, his do not follow a narrative; nonetheless, he is committed to a coherent pictorial logic. His images are not depictions of reality but are rather "digital manifestations" with the artist's imagination as their source.[7] While it might appear that traces of nature and of representation are detectable in the images, they nevertheless remain abstract. However, even though they do not tell any stories, and even though they are neither naturalistic nor realistic, they do not negate the figurative. Rather, they are an expansion of reality, in which the possibilities of a digital world and, with it, differently-evaluated probabilities of the now are formulated. Seidel's images and forms thus simultaneously surmount abstraction because they allow for associations of events which have been experienced and seen. His works fundamentally fluctuate between emotional experientiality and polysemic abstraction.

Seidel uses the computer as a creative tool, enabling him to transcend the physical laws and limits of matter and to create artificial textures and virtual sculptures, as well as immersive landscapes, thereby fundamentally expanding the possibilities of artistic expression.[8] Layer by layer, aided by digital compositing, Seidel superimposes different individually-produced, computer-generated elements onto abstract imaginary worlds.[9] The computer offers him a broad spectrum of possibilities in which a new degree of abstraction of the real ultimately becomes conceivable. Seidel, therefore, leaves not only unavoidable objectification and representation of the world behind, but also, so to speak, abstraction itself. In his films, our gaze gets lost in structures that oscillate between surface and depth, object and idea, future and past.

6 See the interview in this volume: Claudia Tittel, *In the Universe of Digital Images: Robert Seidel interviewed by Claudia Tittel,* in: Robert Seidel. LUX AETERNA. Videoinstallationen, Filme und Zeichnungen, Exhibition Catalogue Kunstverein Gera e.V. and Museum für Angewandte Kunst Gera, Jena 2016, p. 68.
7 Robert Seidel, *Folds,* in: Robert Seidel. Folds, Exhibition Catalogue Lindenau-Museum Altenburg, Altenburg 2011, p. 49.
8 Robert Seidel, *Aftershock into Today,* in: Cindy Keefer and Jaap Guldemond (Ed.), Oskar Fischinger 1900-1967. Experiments in Cinematic Abstraction, Exhibition Catalogue EYE Filmmuseum, Amsterdam/Center for Visual Music, Los Angeles 2013, p. 224.
9 Zsuzsanna Kiràly and Daniel Ebner, *Interview with David OReilly and Robert Seidel,* in: Revolver. Zeitschrift für Film, Vol. 29, 2013, p. 46-71, p. 48.

They can be understood as material discharges of the digital world, which call attributions into question and shape new ways of reading the world. Illusionistic light and shadow spaces emerge, as do imaginary realities, offering manifold spaces of association to be perfected in the mind of the beholder.[10] Seidel's synthetic works create lucid worlds and thus expand not only the realm of art, but also that of the machine. As in other works of abstract art, his images adhere to their own laws and transcend tangible formal vocabulary.[11]

In this sense, Seidel is also close to one of the originators of abstract art, Wassily Kandinsky, who attempted to portray cognitive processes in his images. In his 1911 book *Concerning the Spiritual in Art*, written as a manifesto, he justifies an abstract visual language as a genuine form of thought.[12] However, while Kandinsky and the early modern abstractionists wanted to overcome the object and thus free themselves from any sort of materialism, Seidel's images, consisting of codes and data, are immaterial from the outset and are thus "pure illusions."[13] Seidel's works are first visible and tangible as projections on a surface or as light shining on a screen – however, they are still not material.[14] That quality ascribed to light, as perhaps the most abstract of all visual media, can be experienced here: the immersion into a world not bound to functionality or the mimetic, but rather to aesthetic experience.[15]

II.

In *Abstraction and Empathy* (1907)[16], before the advent of abstraction in art, Wilhelm Worringer located the connection between the abstract and the imagined in the emotional conceptual world, that is, within the pure imagination of the artist. These observations are not only transferrable to the abstract painting of modernism – in 1927 Kazimir Malevich understood abstraction as the "manifestation of perception"[17] – but also nearly a hundred years later to Seidel's works. Associations and emotions are often the point of origin for many of his works, which he first materializes in sketches and later solidifies into synthetic images.[18] In *E3* (2002), he created a digital flow of gouaches that came into being as journal entries during a three-month residence in England. In chromatic progressions and dissolutions, the visual sequences become pulsing mutations in red and black.[19] The flowing images are not just an expression of the artist's inner life, but also, in an abstract form, visualize his life in a foreign environment: From the first explorations and inquisitiveness about others, to beautiful days and gloomy hours, the viewer can experience these events in a time-lapse. Occurrences flow into one another, coalesce, are disrupted and dissolve again. One could say that Seidel's films are animated, abstract-ephemeral paintings without being conclusive visual manifestations.[20] *E3* perpetually progresses – like a rotated infinity symbol: ∞.

E3 (2002), p. 82–83

Seidel's works are more evocative of painting than they are of computer-generated images. While painting however, is static, the artist attempts not to "capture their end-state so much as different stages of their manifestations: the wrestling with each line, the fraying and foliating into complex webs or the dying off of entire ramifications."[21] Seidel's computer-animated paintings, figurations and shapings do not, in the process, fill only one pictorial plane, but can be connected, continually altered, set into flow, and

10 Pennewitz 2011, p. 14.
11 Brigitte Oetker, *Vorwort*, in: Friedrich Meschede (Ed.), Etwas von Etwas. Abstrakte Kunst, Jahresring 52, Jahrbuch für moderne Kunst, Cologne 2005, p. 5.
12 Wassily Kandinsky, *Über das Geistige in der Kunst* (1911), Bern 1980. English version: *Concerning the Spiritual in Art* (1911), Boston 2006.
13 Pennewitz 2011, p. 14.
14 While light provides the basis for all visual media, despite their customarily belonging to separate systems, light itself is created in the form of luminosity by video and cinematic art. This aspect clearly comes to the fore in Seidel's site-specific video installations, in which a new image-space framework is constructed; here space is directly and indirectly shaped by light. See also Joost Rekveld's essay *Viewer in Orbit*, p. 56.
15 Böhme 1996, p. 4.
16 Wilhelm Worringer, *Abstraktion und Einfühlung. Ein Beitrag zur Stilpsychologie* (1907), Amsterdam 1996. English version: *Abstraction and Empathy: A Contribution to the Psychology of Style* (1907), Chicago 1997.
17 Kasimir Malewitsch, *Die gegenstandslose Welt* (1927), Mainz 1980. English version: *The Non-Objective World* (1927), Mineola, NY, 2003.
18 See also the interview with Robert Seidel in this catalogue: Tittel 2016, p. 68.
19 Leah Ollmann, *A fluid stream of consciousness*, in: Los Angeles Times, 29. April 2011, p. 16.
20 Ollmann 2011, p. 16.
21 Seidel 2011, p. 49.

even observed from all sides in his installations. In this way, digital media, based on ephemerality and immateriality, melds with the authenticity of painting. In his films, Seidel lets complex forms and delicate structures come into being: fragmented bodies, organs, and tissues that range through space. He mixes colors as well as forms, resembling digital fluids, without, however, being bound to the world of physics. In this way, many of his works appear as painterly impressions.[22]

With *chiral* (2010), a work that he first exhibited in the Museum of Contemporary Art in Taipei, Seidel surmounted the two-dimensionality of the screen and transferred his work into time and space. The origin of this work was an engagement with the Asian art of calligraphy. He formed fragile nets from handmade paper and suspended them from the ceiling, letting them fuse with the flowing luminous imagery. He thereby lent adequate form to calligraphy, which oscillates between the momentary and the permanent. For the adaptation of *chiral* in Gera, he replaced the original paper sculpture with a wall of staggered plastic surfaces, which rises up in the room like a monumental white cloud. When the fine lines emerge on the projection surface and condense into structures, the whole room seems to vibrate. The projected images, reminiscent of painting, are thus not only reflected by the surface so that the white of the "cloud" appears yet more luminous, but the materiality of the projection sculpture itself also changes with every image. When red light strikes the screen and gushes onto it, associations of bloodstreams, or images of war and battlefield panoramas are aroused – the "cloud" becomes a blood-soaked textile. When Seidel, however, lets delicate clusters of lines glide across the surface, they become a structure field upon which Asian calligraphic art mixes with influences from European Informalist painting.[23] Informalist artists, in particular, declared their method to be "the principle of formlessness caught in an interplay between dissolution and morphogenesis," a principle which also characterizes Seidel's work.[24]

III.

Seidel's abstract pictorial worlds fluctuate between the material as well as the immaterial and are underpinned by a fascination with lucid light images. These images, in their fleeting form, not only create something unique at every moment, but also allow for the transformation of spaces into abstract illusionistic structures. If film, with the Lumière brothers' invention of the cinematograph, became an important (light) medium able to depict reality in a novel way, it above all inspired artists to experiment with the new lighting technologies.[25] Light and movement developed into crucial categories of a new aesthetic experience of modernity, which the artists used to comment on the new world and modern life. In this way, László Moholy-Nagy succeeded in using his *Light-Space-Modulator* to expand space with the aid of light effects, visually transforming it by projecting different forms, colors, shadows and movements onto the walls. In Seidel's more recent works, digital light images traverse the room as well. For some years, his works have ceased to be shown only as one-channel projections and have thus no longer been constrained by monitors or silver screens; rather he interweaves them with sculptural elements in the room. His images traverse the exhibition space and the various surfaces within it. They refract from the ceiling, the floor, and the walls, or from the plastic surfaces which gather together to form a large sculpture, which rises up in the room. They float through the pictorial space, seem to twist and incline, attaching themselves to new structures, and they intermingle anew before dissolving a moment later. Just as in his films, space becomes an abstract-digital landscape, a spatial and pictorial illusion in which new formal systems and viewpoints of the digital are constantly brought forth, encountering and grappling with reality. Like the early experiments of cinematic abstraction, for example those of Oskar Fischinger, Hans Richter and Viking Eggeling, who strove to expand abstract painting on a temporal level, Seidel's films also oscillate between imagination and reality. In his projection sculpture *tearing shadows* (2013), light images transform into an intricate shadow image that interlaces with various levels of reality. Consisting of hand-cut pieces of synthetic foil, the sculpture has the effect of a plexus from one of Seidel's films, manifested in reality.

---

22   Ollmann 2011, p. 16.
23   Seidel himself has suggested this affinity. See for example the artist statement on his homepage: http://www.robertseidel.com (last accessed 20.12.2015).
24   Rolf Wedewer, *Die Malerei des Informel. Weltverlust und Ich-Behauptung,* Munich/Berlin 2007, p. 15.
25   For this reason, at cinema's inception there were fewer narrative structures, since the "visual spectacle" of film was so highly valued. For artists, the qualities and artistic forms of film – the play of light on the surface and with it the new technological possibilities of film itself – were at stake. Tom Gunning thus characterizes early film as "the cinema of attractions," and, in contrast to other critics, sees it not as primitive, but as a highly-valued visual spectacle. See Tom Gunning, *The Cinema of Attractions. Early Film, Its Spectator and the Avant-Garde,* in: Thomas Elsaesser, Early Cinema. Space, Frame, Narrative, Amsterdam 1990, p. 56-62.

Movement already inheres in this sculpturally-drawn gossamer owing to its fragile form. Like Alexander Calder's mobiles, they can be swayed by a slight breeze. The tension of the installation, however, born of fragility, increases even more; silhouettes glide across the surface, and flashes of light are set to rapid rhythms, so that it appears as if the structures are actually moving. The fragile forms themselves simultaneously cast shadows on the walls and the floor, sketching two-dimensional shadow images in the space. These shadowy networks are overlaid with other artificially-created projected shadows. The result is an interplay of reality and imagination, of dimensions of perception and existence, which allows a process of "development, transformation and appropriation to become not only a purely theoretical, but also a visually lived experience."[26]

IV.

Despite technological developments and advances in scientific knowledge, the fascination with light has endured across centuries, even if its nature has changed. Through the harnessing of electricity and above all the invention of the light bulb, attributed to Thomas Alva Edison, light ceased to be simply a natural phenomenon, but became a medium in its own right and changed humankind's realm of experience. Night became day. As darkness encroached upon them, cities were transformed into huge seas of lights, streets and houses shone in the new splendor.[27] While some hailed the aura of artificial light, others, like the sociologist and film theorist Siegfried Kracauer, reacted critically towards the excitement surrounding light: "Light blinds more than it illuminates, and perhaps the abundance of light pouring out lately over our cities serves not least to increase the darkness."[28] With regard to the urban ubiquity of the variegated light spectacles formed by architectonic staging, giant neon signs and media façades, this critique seems, above all, to be relevant to modern-day urban scenarios. With advancing technologization and the digital revolution, the metaphor of light has reached a new pinnacle; owing to its immateriality and ephemerality, light has become a visual hallmark of the digital world.

However, although Seidel works with the same technological sources of light, he creates spaces of deceleration and contemplation within the pulsing cities.[29] By transcoding digital technology and deploying it as a field of possibility to generate new (light) imagery and experiences, his works become a reflection of today. He examines fundamentally different types of light and reflects, as it were, the potential of technological visual media.[30] His transitory images are as breathtaking as they are fascinating. Still, they neither operate with rapid image- or scene changes, nor are they narrative or intrusive; rather, they present an abstraction that sensually subdues the viewer. When contemplating the images, one is caught up in the fragile constellations, the virtual sculptures and the endlessly metamorphosing structures. The images create an undertow from which we, as viewers, can scarcely escape. The flowing forms generate an intense beauty and are, in their lack of referentiality, the epitome of the sublime. They collide with the most diverse surfaces and transform them with light. With the aid of digital technology, Seidel has created spaces of pure perception in which light, color, sound, and movement respond to all of the viewer's senses. Despite their mutability, the artist has created images for eternity, images whose potency and meaning will not have lost their validity a hundred years from now. They are images, resonances of eternal light – LUX AETERNA.

26 Robert Seidel, *grapheme – Raumzeichnungen und Projektion im Museum Wiesbaden,* concept paper about the installation (2013), Archive Museum Wiesbaden, unpublished.
27 See Wolfgang Schivelbusch, *Lichtblicke. Zur Geschichte der künstlichen Helligkeit,* Frankfurt am Main 1986. English version: *Disenchanted Night: The Industrialization of Light in the Nineteenth Century,* Los Angeles 1988.
28 Siegfried Kracauer, *Asyl für Obdachlose (1929),* in: Die Angestellten, Frankfurt am Main 1971, p. 91-101, p. 93. Translation taken from the English version: *Shelter for the Homeless,* in: The Salaried Masses, London/New York 1988, p. 88-95.
29 Seidel has been creating projection mappings in public space and projecting his films onto media façades since 2007. In these, he seeks to juxtapose commercialized urban spaces with alternative images. See the interview in this volume, p. 68.
30 Robert Seidel: *Penetrating Surfaces,* in: filmmuseum, May/June 2014, booklet of the Austrian Film Museum, Vienna 2014, p. 32-35, p. 32.

Betrachter im Orbit.
Zu Robert Seidels
Projektionskunst
—
Joost Rekveld

„Niemals sieht die Sonne einen Schatten", schreibt Leonardo da Vinci um 1500, als er die Umlaufbahnen von Sonne und Mond skizzierte. Eine Feststellung, die, leicht aus dem Kontext genommen und im poetischen Sinne interpretiert, jene Abflachung heraufbeschwört, sobald Lichtquelle und Betrachterstandpunkt genau übereinstimmen. Heute, ein halbes Jahrhundert nach dem Raumfahrtzeitalter, ist es nicht mehr schwer sich vorzustellen, wie die gesamte Erde einer vielfarbigen und flachen Scheibe gleicht – wenn man sie von jenem Stern aus betrachtet, der sie mit Energie versorgt.

Da Vincis Feststellung erinnert daran, dass zu seiner Zeit die Zentralperspektive, jene Kunst der Ausrichtung der Projektionspunkte auf den Betrachterstandpunkt, gerade erst erfunden worden war – eine Methode, mit der die Maler den dreidimensionalen Raum auf einer ebenen Fläche darstellen konnten. Ein perspektivisches Bild ist ein optischer Schnitt durch die Welt, welche in ein virtuelles Fenster eingeebnet wird und nur von einem Standpunkt aus korrekt gesehen werden kann. Ein gutes Jahrhundert später war die Projektionsgeometrie bereits vollständig verinnerlicht, sodass solcherart perspektivische Bilder auch mit ungewöhnlichen Blickwinkeln oder auf gewölbten Oberflächen – und nicht mehr nur auf flachen Wänden und Leinwänden – konstruiert werden konnten. Der französische Mönch Jean-François Niceron nahm diese Konstruktionsmöglichkeit als Ausgangspunkt für eine religiöse Kunst, welche die Nichtigkeit unserer Existenz betonen sollte, indem er die Vergänglichkeit der Bilder hervorhob, welche abhängig von unserem Blickwinkel erscheinen oder verschwinden. In seiner anamorphotischen Kunst sollte die Angleichung von Projektions- und Blickwinkel einer seltenen und erhabenen Erscheinung gleichen, die sich nur aus einem ganz bestimmten Betrachterstandpunkt auf das Fresko ergibt. Ein weiteres Jahrhundert später erreichten die anamorphotischen Bilder ihre Vervollkommnung in den spektakulären Visionen des Malers Andrea Pozzo, die er für die Deckengewölbe von Sant'Ignazio in Rom schuf.

In unserer Zeit sehen wir perspektivische Darstellungen nicht mehr nur als in Farbe ausgeführte geometrische Verfahren, sondern als die Ausgabeleistung von Apparaten, die umherbewegt werden können. In der Virtuellen Realität ist beispielsweise das Zentrum der Projektion portabel, sodass es konstant mit dem Standpunkt des Betrachters, welcher sich ebenfalls während der Navigation durch den virtuellen Raum frei bewegen kann, übereinstimmt, wodurch es immer auf die gleiche Weise erscheint.

Im Sinne Leonardos verhandeln die Werke Robert Seidels den Ursprung jener Schatten, die die Sonne niemals sieht. Wenn Projektions- und Blickwinkel nicht übereinstimmen, dann offenbart sich ein Raum, der nicht illusionistisch ist, sondern das dynamische Ergebnis von beiden bildet – vom Projizierten und dem realen Raum, in dem die Projektion stattfindet. Beginnend mit seiner Installation *chiral* (2010) entwickelte Seidel seine eigene Projektionsmethodik, welche die Körperlichkeit betont und darüber hinaus sein Werk graduell in die Ausstellungssituation einbezieht. „Chiralität" ist ein Begriff, der die Links- oder Rechtshändigkeit von Formen bezeichnet und vor allem in der Chemie verwendet wird, um die Orientierung von Atomen in einem Molekül zu beschreiben. So wie ein linker Fußabdruck in seiner Außenform nur in einen rechten Fußabdruck transformiert werden kann, indem man ihn aus seiner planen Fläche hebt und rotiert, so kann eine chirale Form nur in ihr Gegenstück gedreht werden, wenn man sie durch die nächsthöhere Dimension bewegt. Seidels Werk *chiral* basiert auf ähnlichen Beziehungswandlungen, die eintreten, wenn Formen von der zweiten in die dritte Dimension gebracht werden. Bildfolgen, die Seidel als „Filmische Etüden" [„Cinematic Etudes"] bezeichnet, werden dabei auf eine flache Leinwand sowie auf eine komplexe Struktur, die aus handgeschöpftem chinesischen Papier geschnitten wurde, projiziert und verdeutlichen die gegensätzlichen Erfahrungen beider Situationen. In den projizierten Bildern entstehen Volumen aus geschichteten, flachen Formen, Oberflächen entfalten sich und Partikel treiben scheinbar durch mehrere Flüssigkeitsschichten. Doch die besagte Öffnung in eine höhere Dimension hängt von der Verteilung des Lichtstrahls des Projektors auf der Papierskulptur ab. Die radikale Verschiebung von Betrachterstandpunkt und Projektor lässt den Schnittpunkt von Papier und Licht zu einer selbstleuchtenden Landschaft werden.

In *black mirror* (2011), *tearing shadows* (2012) und *grapheme* (2013) erweiterte Seidel dieses Prinzip der Projektion auf skulpturale Formen. Die grazilen und kunstvoll mit der Hand oder dem Laser geschnittenen Formen der Installationen schaffen ein zusätzliches Gefühl von Transparenz und Schichtung, das der Fülle und dem Reichtum der visuellen Erfahrung hinzugefügt wird. Der Betrachter ist ebenfalls wesentlich aktiver eingebunden: Er kann die Skulptur umrunden und unterschiedliche Blickwinkel erforschen, die alle gleichwertig sind – jede Projektionsansicht und jeder Standpunkt sind gleichermaßen privilegiert. Durch den vereinzelten Einsatz von Spiegeln fängt Seidel jenes Licht ein, welches über die Skulpturen hinausstrahlt und spiegelt es zurück. Dies schafft eine Situation, in der selbst der Luftzug der Betrachter das fragile Arrangement nicht stört, sondern sogar weitere mögliche Konfigurationen erlaubt. Dieselben Spiegel lassen auch den Betrachter zu einem Teil des Werks werden und aktivieren den Ausstellungsraum, indem sie das Licht der Projektionen in ihn reflektieren. Seidels Interesse gilt den weitreichenden Wechselbeziehungen all dieser Parameter und den räumlichen Verhältnissen innerhalb seines Werks, die auch das Publikum, welches in den Raum tritt, zu einem integralen Teil der Raumkonfiguration werden lassen. In seinem Projekt *magnitude* (2015) treibt Seidel dieses Konzept noch weiter, indem er es auf Laserprojektionen an Schauplätze unter freiem Himmel überträgt, die als Video dokumentiert werden. Dort lässt die fehlende Deckungsgleichheit zwischen Kamera und Laser das Oberflächenrelief des von ihm gewählten Ortes zu Tage treten. Als Ergebnis des Dialogs zwischen den Projektionen und den dreidimensionalen Eigenschaften der Landschaft entsteht ein betörend komplexes Lichtspiel.

Seidels Werke stehen in Bezug zur Forschung anderer zeitgenössischer Künstler, die sich ebenfalls mit subtilen Verschiebungen zwischen Projektion, Blickwinkel und projizierten Oberflächen auseinandersetzen. Ein Schlüsselwerk in der jüngeren Geschichte ist die raumgreifende Expanded Cinema-Installation *Displacements* (1980) von Michael Naimark. In diesem Werk werden Farbbilder eines Interieurs, das weiß gestrichen wurde, auf dieses (zurück)projiziert, sodass sich Projektionsbild und Realität überlagern und die Schauspieler, die in der Projektion auftauchen, als flache und flüchtige Geister vorüberziehen – ein interessanter Einklang mit Jean-François Nicerons Ideen über die menschliche Vergänglichkeit. Ein zeitgenössischeres und allgemein bekanntes Beispiel von projizierter Objektverlebendigung wurde von Pablo Valbuena in seiner *Augmented Sculpture Series* (2007) entwickelt. In diesen Arbeiten animiert er virtuelle Lichtquellen, indem er Computeranimationen von wechselnden Lichtsituationen auf digitalen, dreidimensionalen Objekten herstellt und diese auf reale Körper projiziert, die exakt dieselbe Form haben, sodass diese perfekt mit der Projektion übereinstimmen.

Geht man in der Geschichte weiter zurück, war ein wichtiger Teil des Fotografiekurses, den László Moholy-Nagy am Bauhaus entwickelte, die Belebung von Oberflächen durch Licht. In seinem Buch *Vision in Motion* beschreibt er den *Lichtmodulator* als ein Werkzeug zur Herstellung abstrakter Fotografie, mit dem er in seinen Kursen experimentierte: „Jeden anderen Gegenstand mit konkav-konvexen oder faltigen Oberflächen kann man als Lichtmodulator bezeichnen, da er das Licht je nach seiner Beschaffenheit und nach der Hinwendung seiner Oberflächen zur Lichtquelle mit verschiedener Intensität zurückwirft."[1] Ziel dieser Kurse war es, den Studierenden bewusst zu machen, wie Licht unsere Wahrnehmung von Objekten verändern kann, und ihre Sensibilität für die Interaktionen von Licht und Volumen zu schärfen. Nathan Lerner war einer von Moholy-Nagys Studenten am New Bauhaus in Chicago im Jahre 1937 und entwickelte die Aufgabenstellung mit seiner *light box* [Lichtkasten] einen Schritt weiter: Lerner bohrte Löcher in die Seitenwände des Lichtkastens, die ihn wie eine Art Miniaturtheater funktionieren ließen, sodass das Licht genau kontrolliert werden konnte. Moholy-Nagy beschrieb dies als „ein äußerst effizientes *Labor* zur Untersuchung der zurückweichenden und hervortretenden Werte auf den beleuchteten Oberflächen. Diese Erscheinungen bewirken direkte Reaktionen des Gefühls, die sich durch die Kombination der visuellen Grundelemente […] noch steigern lassen. Man kann daher mit Licht ebenso treffsicher malen wie mit Öl oder Farbstoffen."[2]

Zehn Jahre vor Lerners *light box* hatte der Fotograf Francis Bruguière eine sehr ähnliche Methode entwickelt, um in abstrakten Fotografien die Lichteffekte dreidimensionaler Papierausschnitte einzufangen. Im Jahr 1929 drehte er in London zusammen mit dem Filmkritiker Oswell Blakeston den abstrakten Film *Light Rythms*. Ihr Film basiert auf einer Sequenz von Bruguières statischen Papierschnitten, die durch von Hand bewegte Lichtquellen glaubhaft in Bewegung versetzt wurden. An einigen Stellen des Films wurde die Überblendung von zwei Ebenen genutzt, um das Bild räumlich komplexer und mehrdeutig werden zu lassen. Der Film wurde genau auf die Klaviermusik von Jack Ellitt geschnitten und ist ein seltenes Beispiel für den frühen abstrakten, britischen Film.

Eine der von Seidel selbst zitierten Inspirationen ist der Experimentalfilm *Lichtspiel, schwarz-weiß-grau* (1930) von László Moholy-Nagy. Dieser zeigt den zwischen 1922 und 1930 von Moholy-Nagy entwickelten *Licht-Raum-Modulator,* welchen er selbst als „Lichtrequisit einer elektrischen Bühne" bezeichnete. Der Modulator wird im Allgemeinen als eine der ersten kinetischen Skulpturen verstanden und ist zudem ein Schlüsselwerk der Geschichte der Lichtkunst.

1 László Moholy-Nagy: *Light Modulator,* in: ders., Vision in Motion, Chicago 1947, S. 198, zitiert nach der deutschen Ausgabe: László Moholy-Nagy, *Lichtraummodulator* (1947), in: ders., Sehen in Bewegung, Leipzig 2014, S. 198.
2 László Moholy-Nagy 2014, S. 198.

Er besteht aus einer Anordnung von Grundformen, die sich in einem komplexen Ablauf in etwa zwanzig Minuten gegenseitig umkreisen – einem Modell, das dem Sonnensystem ähnelt. Moholy-Nagy beschrieb mehrere Möglichkeiten das Werk auszustellen, jedoch war allen Beschreibungen gemein, dass die Aufmerksamkeit der Zuschauer weniger auf die tatsächliche Skulptur, sondern darauf gelenkt werden sollte, wie die durch die Skulptur entstandenen, sich bewegenden Schatten und Reflektionen mit der räumlichen Umgebung interagieren.

László Maholy-Nagy, Licht-Raum-Modulator (1922–1930)

Im Denken von Moholy-Nagy demonstrieren der *Licht-Raum-Modulator* und die *light box* aber auch das *Lichtrequisit* sein Bestreben, Licht als Medium einzusetzen, um neuartige räumliche Beziehungen zu entwickeln und darzustellen. Diese neuen Verschränkungen beziehen sich auf Konzepte wie Dynamik, Energie und gegenseitige Durchdringung – Konzepte, die Moholy-Nagy letztlich als essentiell für eine vernünftigere, „biologischere" Einstellung zur technischen Gesellschaft betrachtete.

Ein Schlüsselwerk der künstlerischen Entwicklung Robert Seidels ist der Film _grau (2004), der zu einem persönlichen Zugang zu synthetischen Bildern führte und alle seine späteren Arbeiten durchdringt. So schreibt er, dass er in dieser Zeit von der Vielfalt unterschiedlicher wissenschaftlicher Bild- und Visualisierungstechniken inspiriert wurde, beispielsweise in Form von Magnetresonanz- oder Computertomografieaufnahmen.[3] Diese brachten ihn dazu, andersartig über mögliche Wechselbeziehungen von Zeit, Bewegung, Raum und Gestalt in Verbindung mit einer gestischen Qualität und materiellen Texturen nachzudenken, die seinem fortwährenden Interesse am Zeichnen entsprangen. Von diesem Moment an bezeichnet Seidel seine Arbeiten häufiger als „virtuelle Skulpturen". Eine weitreichende Konsequenz dieser Idee digital erschaffener Skulpturen ist deren grundverschiedene Ausarbeitung und Umsetzung. Einige Arbeiten Seidels existieren in unterschiedlichen Versionen – sie wurden sowohl auf großformatigen Medienfassaden, als auch an traditionelleren Ausstellungsorten und als Screenings gezeigt. Ein Beispiel für diese Formbarkeit ist *vellum* (Art Center Nabi Seoul, 2009), eine Installation für mehrere, verschiedenformatige LED-Screens innerhalb und außerhalb eines Gebäudes, bei der jeder Screen einen Blick auf dieselbe gigantische „virtuelle Skulptur" von 100 × 125 × 80 Metern freilegt. Eine spätere Version wurde an drei Filmleinwände (SESC Sao Paulo, 2010) und fünf Bildschirme (MOCA Taipei, 2010) in sehr unterschiedlichen Kompositionen angepasst.

Die Bildsprache vieler seiner Animationen reflektiert gerade auch diese Idee der Aktualisierung einer „virtuellen Skulptur". Manche von Seidels Arbeiten haben eine Ähnlichkeit zu Francis Bruguières Ansatz, Papierskulpturen mit bewegten Lichtern zum Leben zu erwecken, selbst wenn in Seidels Animationen die Lichtquellen virtuell sind. Viele der Bilder und Bewegungsmomente erinnern an die Schnittdarstellungen wissenschaftlicher Visualisierungstechniken, allerdings in einer deutlich komplexeren Weise – so als würden wir dreidimensionale Schnitte durch eine verschlungene vierdimensionale Form sehen. Beide Arten der Umsetzung legen nahe, dass derselbe Datensatz auf viele Weisen dargestellt und aufgerollt werden kann und verschiedene Blicke auf dasselbe Ereignis oder dieselbe Anordnung ermöglicht. Eine Charakteristik wissenschaftlicher Bildverfahren, aus denen Seidel Inspiration schöpft, ist, dass sie weniger aus Abbildungen von Objektoberflächen resultieren, sondern Datenmengen produzieren, die Beziehungen und Volumen repräsentieren. Wissenschaftler verwenden routinemäßig Schnittverfahren, Mehrfachprojektionen, Korrelationen und andere Methoden, um die darin enthaltenden Informationen zu entschlüsseln. Das bedeutet, dass es nicht einen bevorzugten Blickpunkt oder eine „wahre" Darstellung der Informationen gibt, sondern alle Sichtweisen gleichermaßen gültig und alle Darstellungsmethoden potentiell interessant sind. So entsteht ein Raumkonzept, das zwar nicht mit den Vorstellungen Moholy-Nagys vergleichbar, aber in seiner Offenheit ebenso reichhaltig an Dynamik und Wechselbeziehungen ist.

3   Robert Seidel, _grau - an organic experimental film, in: Animation: An Interdisciplinary Journal, ed. by Suzanne Buchan, H. 2, Nr. 1, März 2007, S. 77–84, S. 78.

Viewer in Orbit.
Around Robert Seidel's
Art of Projection
—
Joost Rekveld

"The sun never sees any shadow," wrote Leonardo Da Vinci around the year 1500, when he was sketching the orbits of sun and moon. A statement that, when taken gently out of context, poetically evokes the flattening that occurs when light source and viewpoint perfectly coincide. Nowadays, half a century after the Space Age, it is not hard to imagine how the whole earth, with its mountains, trees, cities and people, would look like a flat disk with different colours when viewed from the star that powers it.

Da Vinci's statement also brings to mind how in his time the central perspective, the art of aligning points of projection and points of view had just been developed, as a method for painters to suggest three-dimensional space on a flat surface. A perspective image is an optical slice of the world flattened into a virtual window that can only be correctly seen from one point. A good century later, projective geometry had been completely figured out, so that such images could also be constructed from unlikely angles, or on vaulted surfaces instead of on a flat wall or canvas. The French monk Jean-François Niceron took this possibility as the starting point for a religious art that would emphasize the vanity of our existence by dramatizing the transience of images that appear and disappear depending on our viewpoint. In his art of anamorphosis, the alignment between projection and viewpoint was to be turned into an experience by making it a rare and privileged occurrence, only happening at a very specific location relative to a fresco. Again a century later, anamorphosis in painting reached its apotheosis in the spectacular visions painted by Andrea Pozzo on the ceiling of the Sant'Ignazio in Rome.

In our age, we see projections not as geometrical procedures executed in paint, but as the output of machines that can be moved around. In virtual reality for instance, the center of perspective projection is made portable, so that it remains constantly aligned with the viewpoint of the user, who is then free to move and navigate a virtual space that is always revealed in the same way.

In Leonardo's terms, the work of Robert Seidel deals with the cause of those shadows that the sun never sees. When point of projection and point of view are not aligned, a space is revealed that is not illusionistic, but the dynamic result of both what is being projected and the real space in which this projection is taking place. Starting with his installation *chiral* (2010), Seidel developed his own approach to projection that emphasizes its physicality and gradually opened up his work to encompass in the situation of exhibition.

"Chirality" is a term that is used to refer to the left- or right-handedness of shapes and is commonly used in chemistry to describe the orientation of molecules. Just as a left footprint can only be turned into a right footprint by lifting it out of the plane and turning it over, a chiral form can only be rotated into its counterpart through the next higher dimension. Seidel's work *chiral* is based on similar changes in relationships when shapes are moved from two to three dimensions. Visual sequences that Seidel refers to as "Cinematic Etudes" are projected onto a flat screen as well as onto a complex sculpture that is made from cut-outs in handmade chinese paper, in order to show the difference of experience in the two situations. In the projected imagery, volumes are constructed from stacks of flat shapes, surfaces fold open or particles seem to move through multiple layers of liquid, but the opening up to a higher dimension really happens in the way the projector beam is distributed across the paper sculpture. The radical disalignment of viewpoint and projector turns the intersection of paper and light into a luminous landscape.

black mirror (2011), p. 114–117

Seidel expanded on this principle of projection on sculptural forms in *black mirror* (2011), *tearing shadows* (2012) and *grapheme* (2013). In these installations, the even more delicate and elaborate hand- or laser-cut shapes create an extra sensation of transparency and layering that adds to the richness of the visual experience. The spectator's role has also become much more active; the spectator is able to move around the sculpture and explore different points of view that are all equally valid – every constellation of projections and viewpoint is as privileged as every other one. By his occasional use of mirrors, Seidel captures the light that spills around the sculptures and reflects it back. This creates a situation in which for instance the flow of air generated by the spectators does not disturb the fragile alignment, but is welcomed as helping to reveal another possible configuration. The same mirrors make the viewer a part of the work and activate the exhibition space by reflecting the light of the projections into it. Seidel is interested in the lush interactions of all these parameters, being as focused on the spatial relations within his work as in making the audience an integral part of the spatial configuration they have entered. In his project *magnitude* (2015), Seidel takes this concept further by applying it to laser projections in outdoor settings, documented on video. This time, the non-alignment between camera and laser gives a voice to the relief present in the particular locations he chose. The beautifully complex light play that results is the outcome of a dialogue between the projections and the three-dimensional features of the landscape.

These works of Seidel resonate with the research of other contemporary artists who are also working with the subtle disalignments of projection, viewpoint and projection surfaces. A key work in this recent history is the expanded cinema installation *Displacements* (1980) by Michael Naimark. In this work, colour images of an interior are projected back upon that same interior painted white, so that the actors that appear in the projection pass through as flat and fleeting ghosts, in an interesting resonance with Jean-François Niceron's thoughts about human ephemerality. A more contemporary and well-known example of projecting life into objects was developed by Pablo Valbuena in his *Augmented Sculpture Series* (2007). In these works, he animates plays of virtual light sources by making computer-animations of changing light on digital, three-dimensional objects, and by projecting these on real objects that have exactly the same shape and are perfectly aligned with the projection.

If we go further back in history, this power of light to bring surfaces to life was an important part of the photography course László Moholy-Nagy developed at the Bauhaus. In his book *Vision in Motion*, he describes the *light modulator* as a tool for an abstract photography assignment: "… any object with combined concave-convex or wrinkled surfaces may be considered a light modulator since it reflects light with varied intensity depending upon its substance and the way its surfaces are turned towards the light source."[1] The goal of this assignment was to make students aware of the extent to which light can change our perception of objects, and to develop their sensitivity to the interactions of light and volumes that could be applied to all kinds of photography. Nathan Lerner was one of Moholy-Nagy's students at the *New Bauhaus* in Chicago in 1937, and took this assignment a step further by developing the *light box*. The holes in the sides of this box made it function as a kind of miniature theatre in which the light on the *light modulator* could be carefully controlled. Moholy-Nagy described this as "a particularly effective laboratory for the study of receding and advancing values of the lit surfaces. These effects produce direct emotional reactions which can be enlarged upon through the combinations of visual fundamentals [...]. Thus, one may paint with light as surely as one can paint with oil and pigment."[2]

Ten years before Lerner's *light box*, the photographer Francis Bruguière had developed a very similar method of making abstract photographs of the effects of light on three-dimensional paper cut-outs. In 1929 he realized an abstract film called *Light Rhythms* in London, together with film critic Oswell Blakeston. Their film was based on a sequence of Bruguières' static cut-outs, set into convincing apparent motion by light sources that were moved by hand. In some parts of the film, superimposition of two layers was used to make the image more spatially complex and ambiguous. The film was skilfully edited to piano music by Jack Ellitt and is a rare early example of abstract film made in Britain.

One of the inspirations cited by Seidel is the experimental film *A Lightplay : Black White Grey* (1930) featuring the *Light-Space-Modulator* that Moholy-Nagy developed between 1922 and 1930, which he himself referred to as the "Light Prop for an Electric Stage." The modulator is generally seen as one of the first kinetic sculptures and is an especially important piece in the history of light art. It consists of a set of elementary shapes that revolve around each other in a complex cycle of about twenty minutes, almost like a model of the solar system. Moholy-Nagy described a number of ways to show this piece, but what is essential in all of them is the intention to focus the attention of the viewer not so much on the actual sculpture itself, but on how the moving shadows and reflections produced by the piece interact with the space around it. In the thinking of Moholy-Nagy, both the *light modulator* and *light box* assignments as well as the *Light Prop* demonstrated his commitment to using the medium of light to develop and depict new kinds of spatial relations. These new relations were based on concepts such as dynamism, energy

---

1 László Moholy-Nagy, *Light Modulator*, in: László Moholy-Nagy, Vision in Motion, Chicago 1947, p. 198.

2 László Moholy-Nagy 1947, p. 198.

and interpenetration, concepts that Moholy-Nagy ultimately considered essential for a more sound, "biological" approach to technological society.

A key work in the artistic development of Robert Seidel was the film _grau (2004), which led to a personal approach to synthetic imagery that permeates all of his later projects. He writes that at the time he was inspired by a variety of different scientific imaging and visualization techniques, such as Magnetic Resonance Imaging and Computed Tomography.[3] These triggered him to think differently about the possible interrelations between time, movement, space and form, in combination with the gestural quality and material textures that remained from his continued interest in drawing. Also from that time on, Seidel often refers to his work as "virtual sculptures." An extensive implication of this idea of digitally transformed sculptures is that these can be rendered in many ways. Several works by Seidel exist in different versions or have been shown on gigantic media facades as well as in more traditional settings for exhibition or screening. An example of this malleability is *vellum* (Art Center Nabi Seoul, 2009), a piece that at first existed as an installation made for multiple led-screens of radically different dimensions in and on a building, with each screen slicing a view of the same gigantic "virtual sculpture" of 100 × 125 × 80 meters. A later version was rendered for three silver screens (SESC Sao Paulo, 2010) and five screens (MOCA Taipei, 2010) in a very different arrangement.

vellum (2009)

The visual language of many of his animations also reflect this idea of actualizing a "virtual sculpture." Some of Seidel's works have a resemblance to the way Francis Bruguière activated his paper sculptures by way of moving lights, even though in Seidel's animations these light sources are virtual. Many of the images and movements evoke the kinds of slicing that we know from scientific visualisation techniques, but in a much more complex way – as if we are seeing three-dimensional slices through a intricate four-dimensional shape. Both these ways of rendering suggest that there are many ways to show or traverse the same dataset, giving different views on the same event or configuration. One characteristic of the scientific imaging methods Seidel draws inspiration from, is that they do not so much result in images of the surface of things but produce datasets that represent relations and volumes. Scientists routinely use techniques of slicing, multiple projections, correlations and other ways to decipher the data contained in these sets. This means that there is not one viewpoint that is privileged or one "true" way of rendering the data, but all viewpoints are equally valid and all rendering methods are potentially interesting. This gives rise to a conception of space that is certainly not the same as what Moholy-Nagy envisioned, but similar in its openness to dynamism and interrelations.

3   Robert Seidel, _grau - an organic experimental film, in: Animation: An Interdisciplinary Journal, ed. by Suzanne Buchan, Vol. 2, No. 1, March 2007, p. 77–84, p. 78.

Im Universum digitaler Bilder

—

Robert Seidel
im Interview mit
Claudia Tittel

CT Deine Experimentalfilme werden nicht nur auf Festivals gezeigt, sondern auch auf Medienfassaden und in musealen Einrichtungen. Wie verändern sich deine Filme durch neue räumliche Kontexte?

RS Bis ungefähr 2008 habe ich mich vornehmlich auf Filme konzentriert, die auf Filmfestivals und in Ausstellungen als Einkanal-Arbeiten gezeigt wurden. Dann habe ich die erste größere Gebäudeprojektion *processes: living painting* realisiert und ein Jahr später, also 2009, entstand die erste Projektionsskulptur im Museum of Contemporary Art in Taipeh, Taiwan. Ich habe mich damals mit realen räumlichen Strukturen auseinandergesetzt und wollte projizierte Formen und Farben mit der Oberfläche von Papier interagieren lassen. Deshalb habe ich die klassische Projektion verlassen und eine schwebende Skulptur aus handgeschöpftem Papier entwickelt, auf die der Film *chiral* projiziert wurde. Im Raum gab es eine Gegenüberstellung von der bespielten Papierskulptur und dem Film selbst, der auf einem flach aufgespannten Papier präsentiert wurde. So konnten die Besucher die Brücke von der Zweidimensionalität der Projektion in die räumliche Dimension selbst schlagen. *chiral* ist auch der erste Film, den es in verschiedenen Iterationen und Variationen gibt. Meine älteren Filme zeige ich dagegen nie als Projektionsskulpturen, weil sie als Filme entstanden sind und andere Anforderungen an das filmische Gefüge stellen.

CT Wäre es für dich denkbar, dass du deine Filme in andere räumliche Kontexte überträgst?

RS Natürlich, aber _grau ist zum Beispiel ein sehr konzentrierter Film, der die Bildfläche aufdehnt. Er erzeugt einen Sog, der bei einer Installation nicht existiert. In den Installationen sind die Betrachter integraler Teil der Bild-Raum-Konstruktion. Sie nehmen nicht nur den Film, sondern auch die Umgebung wahr. Das ist einerseits verlockend, aber es fehlt andererseits die Fokussierung. _grau ist kein Film, an dem man einfach vorbeilaufen sollte.

CT Heißt das, dass jede Arbeit eine bestimmte Rezeptionssituation verlangt?

RS Es wäre natürlich schön, wenn meine Filme, die speziell als solche entwickelt wurden, konzentriert betrachtet werden könnten. Eine fokussierte Betrachtung ist jedoch fast unmöglich. Im Festivalkontext werden meine Filme gern irgendwo in ein 60- bis 80-Minuten-Programm zwischen Experimentalfilme oder Animationen gepresst. Da gibt es diesen Moment der Kontemplation selten. Auch im Internet – eine für mich wichtige Plattform – klicken die Zuschauer durch die Filme und springen von einem zum nächsten Reiz. Selbst im Museum kann man die meisten Filme nicht ohne Ablenkung sehen. Es gibt zwar große Ausstellungen mit aufwendigen Black-Box-Architekturen und festen Zeitplänen, die für eine konzentrierte Betrachtung den idealen Rahmen bieten, aber in kleineren Ausstellungshäusern ist das fast nie der Fall. Dann ist man darauf angewiesen, dass sich der umherschweifende Flaneur für einen Moment festhalten lässt.

CT Deine Filme funktionieren im übertragenen Sinne wie Malerei, nicht nur weil sie malerisch wirken, sondern weil es – wie ich finde – keinen Anfang und kein Ende, keine abgeschlossene Geschichte und keine Protagonisten gibt.

RS Meine Filme, da hast du sicher recht, wirken malerisch. Ich arbeite mit Schichtungen von Texturen, Farben und Stimmungen. Es tauchen Momente des Stillstands, aber auch sich kontinuierlich verändernde Strukturen auf. Mir geht es genau um diese Veränderungen. Insofern wäre es optimal, wenn die Filme von Anfang bis Ende konzentriert betrachtet werden könnten. Das lineare Sehen ist wichtig, da den Arbeiten zwar kein narratives Gerüst, aber eine Art Partitur zugrunde liegt. Deswegen verwehre ich mich auch meist gegen Mehrkanal-Arbeiten. Man steht manchmal etwa hilflos davor, hat eine Vielzahl von Screens und weiß nicht, auf welchen man zuerst schauen soll. Mit dieser Überforderung kann man natürlich arbeiten, aber die von mir favorisierte Aufmerksamkeit ist häufig an einen Screen gebunden. Es gibt natürlich auch Gegenbeispiele: *vellum* ist eine virtuelle Skulptur, die auf mehreren Screens und auf einer Medienfassade gleichzeitig lief. Somit war dasselbe Objekt aus verschiedenen Schnittebenen und Blickwinkeln zu sehen. Komplizierter wird es, wenn man skulptural arbeitet, den Raum auffächert und auf eine rechteckige Projektionsfläche verzichtet. Dann sind die Zuschauer zunächst verunsichert, aber sie verstehen schnell, dass es nicht notwendig ist, die Bilder einzeln auf sich wirken zu lassen, sondern dass sie sich selbst bewegen müssen. Ich hoffe, dass die Funken der Skulpturen auf die Betrachter überspringen und diese auf Entdeckungsreise gehen.

CT Wie entwickelst du deine Formen? Was ist der Ausgangspunkt deiner Arbeiten?

RS Das kann ich nicht eindeutig beschreiben, denn es sind eher Empfindungen, Assoziationen, die ich versuche darzustellen. Meist sind Zeichnungen der Ausgangspunkt meiner Arbeiten. Ein paar davon sind erstmalig in der Ausstellung zu sehen, beispielsweise Ideenskizzen für meinen nächsten Film. Die Zeichnungen bilden eine Art lose Grundstruktur und

Ideenkonvolut, welche dann in den Projektionen oder Skulpturen weiter ausformuliert werden.

CT Bei fast allen deiner Arbeiten hat man das Gefühl, dass du Zeichnung oder Malerei in ein filmisches Medium überführst. Du schaffst bewegte Malerei. In dieser Hinsicht korrelierst du mit den Ideen der Avantgardisten, die den Film als neues Medium der Malerei betrachteten. Walter Ruttmann, Viking Eggeling oder Hans Richter meinten, dass der Film „Malerei mit Zeit" sei und die Malerei aus ihrer statischen Enge befreit werden müsse.

RS In der Tat, sie alle haben gemalt, waren erfinderisch und konnten mit den Möglichkeiten der Zeit neuartige Bilder erzeugen. Oskar Fischinger hat beispielsweise Apparate entwickelt, László Moholy-Nagy hat kinetische Objekte gebaut, und trotzdem bleibt es geheimnisvoll, wie die filmischen Bilder letztendlich entstanden sind. Ich habe mir vor Kurzem die Neuauflage des Buches *Vision in Motion* von Moholy-Nagy besorgt. Für mich ist das Buch immer noch relevant. Man sollte nicht unterschätzen, dass wir die ganze Zeit von bewegten Bildern umgeben sind und dass die Fragen von damals auch heute noch nicht vollständig beantwortet sind. Früher standen recht primitive Mittel zur Verfügung. Heute gibt es viel mehr Möglichkeiten, denn das Digitale hat den Alltag vollständig durchdrungen. Aber diese technische Freiheit überfordert uns und verhindert vielleicht ein tatsächliches Hinterfragen. Man sollte nicht vergessen: Der abstrakte Film hat zunächst keine Funktion. Man muss seine Komplexität aus eigenem Antrieb erforschen und verstehen wollen, sich der reinen Bewegung annähern und der zeitlichen Veränderung zuwenden. Marcel Duchamp ließ zum Beispiel bemalte Scheiben rotieren, sodass sich die Malerei nicht nur bewegte, sondern durch die Bewegung auch eine neue Räumlichkeit entstand. Ich habe manchmal das Gefühl, dass es vermeintlich schon alles gegeben hat, aufgrund der technischen Hürden aber eine weiterführende Auseinandersetzung selten geworden ist. Deshalb hatte ich beispielsweise 2014 das Filmprogramm *Penetrating Surfaces* für das Österreichische Filmmuseum kuratiert, welches das materialinhärente ästhetische Potential des Digitalen reflektieren sollte.

CT Im Umfeld Marcel Duchamps haben ab 1909 Georges Braque und Pablo Picasso den Raum gesprengt und aufgefächert, verschiedene Perspektiven im Raum dargestellt und damit den Kubismus erfunden. Die Kubisten sind zwar im Medium der Malerei geblieben, haben aber trotzdem Zeitlichkeit auf der Leinwand abgebildet oder wenn man an die Futuristen denkt wie beispielsweise Umberto Boccionis *Die Straße dringt in das Haus* [La strada entra nella casa, 1911] – da spürt man regelrecht die Bewegung.

RS Ich habe von den Kubisten und Futuristen gelernt, das Sehen als Sinnes- und Bewusstseinsakt zu hinterfragen, die Linearität von Perspektive und Form aufzubrechen. Ich kann mich erinnern, dass ich im Alter von ungefähr sechzehn Jahren Marcel Duchamps *Akt, eine Treppe herabsteigend, Nr. 2* [Nu descendant un escalier, no. 2, 1912] gesehen habe. Ich war fasziniert, wie Duchamp die Figur darstellt und die Bewegung in Facetten zerfallen lässt. Die Zeitsequenz wurde aufgespannt und gleichzeitig so frei gestaffelt, dass es entfaltete Architektur sein könnte. Der große Anknüpfungspunkt ist und war, dass Duchamp etwas darstellt, was einen direkten Bezug zur Realität hat, unmittelbar von den Betrachtern verstanden wird und es trotzdem abstrakt, also nie in dieser Form zu sehen ist.

CT Wie kam es dazu, dass du dich Filmen, insbesondere abstrakten Filmen gewidmet hast?

RS Film war für mich immer eine sehr zeitgemäße Form, Gefühle und Stimmungen zu transportieren. Ich habe anfangs viel gezeichnet, sowohl auf Papier als auch am Computer. Aber ich empfand die Ergebnisse nie so fesselnd wie ein bewegtes Bild. Im Film kannst du unterschiedliche Momente aneinanderreihen und diese Verdichtung immer wieder ohne Aufwand ansehen. Die Zeichnungen kommen in einen Fluss und verlieren ihre Eigenständigkeit. Der Computer ist für mich eine Art Archiv. Ich sammle dort Ideen und durchschreite sie immer wieder.

Unsere Welt ist extrem funktional geworden. Alles muss eine Bedeutung haben, alles muss kategorisiert werden. Die Abstraktion ermöglicht mir eine Entfunktionalisierung, die mir einen neuen Blick auf die Welt, aber auch auf die Persönlichkeit eines Menschen und schlussendlich auch auf meine eigene erlaubt. Manchmal kommentieren Zuschauer, die wenig Bezug zu Kunst haben, meine Arbeiten. Sie beschreiben ihre ganz eigenen Erlebnisse, die für mich häufig völlig überraschend sind. Es ist unglaublich bereichernd, wenn jemand einen so persönlichen Moment mit mir teilt. Es ist dabei vollkommen egal, welchen Hintergrund derjenige besitzt. Jeder kann über das Leben abstrakt nachdenken. Und ich habe Menschen getroffen, die eine komplexe Arbeit von mir so zusammengefasst haben, wie es nachdenklicher und poetischer nicht sein könnte. Ich habe oft das Gefühl, dass ich „die Menschen" nicht richtig verstehe, aber durch diese Reaktionen lerne ich auf einer sehr persönlichen Ebene dazu. Die Funktionalisierung von allem, von und in der Welt, bestürzt mich und auch die Notwendigkeit, klare Antworten geben zu müssen. Die Welt ist viel zu komplex, als dass es eindeutige Antworten auf jede Frage geben könnte. Natürlich möchte man im Leben in vielen Bereichen Klarheit, Struktur oder gar Zuversicht, aber genauso möchte ich einfach überwältigt, überrascht oder verwirrt sein dürfen. Am Ende kommt es vielleicht nur darauf an den Alltag zu unterbrechen.

CT Bist du deshalb so fasziniert von der Natur?

RS Die Natur ist unendlich vielfältig. Ich glaube, dass wir – dass ich – dort die reizvollsten Momente finde. Mich interessiert das Prozesshafte der Natur. Alles wächst und verändert sich stetig, stirbt, wächst wieder. Die Natur hat sich in grundverschiedenen Zeiträumen auf mannigfaltige Art ausgeprägt. Man findet ein unglaubliches Spektrum an Zeitdimensionen – von der Eintagsfliege bis zu Gebirgen, die sich in Jahrmillionen herausgebildet haben und sich auch weiterhin transformieren. Heutzutage gibt es in der Wissenschaft unterschiedliche Verfahren, sich diesen verschiedenen Zeiten zu nähern – vom Mikroskop über das Teleskop bis hin zu archäologischen Grabungen. In den Sedimenten sind sowohl Landschafts- als auch Gesellschaftsveränderungen gespeichert, die uns heute Auskunft über die Erdentwicklung oder das Klima vor Millionen Jahren geben. Mit den unterschiedlichsten Mikroskopen wiederum kann man Dinge sehen, die aufgrund ihrer Größe mit dem bloßen Auge nicht zu erkennen sind oder gar außerhalb des sichtbaren Spektrums liegen. Ich komme aus einer naturwissenschaftlich interessierten Familie. Mein Vater ist Physiker, ich hatte einen naturwissenschaftlichen Fokus in der Schule und habe ein Jahr Biologie studiert. Mir ist immer wieder aufgefallen, dass die Naturwissenschaftler Bilder hervorbringen, die wir in der Kunst noch nicht gesehen haben. Für die Wissenschaftler sind diese Bilder in erster Linie ein Analyseinstrument. Sie liefern eine Übersicht, ein Schema oder ein Indiz. Die ästhetische Seite dieser Bilder bleibt den meisten Wissenschaftlern verborgen, auch wenn die Notwendigkeit zur Publikation ihr Auge schärft. Ich möchte diese Filterungen der Natur dekonstruieren und deren poetische Seite zeigen. Das Allerwichtigste ist dabei, eine beinahe archaische Struktur zu finden, in der sich der Betrachter verlieren kann und die ständigen Ablenkungen des Alltags in den Hintergrund treten.

CT Wo beginnt dein Schaffensprozess? Zeichnest du immer zuerst auf Papier?

RS Ja, es sind meistens keine „perfekten" Zeichnungen, sondern eher Skizzen. Es sind zunächst grobe Verdichtungen von Ideen, die am Computer komplexer werden. Der Stift, die Hand, das Papier fließen beim Zeichnen scheinbar ineinander. Die Zeichnung ist ein schnelles Medium – Ideen können sich ohne Kontrollzwang auf einem simplen Blatt manifestieren. Es sollen vor allem erst einmal Ideen festgehalten und der Schaffensprozess angeregt werden. Das kann ich am besten auf Papier. Sobald man den Computer anschaltet und wartet, bis die Programme gestartet sind, befindet man sich meistens schon in einem anderen Modus. Der Ideenfluss geht dann erst einmal verloren. Sehr oft ist es am Rechner ein Abarbeiten von diesen spontan festgehaltenen Ideen.

fulcrum #1 (2015), S. 180–183

CT Aber es gibt doch auch Zeichenprogramme?

RS Natürlich gibt es Zeichentabletts und Software, mit denen man wie mit einem Stift zeichnen kann. Die verwende ich auch, denn Papier kann genau wie die Arbeit mit der Maus ermüden. Doch auch wenn die Metaphern hinter der Soft- und Hardware häufig realen Werkzeugen oder Prozessen nachempfunden sind – dem Stift, der Ebene, dem Koordinatensystem – ist, dessen ungeachtet, die Geste, die dahinter steckt, eine andere. Digitale Werkzeuge sind in ganz andere Bahnen zu lenken. Beispielsweise ist es einfach, die Bewegung eines Objektes mit der Intensität einer Lichtquelle zu verknüpfen. Und selbstverständlich kann man dreidimensional modellieren, also virtuell wie ein Bildhauer Objekte bearbeiten. Der große Vorteil sind die frei skalierbaren Größenverhältnisse. Man kann mit demselben

Vorgang ein Sandkorn oder eine riesige Landschaft erschaffen. Diese verschiedenen Prozesse greifen ohne physikalische Grenzen ineinander. Es kann passieren, dass ich zuerst eine Form entwickle, die dann später die Grundlage für die Farbigkeit eines Hintergrundes wird. Das Besondere am Computer ist, dass es keinen Endzustand und keinen Qualitätsverlust gibt, sondern er die kontinuierliche Transformation als Arbeitsmetapher in sich trägt.

CT Wie muss man sich das vorstellen? Es wird Künstlern, die mit dem Computer arbeiten, ja häufig vorgeworfen, dass der Computer beziehungsweise dass die Programme die Arbeit übernehmen würden.

RS Der Computer „erschafft" selbstverständlich nichts alleine. Ich breche es immer auf ein einfaches Beispiel herunter: Auch ein Textverarbeitungsprogramm ist nur ein Hilfsprogramm, ein Werkzeug. Das Programm funktioniert letztendlich wie eine komfortable Schreibmaschine, aber sie schreibt nicht automatisch einen interessanten und eleganten Text. Man muss schon selbst denken und schreiben. Bei mir beginnt die Arbeit immer mit einer Sammlung von Ideen und Skizzen, die ich dann mit Programmen und eigenen Werkzeugen bearbeite. Der Computer und die Programme sind nur ein weiteres Hilfsmittel wie Bleistift und Papier, um meine Ideen auszuformulieren. Manche Programme fügen sich gut in meinen Ansatz. Sobald ich aber an Grenzen stoße, verändere ich den Arbeitsweg und nähere mich meiner Idee auf einem anderen Pfad.

CT Weißt du immer genau, wohin dich deine Ideen führen oder verändern sie sich während des Arbeitsprozesses massiv?

RS Meine Arbeit ist schon wesentlich vom Computer und seinen Prozessen inspiriert, aber ich habe eine feste Vorstellung, wenn ich mit einer neuen Arbeit beginne. Dennoch ergibt es oft keinen Sinn, erste Ideen zu zeigen, denn die Arbeit unterscheidet sich von den Skizzen über den Film bis hin zur Installation schon sehr. Wenn ich eine neue Arbeit vorbereite und das Museum möchte zum Beispiel für die Presse ein Vorschaubild, dann ist dieser Wunsch häufig schwer einzulösen. Natürlich könnte ich ein Standbild aus einem Film extrahieren, aber erstens würde ich dann dieses gegenüber tausend anderen Bildern favorisieren und zweitens weiß ich meist vorher nicht, wie der Film auf der Skulptur im Raum wirken wird. Ich habe zwar ein konkretes Bild im Kopf, aber die Unzahl der Parameter an einem realen Ort lässt sich vorher schwer vorhersehen und in ein ausgewogenes Verhältnis bringen. Auf dem Papier blätterst du auf die nächste Seite und fängst von vorn an. Eine ähnliche Freiheit und Offenheit in der Verwirklichung meiner Ideen möchte ich mir auch erhalten. Ich kenne viele Künstler, die ihre Idee nicht ändern und alles bis ins letzte Detail durchplanen. Sie haben oft gar nicht die Möglichkeit in Arbeitsprozesse einzugreifen, zum einen aus Zeitgründen, aber auch weil ein ganzes Team in der Produktionskette hängt. Sie lassen große Skulpturen gießen und Oberflächen polieren. Jeder, der mit seinen eigenen Händen das Kunstwerk erschafft, wird am Ende Abweichungen von seiner Ausgangsidee feststellen. Wenn nun ein ganzes Team daran arbeitet, wird diese Abweichung noch größer sein. Alles was wir tun, unterliegt gewissen Entscheidungs- und Formulierungsprozessen, die bis zum Ende wirken. Meine Arbeiten sind keine digitalen Ready-mades.

CT Ich würde sagen, dass es so etwas wie eine Robert-Seidel-Handschrift gibt und ich würde auch behaupten, dass ich deine Arbeiten erkennen würde. Gibt es etwas, was alle deine Arbeiten auszeichnet?

RS Es ist schwer zu sagen, ob es eine Art übergeordnetes Thema gibt. Es gibt Arbeiten, vor allem die ortsspezifischen, die ich für bestimmte Konstellationen entworfen habe. Nehmen wir etwa die eingangs erwähnte Arbeit *processes: living paintings* für das Phyletische Museum in Jena. Dort war das Thema durch das Gebäude und die Sammlung vorgegeben. Es ist das bekannteste Museum der Evolutionstheorie und zeigt die Entstehung des Lebens sowie die Entwicklung des Menschen in allen Facetten. Martin Fischer, Professor für Evolutionsbiologie und Direktor des Museums, hat viel zum Thema Bewegung geforscht und beispielsweise mit Röntgen-High-Speed-Aufnahmen gearbeitet, was mich schon während meines Studiums fasziniert hat. Diese Erforschung von Bewegung verbindet meine Arbeit mit Marcel Duchamp, aber eben auch mit den Fotografen Eadweard Muybridge und Étienne-Jules Marey. Deren Aufnahmen von Bewegungsabläufen entstammen einer Zeit, in der auch Künstler versuchten, Vorhandenes neu zu bewerten und ihr Blickfeld zu erweitern. Es war eine Aufbruchsphase. Duchamp oder auch Max Ernst haben in vielen Richtungen experimentiert, von der Frottage über fotografische Experimente bis hin zu transportablen Ausstellungen im Kofferformat. Diese universellen Ideen und die Möglichkeiten der heutigen Wissenschaft habe ich auf das Jenaer Museum in Form von abstrahierten, biologischen Prozessen projiziert. Sie bilden einen Teil des Themenspektrums ab, mit dem ich mich auseinandersetze und welches man vielleicht als Handschrift lesen kann.

CT Du hast nicht nur diese Arbeit auf dem Phyletischen Museum realisiert, sondern auch Medienfassaden in der ganzen Welt bespielt. Wie wichtig ist für dich die Integration der architektonischen und räumlichen Umgebung in die Projektionsfläche?

RS Ich versuche mich zunächst dem Ort und seinen Geschichten zu nähern, aber nicht in einem didaktischen Sinn. Ich möchte nichts erklären, sondern ich versuche einen Moment zu finden, der mich persönlich fasziniert. In Korea habe ich beispielsweise eine Medienfassade bespielt, die kaum architektonische Besonderheiten aufwies. Sie befindet sich mitten in einem belebten Areal, indem es überall flimmert, glitzert und blinkt. Seoul ist voller Medienfassaden, auf denen aber meistens nur Werbung läuft. Der Ort selbst, aber auch das Gebäude und die Fassade waren recht unspezifisch, dafür aber sehr einnehmend – einer der momentan größten LED-Flächen weltweit. Die entstandene Arbeit *scrape* bindet am Ende die komplette Umgebung ein ohne deren Besonderheiten zu betonen. Der Film zeigt Formen, die sich langsam aus der Dunkelheit lösen, sich verzweigen und das urbane Chaos in sich binden – eine maritime Erhabenheit, welche die Stadt entschleunigt.

CT Wie stark sind deine Fassadenprojekte an den Ort gebunden? Können sie auch woanders gezeigt werden?

processes: living paintings (2008), S. 96–99

RS *processes: living paintings* ist auf jeden Fall so stark mit dem Phyletischen Museum verwachsen, dass ich sie nicht woanders zeigen wollte und auch gar nicht könnte. Aber es gibt andere Arbeiten, wie zum Beispiel *recoil* und *ligature*, in der ich gestisch über die Architektur hinweggearbeitet habe, sie also nur als räumliche Leinwand begreife. Das ist Katharina Grosses malerischer Arbeitsweise nicht unähnlich. Es gibt natürlich kommerzielle Projection Mappings, die noch bunter, noch lauter und noch schneller sein wollen und sich nicht von der Architektur lösen können, weil sie auf der Illusion von perfekter Übereinstimmung der Projektion mit dem Gebäude beruhen. Dem versuche ich entgegenzusteuern. Man muss nicht unbedingt immer wieder die gleichen Ideen mit besserer Technik durchspielen. Bei Projektionsarbeiten hat man eigentlich große Freiheiten, die „Tradition" des Projection Mappings ist noch sehr jung. Natürlich kann man auf die Architektur eingehen, aber genau so gut kann man alles überschreiben, übermalen, ausradieren. Das sind Prozesse, die in der Malerei schon lange verfolgt werden, etwa bei *Erased* von Robert Rauschenberg. Rauschenberg hat die Zeichnungen von Willem De Kooning komplett ausradiert, also muss ich auch keinen Stein auf dem anderen lassen.

CT Wie wichtig sind für dich zeitgenössische Tendenzen, etwa die abstrakte Fotografie? Ich habe das Gefühl, dass die abstrakte Fotografie in den letzten Jahren unglaublich wichtig geworden ist, beispielsweise bei Wolfgang Tillmans.

RS Die Arbeit mit Foto-Chemikalien oder gefalteten Papieren finde ich auf jeden Fall spannend, aber auch die frühen Fotogramme von Henry Fox Talbot. Tillmans arbeitet mit den Möglichkeiten des Fotografischen und entnimmt Ausschnitte aus diesen Veränderungen. Aber Tillmans Ideen kann man schwerlich als Film darstellen, weil es nur einen kleinen Moment gibt, in dem das Bild funktioniert – es darf nicht zu leer und nicht zu überladen sein. Genau in diesem Sekundenbruchteil müsste man den Moment aufnehmen und zeitlich strecken. In einer Ausstellung in Los Angeles [Young Projects, 2011] meinte ein Besucher, dass meine Filme tausend abstrakte Gemälde pro Minute wären – in dem Sinne, dass jedes als einzelnes Bild für sich stehen könnte. Ich habe mich über diesen Satz sehr gefreut, denn das ist tatsächlich eine Grundidee meiner Arbeit. Ich versuche sehr stark verdichtete Bilder zu schaffen. Insofern kann man einen dreiminütigen Film vielleicht als eine komprimierte Ausstellung verstehen.

CT Manche Sequenzen von _grau kann ich mir unglaublich gut als großen Farbabzug vorstellen.

RS In _grau stecken neun Monate Arbeit. Das Isolieren von Einzelbildern ist für mich nicht wirklich reizvoll, denn das Herausfordernde an der Projektion ist doch, dass die Bilder jede Größe einnehmen und bei den Installationen auf jedes Material projiziert werden können. Daher verwende ich auch Papier oder Kunststoff als Projektionsfläche, denn sie bieten eine hohe Flexibilität. Dem Licht ist es per se egal, ob es auf ein Haus, eine Leinwand oder gefaltetes Papier projiziert wird. Da das Projektorlicht diese Materialien nicht durchdringen kann, hat es diese hochillusionistische Wirkung. Das projizierte Bild wird von 0,1 Millimeter Papier aufgehalten, wirft Schatten und kann zudem wie in *tearing shadows* mit künstlichen Schatten erweitert werden. Warum braucht man ein Einzelbild, wenn eine Papierhülle zu einer eigenen Welt werden kann?

CT In der Ausstellung LUX AETERNA stellst du das erste Mal Zeichnungen aus, baust Lichträume und zeigst Dokumentationen, etwa von der Performance *magnitude*, die nicht unbedingt filmisch, sondern deren Medium der Laserstrahl ist. In dieser Arbeit „malst" oder „zeichnest" du mit Licht. Interessiert dich generell die Arbeit mit Licht oder wolltest du die Möglichkeit nutzen, etwas Neues auszuprobieren?

magnitude (2015), S. 150–153

RS Zum einem interessiert mich ganz klar das Experiment. Für die Ausstellung habe ich kleine Lichtobjekte gebaut, als eine Art Ergänzung zu den vielen Ideen, die nur auf Papier existieren. Natürlich ist ein Film sehr viel durchdachter, aber in der umfangreichen Ausstellung ist es das Schöne, dass mein Arbeitsprozess in den Fokus rückt und nicht nur die finalen Ergebnisse. Zum anderen erlauben mir die Räume meine eigene Geschichte mit der des Mediums Licht zu verknüpfen, beispielsweise bei der Installation *mold* mit den Overhead-Projektoren, die ich noch aus Schulzeiten kenne und die früher Polyluxe genannt wurden. In der Schule wurden sie nur als technisches Hilfsmittel eingesetzt und sind nun längst von Videoprojektoren verdrängt worden. Ich hatte nun die Möglichkeit, ihr künstlerisches Potenzial zu untersuchen, mit ihnen zu experimentieren und die Wände mit Lichtzeichnungen zu versehen. Diese verschiedenen Situationen im Museum und Kunstverein sollen auch verschiedene Qualitäten des Lichts widerspiegeln. *lux aeterna*, eine Skulptur, die ich im Kunstverein ausstelle und die gleichzeitig den Namen der Ausstellung trägt, besteht aus alten Röhrenfernsehern. Hier finden grundverschiedene Arbeiten sowie Experimente erstmalig zusammen und verschmelzen zu einem vertrauten Röhrenflimmern, welches sich vom sterilen Look moderner Fernsehgeräte unterscheidet. Und ich greife endlich wieder eine Idee auf, die ich vor einigen Jahren während einer Residency im MuseumsQuartier Wien in Miniatur erprobt habe: Mein neuester Film *vitreous* verschränkt sich dabei mit einer durch einen Luftstrom bewegten Folie und lässt diesen fast kreatürlich werden. Für mich ist die Ausstellung sowohl ein emotional-persönliches Durchschreiten meiner eigenen Entwicklung, als auch der Zustände von Licht. Nur die Arbeit *sputter* fällt ein wenig aus der Reihe, da hier der Elektronenstrahl des Rasterelektronenmikroskops die Aufnahmen entstehen ließ.

CT Und was wird danach kommen?

RS Ich freue mich an einem neuen Film arbeiten zu können und alle Hindernisse der Realität hinter mir zu lassen. Die in der Ausstellung gezeigten Skizzen und viele Ideen, die sich in Installationen nicht umsetzen ließen, werden von mir neu bewertet werden können und in diesem Experimentalfilm zusammenfinden. Aber der Rückzug ins Virtuelle wird nur von kurzer Dauer sein, einige in Planung befindliche Projekte werden mich wohl bald wieder aus dem Studio locken.

In the Universe of Digital Images
—
Robert Seidel
interviewed by
Claudia Tittel

CT Your experimental films are not only shown at festivals, but also on media façades and in museum exhibitions. How are your films changed by new spatial contexts?

RS Until approximately 2008, I concentrated primarily on films that were shown as single-channel works at film festivals and exhibitions. In 2008, I created my first larger building projection, *processes: living painting.* One year later, my first projection sculpture appeared at the Museum of Contemporary Art in Taipei, Taiwan. At the time, I was dealing with actual spatial structures and wanted to let projected forms and colors interact with paper surfaces. Because of this, I abandoned traditional projection and created a suspended sculpture from handmade paper, upon which the film *chiral* was projected. In the space, there was a juxtaposition of the projected-upon paper sculpture and the film itself, which was shown on evenly-stretched paper. In this way, visitors were able to build a bridge on their own from the two-dimensionality of the projection to the spatial dimension. *chiral* is also the first film that exists in different iterations and variants. I never show my older films as projection sculptures because they came into being as films and thus place different demands upon the filmic framework.

CT Would it be conceivable for you to transfer your films into different spatial contexts?

RS Of course, but *_grau,* for instance, is quite a concentrated film that expands the screen. It produces an undertow that doesn't exist within an installation. In the installations, the viewers are an integral part of the image-space construction. They are perceiving not only the film, but also the surrounding environment. On the one hand, that is appealing, but on the other hand, the focus is missing. *_grau* isn't a film that one should just rush past.

CT Is that to say that every work demands a particular mode of reception?

RS Of course it would be great if my films, which are developed specifically as such, could be viewed intently. A focused viewing is, however, nearly impossible. Within the context of a festival, my films are often squeezed into a 60 to 80 minute program between experimental films or animations. This contemplative moment rarely occurs. Also, on the internet – an important platform for me – viewers click through the films and jump from one stimulus to the next. Even within a museum, it's not often possible to experience films without distraction. There are indeed large exhibitions with elaborate frameworks for a concentrated viewing, but this is seldom the case in smaller exhibition spaces. There you're dependent upon the wandering flâneur being stopped for a moment.

CT In an exaggerated sense, your films function like painting, not only because they have visual similarities, but rather because – as I see it – there's no beginning and no end, no story and no protagonists.

RS You are definitely correct that my films come across as painterly. I work with layers of textures, colors, and atmospheres. Moments of stasis emerge, but so do continually changing structures. It is precisely these changes with which I'm concerned. In this respect, it would be ideal if the films could be viewed intently from beginning to end. A linear viewing of the films is important since a type of notation, rather than a narrative structure, forms the basis of the works. It's for this reason that I generally resist multi-channel works. Sometimes one stands somewhat helpless before such pieces; there are a number of screens and you don't know which one you're supposed to watch first. Of course, one can work with this overload, but the attentiveness that I prefer is oftentimes bound to one screen. There are also examples which contradict this: *vellum* is a virtual sculpture that ran simultaneously on multiple screens and media façades. Thus, the same object could be seen from different intersecting planes and viewing angles. It gets more complicated when one works sculpturally, expanding the space, doing so without a rectangular projection surface. Then the audience is initially bewildered, but they quickly understand that it's not necessary to let the images sink in one after another, but rather that they themselves need to move actively. I hope that the sculptures ignite the viewers' curiosity, inspiring them to go on their own exploratory journey.

CT How do you develop your forms? What's the point of origin for your works?

RS That's something I can't clearly describe, since it's rather sensations and associations that I'm trying to present. Drawings are usually the starting-point for my works. A few of them are being exhibited for the first time; for instance, the preliminary sketches for my next film. The drawings form a sort of loose basic framework and bundle of ideas that will then be further formulated in the projections or sculptures.

CT In nearly all of your works, one gets the impression that you are translating drawing or painting into a cinematic medium. You are creating moving paintings. In this regard, you're correlating with the ideas of the avant-gardists who conceived of film as a new painterly medium. Walter Ruttmann, Viking Eggeling, or Hans Richter were of the opinion that film was "painting with time" and that painting needed to be freed from its static constraints.

RS As a matter of fact, they all painted, they were inventive, and they all used the possibilities of the time to create novel images. Oskar Fischinger, for example, developed devices; László Moholoy-Nagy constructed kinetic objects; and it, nonetheless, remains partly a mystery how the cinematic images were created in the end. I recently purchased the new edition of Moholy-Nagy's book *Vision in Motion*. For me, the book is still relevant. One shouldn't underestimate the fact that we're constantly surrounded by moving images and that questions which arose then still haven't been completely answered. Earlier, there were only very primitive tools available. Today, there are many more possibilities; the digital has completely permeated everyday existence. But this technological freedom is overwhelming and perhaps prevents us from trying to get to the bottom of things. We shouldn't forget that, initially, abstract film has no function. A person has to have the desire to explore and understand its complexity, approaching pure movement and focusing on temporal transformation. Marcel Duchamp, for example, let painted disks rotate, not only so that paintings moved, but also so that the movement created a new dimensionality. Sometimes I get the feeling that everything has seemingly already existed, but that a detailed analysis of things has seldom come about due to technological barriers. That's why, for instance, I curated the film program *Penetrating Surfaces* for the Austrian Film Museum in 2014, which aimed to reflect the materially-inherent aesthetic potential of the digital.

CT Starting in 1909, while working around Marcel Duchamp, Georges Braque and Pablo Picasso burst open and expanded the boundaries of space, depicting different spatial perspectives, thereby inventing Cubism. The Cubists, although they remained within the medium of painting, nonetheless portrayed temporality on the canvas. And when we think of the Futurists and their works, for example, Umberto Boccioni's *The Street Enters the House* (La Strada entra nella casa, 1911), you can really sense movement.

RS From the Cubists and Futurists, I learned to question seeing as a sensory act and to break up the linearity of perspective and form. I can remember seeing Marcel Duchamp's *Nude Descending a Staircase No. 2* (Nu descendant un escalier, no. 2, 1912) when I was around 16 years old. I was fascinated by how Duchamp depicted the figure, letting the movement dissolve in facets. The temporal sequence was stretched out and, at the same time, staggered so freely that it could have been unfolded architecture. The biggest link is and was that Duchamp depicts something with a direct connection to reality, something which is immediately understood by viewers and which is, nonetheless, abstract and thus never to be seen in this form.

CT How did you come to devote yourself to films, especially to abstract films?

RS For me, film was always a very contemporary way of conveying emotions and atmospheres. Initially, I drew a lot, both on paper and with the computer, but I never found the results to be as captivating as a moving picture. In film, you can connect different moments with one another and examine this conglomeration over and over again without any effort. With the drawings, a flow is established, and they lose their autonomy. For me, computers are a type of archive. I collect ideas there and continually scan through them.

Our world has become extremely functional. Everything has to have a meaning; everything has to be categorized. Abstraction enables a defunctionalization, which allows me to cast a new glance upon the world, but also at someone else's personality and, in the end, at my own as well. Sometimes viewers who have little relation to art comment upon my works. They describe their individual experiences, which are oftentimes completely surprising. It's unbelievably rewarding when someone shares such a personal moment with me. In doing so, it makes no difference at all what kind of background they have. Everyone can contemplate life abstractly. And I've met people who have summed up a complex work of mine in the most thought-provoking and poetic ways possible. I oftentimes have the feeling that I don't really understand "people," but through these reactions I learn something on a very personal level. The functionalization of the world and everything in it and the need always to have a clear answer is dismaying. The world is far too complex for it to be possible to distinct answers to every question. Of course one would like to have clarity, structure, or even reliance in many areas in life, but I'd just as much like to be allowed to simply be overwhelmed, surprised, or confused. In the end, maybe it's just important to interrupt the routine of everyday life.

CT Is that why you're so fascinated by nature?

RS Nature is infinitely varied. I believe that it's there that we – that I – find the most appealing moments. The processual character of nature is interesting to me. Everything grows and changes constantly, dies and regrows. Nature has, in fundamentally different periods, expressed itself in the most manifold ways. One finds an unbelievable spectrum of temporal dimensions – from the mayfly, which lives for a day, to the mountains, which have evolved over millions of years and that continue to change as well. In science today, there are various processes that can draw nearer to these different temporalities – from the microscope, to the telescope, to archaeological excavations. Within the sediment, changes in the landscape, as well as societal changes, are stored, changes that can provide us with information about the earth's development or about the climate millions of years ago. In turn, with the aid of different microscopes, you can see things that are invisible to the naked eye due to their size, or even things that are outside the visible spectrum. I come from a family that is interested in the natural sciences. My father is a physicist, I specialized in science at school and studied biology for a year. It has continually occurred to me that scientists create images that we have yet to see in art. For scientists, these images are primarily analytical tools, providing an overview, a scheme, or an indicator. The aesthetic side of these images remains hidden to most scientists, even when the necessity of publishing them sharpens their focus. I'd like to deconstruct these filterings of nature and show their poetic side. The most important thing is to find an almost archaic structure in the process, a structure in which the viewer can lose her- or himself, letting the constant distractions of everyday life recede into the background.

CT Where does your creative process begin? Do you always draw on paper first?

RS Well, mostly it's not "perfect" drawings, but rather sketches. First of all, there's a rough agglomeration of ideas which become more complex on the computer. The pencil, the hand and the paper seem to flow into one another while drawing. It's a quick medium – ideas can manifest themselves on a simple piece of paper without any compulsion to control them. The main thing is that, first of all, ideas are recorded and the creative process is stimulated. I can best do that on paper. As soon as the computer is turned on and you're waiting until the programs have started, you're already in a different mode. Then the flow of ideas is suddenly lost. On the computer, it's oftentimes a process of working through these spontaneously recorded ideas.

CT But there are drawing programs, right?

RS There are certainly drawing tablets and software with which you can draw as if you were using a pencil. I use those too, since using paper can tire exactly like working with a mouse can. But even the metaphors behind software and hardware are often based on actual tools – the pencil, the surface plane, the coordinate system – the gesture behind it is nevertheless something else. Digital tools can be navigated in very different ways. For example, it's simple to link the movement of an object with the intensity of a light source. And of course you can model three-dimensionally, working virtually with objects like a sculptor. The biggest advantages are the freely scalable proportions. With the same procedure, you can create a grain of sand or a giant landscape. These different processes intertwine without physical borders. It might be that I first develop a form that then later becomes the basis for the color of a background. The special thing about the computer is that there's no defined final state and no loss of quality; rather, this continual transformation as a working metaphor is carried within it.

CT How can one conceive of that? There are artists who work with computers who are often criticized for the fact, that it's the computer, or rather programs, which are doing the work.

RS The computer of course "creates" nothing on its own. I always break it down to a simple example: A word-processing program is also just a utility, a tool. In the end, the program functions like a comfortable typewriter, but it doesn't automatically write an interesting and elegant text. You yourself have to think and write. With me, the work always starts with a collection of ideas and sketches, which I then work with using programs and my own tools. The computer and the programs are just another tool, like pencil and paper, to use in order to formulate my ideas. Some programs fit well into my approach. However, as I run up against their limitations, I change my way of working and approach my ideas via another path.

CT Do you always know exactly where your ideas are leading you, or do they change massively during the working process?

RS My work is essentially inspired by the computer and its processes, but I have a clear conception when I start on a new work. Nevertheless, it often doesn't make sense to present initial ideas, since the work changes quite radically from the sketches to the film on to the installation. When I prepare a new work and the museum would like to have, for example, a preview image for the press, it's often hard to honor the request. I could, of course, pull a still from a film, but I would first of all have to favor one image over thousands of others, and secondly I usually don't know beforehand how the film is going to work on the sculpture in the space. I do indeed have a specific image in my head, but the vast number of parameters in the actual place makes it difficult to anticipate beforehand and to preconceive it in a balanced way. On paper, you turn the page and start over again. I'd like to retain a similar freedom and openness in the realization of my ideas as well.

I know many artists who don't change their ideas and who plan everything out down to the last detail. Often, they don't even have the opportunity to intervene in the working process owing, for one thing, to time considerations, but also because a whole team is tied up in the chain of production. They have huge sculptures cast and surfaces polished. Everyone who fabricates a piece of art with his own hands notices, in the end, deviations from his initial idea. Now, when a whole team works on it, this deviation is even greater. Everything we do is subject to certain processes of decision making and formulation, which are in effect up until the end. My works are not digital readymades.

CT I would say that there's something like a "Robert Seidel signature" and I'd also claim that I would recognize your works. Is there something that characterizes all of your works?

RS It's difficult to say if there's a kind of overarching theme. There are works, above all the place-specific ones, that I designed for particular constellations. Take, for example, the previously mentioned work, *processes: living paintings,* for the Phyletic Museum in Jena. In that case, the theme was predetermined by the building and the collection. It's the most well-known museum of evolutionary theory and shows the genesis of life as well as the development of humankind in every aspect. Martin Fischer, professor of Evolutionary Biology and director of the museum, has done a great deal of research on movement, and has worked, for example, with high-speed X-ray-captures, which already fascinated me during my university studies. This research on movement connects my work with Marcel Duchamp, but also with the photographers Eadweard Muybridge and Étienne-Jules Marey. Their photographs of motion-sequences descend from a time during which artists as well attempted to reevaluate the status quo and to expand their field of vision. It was an atmosphere of departure. Duchamp, or Max Ernst as well, experimented in many areas, from frottage, to photographic experiments, to suitcase-sized transportable exhibitions. These universal ideas and the possibilities of modern science are what I projected onto the Jena-based Museum in the form of abstracted biological processes. They depict part of the range of themes that I deal with, and that is something one could perhaps read as my signature.

CT You not only produced this kind of work at the Phyletic Museum, but also created art for media façades all over the world. How important is integrating the architectonic and spatial surroundings into the projection surface?

RS I first try to approach the location and its histories, but not in a didactic sense. I don't wish to explain anything, rather I try to find a moment that fascinates me personally. In Korea, for example, I projected onto a media façade that had hardly any unique architectonic features. It's located in the middle of a busy area where everything is flickering, twinkling and flashing. Seoul is full of media façades, but most of them just show advertisements. The location itself, but also the building and the façade, were unspecific but, on the other hand, quite engaging – it's one of the largest LED-surfaces in the world at this point. The resulting work, *scrape,* integrates, in the end, the complete surrounding area without emphasizing its particular features. The film shows forms that slowly drift out of the darkness, ramify, and absorb the urban chaos into themselves – a maritime sublimity that decelerates the city.

CT How strongly are your façade projects bound to a place? Can they also be shown somewhere else?

RS *processes: living paintings* is, at any rate, so connately intertwined with the Phyletic Museum that I wouldn't want to show it anywhere else, and indeed couldn't anyway. But there are other works, such as *recoil* and *ligature,* in which I gesturally work beyond the architecture, understanding it simply as a three-dimensional screen. That's not unlike Katharina Grosses' painterly way of working. There are, of course, commercial projection mappings which try to be even more colorful, louder as well as faster, and that are unable to detach themselves from the architecture because they depend upon the illusion of perfect congruence of the projection with the building. I try to steer away from that. One doesn't necessarily have to play out the same idea again and again with better technology. There's actually a lot of freedom in projection works; the "tradition" of projection mapping is still very young. Of course, one could react to the architecture, but one can just as easily write or paint over, even erase everything. Those are processes that have been pursued in painting for a long time now, such as in Robert Rauschenberg's *Erased*. Rauschenberg completely erased Willem de Kooning's drawings, so I'm free to construct as I choose as well.

CT How important are contemporary trends, like abstract photography, to you? I have the impression that abstract photography, for example, like that of

Wolfgang Tillmans, has become unbelievably important in recent years.

RS I certainly find working with photographic chemicals or folded papers exciting, but I'm also thrilled by Henry Fox Talbot's early photograms. Tillmans works with the possibilities of the photographic and excerpts sections from these transformations. But it would be very difficult to show Tillmans' ideas filmically, because there's only a short moment in which the picture satisfies – it can't be too empty or too overloaded. At exactly this split-second, the moment has to be captured and temporally stretched out. In an exhibition in Los Angeles [Young Projects, 2011], a visitor voiced his opinion that my films were a thousand abstract paintings per minute – in the sense that every single image could stand alone as such. This sentence made me incredibly happy, because that is, in fact, a fundamental idea of my work. I attempt to create very strongly condensed images. In this sense, a 3-minute film could perhaps be understood as a compressed exhibition.

CT I can incredibly easily imagine some of the sequences of _grau as large color prints.

RS Nine months of work reside within _grau. Isolating individual images isn't really attractive to me because the challenging part of the projection is that the images can be any size and can be projected onto every material in the installations. That's also why I use paper or plastic as projection surfaces – they offer a high degree of flexibility. For light, per se, it doesn't matter if it's projected on a house, on a screen, or on folded paper. Since the light of the projector is unable to penetrate these objects, it has this highly illusionistic effect. The projected image is stopped by 0.1-millimeter-thick paper, casts shadows, and can moreover be enhanced by artificial shadows, as it is in tearing shadows. Why do we need a single image, when a paper shell can become a world of its own?

CT In the exhibition LUX AETERNA, you're exhibiting drawings for the first time, constructing illuminated rooms and showing documentaries, for example from the performance magnitude, which is not necessarily filmic, but rather whose medium is the laser beam. In this work, you "paint" or "draw" with light. Does working with light in general interest you, or did you want to use the opportunity to try out something new?

RS For one thing, I'm definitely interested in the experiment. For the exhibition, I built small light objects as a type of expansion of the many ideas that just exist on paper. Film is naturally much more deliberated, but the beautiful thing about the comprehensive exhibition is that it focuses on my working process and not just the final results. For another thing, the rooms allow me to connect my own history with the medium of light, for example, in the installation *mold* with the overhead projectors, which I'm still familiar with from my school days and which used to be called Polylux. In school, they were just used as technological aides and were replaced long ago by video projectors. I then had the opportunity to investigate their artistic potential, to experiment with them, and to cover the walls with light drawings. These different settings in the museum and the Kunstverein are also meant to reflect different qualities of light. *lux aeterna,* a sculpture that I am exhibiting in the Kunstverein and which at the same time bears the name of the exhibition, consists of old cathode-ray-tube televisions. Here, fundamentally different films, as well as experiments, come together for the first time, melting in a familiar flickering of the tubes, which differs from the sterile look of modern televisions. And I have finally picked up an old idea again, which I tried out in miniature some years ago during a residency at the MuseumsQuarter Wien: My latest film, *vitreous*, merges with a synthetic sheet moved by an air current, allowing it to become almost creaturely. For me, the exhibition is an emotional-personal passage through both my own development as well the conditions of light. Only the work *sputter* diverges somewhat from this, since here the electron beam of the scanning electron microscope produces the images.

CT And what comes next?

RS I'm happy to be able to be working on a new film and to leave all of the limitations of reality behind me. The sketches shown in the exhibition and many ideas that were unable to be translated into the installations will be re-evaluated and will come together in this experimental film. But the retreat into the virtual will be short-lived; some projects in their planning stages will probably lure me out the studio again soon.

Geraffte Zeit.
Robert Seidel und die Alten Meister
—
Peter Forster

Für das Museum Wiesbaden schuf Robert Seidel 2013 anlässlich der Neupräsentation der Abteilung „Alte Meister" die Rauminstallation *grapheme*. Sie befindet sich im zweiten Obergeschoss des Hauses und ist der Kunst der Alten Meister als Entrée vorgelagert. Im Zuge der Neupräsentation hatte man sich im Museum seinerzeit gegen das Konzept der „geschichteten Zeit" entschieden. Diese im 19. Jahrhundert entwickelte Idee einer linear verlaufenden Geschichte und einer damit verbundenen chronologischen Präsentation ihrer künstlerischen Zeugnisse – wie sie für einen Großteil der Museen noch heute verbindlich ist – wurde bewusst vermieden. Stattdessen beschloss man, die in Frage kommenden Werke, welche einen Zeitraum vom frühen Mittelalter bis ins 19. Jahrhundert umfassen, in einen thematischen Zusammenhang zu stellen. In sieben Themenräumen werden die künstlerischen Prozesse innerhalb der jeweiligen Gattungen verhandelt, wobei zeitlich große Distanzen zu überbrücken sind. Die Jahrhunderte zwischen der Entstehung von Werken Domenico Tintorettos über Pietro Liberis bis hin zu Anselm Feuerbach werden auf diese Weise durchlässig, verbinden und vermischen sich auf inhaltlicher Ebene.

Für dieses Konzept sollte ein schlüssiger Einstieg mit einer künstlerischen Intervention geschaffen werden. Die Gefahr, über eine rein formelhafte oder gar illustrative Beziehung zwischen „alter" und „neuer" Kunst ein additives Verhältnis entstehen zu lassen, war groß. Seidels mediale Arbeit bringt die richtige Lösung, denn es gelingt ihm, mit seinem Werk eine Zeitlosigkeit zu erzeugen, die Raum für Assoziationen lässt. Dabei wirkt *grapheme* sowohl zukunftsweisend als auch rückblickend, Kunstgeschichte verhandelnd und extrahierend. Seidels Farb- und Formenwelt gibt sich offen gegenüber kunsthistorischen Kontexten. Um den Raum zu erweitern und um das Publikum einzubeziehen, ließ Seidel die rückwärtige Wand flächendeckend mit einem Spiegel überziehen. Unmittelbar davor installierte er eine Fülle von weißen Folienskulpturen, die von der Decke herabhängen und die Projektionsflächen für seine Filme bilden. Die animierten Projektionen auf den unregelmäßigen Skulpturoberflächen wachsen zudem auf dunkelgrünem Grund über die beiden Seitenwände – monochromen Wandzeichnungen gleich – weiter. Das dramatische Soundgeflecht von Heiko Tippelt vollendet die Arbeit und ergibt eine Totalinstallation, die alle Sinne anspricht.

Neben dieser komplexen inhaltlichen Aufladung ist der Raum auch wegen seiner eigenwilligen und gedrungenen Proportionen ein schwer zu bespielender Ort: Ohne Begrenzung schließt er unmittelbar an einen hellen Treppenaufgang an und weist in seinem Inneren zwei weitere große Öffnungen auf – eine äußerst schwierige Ausgangssituation, um ein konzentriertes Raumgefüge für eine Videoskulptur zu erzeugen. Ferner gilt es, eine sicht- und fühlbare Zäsur zum übrigen Museumsbetrieb herzustellen. Der Raum soll einem „Zeittunnel" gleichen, die Besucher zunächst irritieren, sie aus ihren vertrauten Sehgewohnheiten lösen und ihre Erwartungshaltung auf ihrem Weg zu den Alten Meistern unterlaufen. Auch wenn diese Aufgabenstellung zunächst schwer einlösbar schien, zeigt sich, dass Seidels Kunst genau hier ansetzt. Ihre Stärken sind die Bewegungen und fließenden Übergänge, die Verbindung vom Immateriellen und Materiellen, die sich aus der formalen und inhaltlichen Gestaltung der Arbeiten ergeben sowie Bezüge zur Flüchtigkeit und dem Zufälligen der Moderne aufweisen. Doch gerade dieses für die Moderne so exemplarische kontingente Fließen findet sich seit alters her auch in anderen Epochen, jedoch mit anderen formalen Mitteln dargestellt. Seidels Installation verdichtet diese künstlerischen Ausdrucksmöglichkeiten und Aussagen der Alten

Meister über Farbe, Form und Raum. In einer Art Reise durch die Jahrhunderte versetzt er sie in Bewegung und verlebendigt den ihnen eigenen Impetus. Im Museum Wiesbaden arbeitet er mit der Essenz alter Kunst, indem er sich ausschnitthaft auf Farbverdichtungen, Texturen, Falten und Gesten konzentriert. Er legt somit die abstrakten und zeitlosen Qualitäten von Kunst frei und stellt deren geistige sowie technische Verwandtschaft dar. Sie gehen im Goetheschen Sinne *Wahlverwandtschaften* ein – allerdings ohne deren tragisches Ende.

Übertraf die altmeisterliche Bilderwelt bereits die Vorstellungskraft ihrer Zeitgenossen, so fügt Seidel mit dem ihm ganz eigenen Bilderkosmos seiner Filmsequenzen unserer Vorstellungskraft und unseren Sehgewohnheiten ein neues Kapitel hinzu. Dennoch finden sich im Kern kurzzeitig verifizierbare Formen der Vergangenheit, insbesondere Faltenbildungen, die sich kaskadenartig ausbreiten, um sich im nächsten Moment endgültig zu verflüssigen. Die kunsthistorischen Vorbilder dieser Arbeiten lassen sich malerisch bei Rogier van der Weyden und Giovanni Bellini verorten. Auch sie füllten den gesamten Bildraum und erreichten eine perspektivische Intensivierung durch Falten- und Farbwürfe, die das Blickfeld auf die Szenerie und die Figuren fortlaufend erweitern. Es ist aber vor allem die griechische Klassik, die eine gewisse Vorbildfunktion ausübt, wie sie beispielsweise durch die *Tauschwestern* vertreten wird, einer Skulpturengruppe im Ostgiebel des Parthenons. Seidel näherte sich dieser Figurengruppe schon in der Arbeit *folds* im Jahre 2011.

Den mehrfach beschädigten und umkopierten Skulpturen wohnt in der Detailbetrachtung ein Abstraktionsgrad inne, der in der Überformung durch Seidels Projektion zur vollständigen Abstraktion ausreift. Fast metaphorisch rafft Seidel die Zeit und deren Folgen für die Skulpturen filmisch zusammen. Der reale Deformationsgrad der Oberflächenstruktur durch Zerstörung und Verwitterung gerät bei ihm im übertragenen Sinne zu einem kontinuierlichen natürlichen Fluss der Veränderungen: einem unausweichlichen und folgerichtigen Prozess, der sich aus Werden und Vergehen speist.

Obwohl Seidels Arbeiten häufig keine reale bildhafte Wiedererkennbarkeit erzeugen, beinhalten sie seine persönliche „Summe aller Bilder" der Alten Meister. Dabei setzt Seidel weniger auf die reine Bildhaftigkeit, sondern auf die Assoziationskraft, die den Charakter der alten Kunst widerspiegelt. Voraussetzung hierfür ist ein Verständnis dieser Kunst und das Einfühlungsvermögen in deren Techniken und Entstehungsgeschichten. Die Basis hierfür bildet die Zeichnung – sowohl bei Seidel als auch bei den Alten Meistern. Während die „Alten" der Zeit entsprechend auf das Trägermaterial Papier zeichneten und ihre Ideen auf diesem Medium bannten, bewegen sich Seidels Zeichnungen in der Gegenwart und werden neben klassischen Materialien wie Bleistift vor allem mit den technischen Mitteln des Jetzt erzeugt. Am und mit dem Computer entstehen Seidels einzigartige Bildtransformationen auf der Grundlage dieser zeichnerischen Findungen. Sie sind schwer zu beschreiben, weil ihnen etwas Amorphes oder gar Kalligrafisches anhaftet, so als würde man einem Aushärtungsprozess beiwohnen. Vielschichtig reihen sich die Szenen aneinander, fließen und mäandern zu bislang ungeahnten Formenwelten zusammen, um sich im nächsten Augenblick in zarte Gespinste aufzulösen.

Hier findet sich die erkennbarste Nähe zu den Künstlern vergangener Epochen, weil es sich um „Geistes-Gebilde" handelt, die neue Horizonte öffnen und sich von der realen Abbildung lösen. Auch die Alten Meister beabsichtigten nicht, die Welt so darzustellen, wie sie sie vorfanden. Vielmehr wollten sie diese um neue symbolische und religiöse Ebenen erweitern und gingen dabei über das rein Abbildhafte hinaus. Robert Seidel entwickelt ein zeit- und raumloses Geflecht bewegter Farb- und Figurenkonstellationen, das wie eine illusionistische Weiterführung vorangegangener Kunst wirkt. Seine Palette ist der Computer, hier finden Mischungen aller Techniken und Gattungen statt. Wo die Alten Meister in ihrer Lasurtechnik Schicht um Schicht auftrugen, projiziert Seidel Farbe auf Farbe, Bewegung auf Stille, Relief auf Fläche. In beinahe barocken Überladungen ergibt sich eine teilweise dramatisch gebärdende Farbenpracht. Sie erinnert etwa an Caravaggios Enthauptungsszenen, bei denen das tiefrote Blut den Betrachtern förmlich ins Gesicht zu spritzen scheint. Seidels „digital drippings" scheinen auch die eruptiven Gesten Jackson Pollocks aufzunehmen und erweitern die auf Leinwand gebannte malerische Bewegung zu kontinuierlich sich neu konstituierenden Bildern. Die Dynamisierung der erstarrten Farbflüsse ist eine Weiterführung von Malerei mit anderen Mitteln. Während van Gogh behauptete: „Aber der Maler der Zukunft ist ein Kolorist, wie es noch keinen gegeben hat", so ist Seidel Künstler jenes Futur. Nicht weil er mit zeitgenössischen Medien arbeitet, sondern weil er es versteht, die Kunst selbst neu zu definieren und mit dem Wissen um die Vergangenheit ins Jetzt zu überführen.

Nested time. Robert Seidel and the Old Masters
—
Peter Forster

In 2013, Robert Seidel created the spatial installation *grapheme* for the Museum Wiesbaden on the occasion of the new presentation of the "Old Masters" section. It is located on the building's second upper storey and situated as an entryway in front of the Old Masters. In the course of the extension, the museum decided against the concept of "layered time." Developed in the 19th century, this idea of a linearly proceeding history and, tied to it, of a chronological presentation of its artistic evidence – still mandatory today for a majority of museums – was intentionally avoided. Instead, it was decided to set the works in question, which cover a period from the early Middle Ages to the 19th century, into a thematic context. In seven thematic rooms, the artistic processes within the respective genres are negotiated, with large temporal distances having to be bridged in the process. In this way, the centuries from the creation of the works of Domenico Tintoretto, to Pietro Liberi, to Anselm Feuerbach become permeable, connecting and mingling on the level of content.

For this concept, a coherent point of entry was supposed to be created via an artistic intervention. There was considerable risk that an additive relation could arise through a purely formal or even illustrative relationship between "old" and "new" art. Seidel's media composition features a fitting solution; with this work, he succeeds in creating a timelessness that allows space for associations. In doing so, *grapheme* operates both in a forward- and backward-looking manner, negotiating and abstracting art history. Seidel's world of colors and forms conducts itself openly in relation to art-historical contexts. In order to enlarge the space and involve the public, Seidel completely blankets the rear wall with a mirror. Immediately in front of this, he installs an abundance of white sculptures made from white synthetic film, which hang down from the ceiling and on which the films are projected. The animated projections on the irregular sculptural surfaces also spread further across the two sidewalls, resembling monochrome wall drawings. The dramatic sound-web by Heiko Tippelt completes the work and yields a total installation speaking to all the senses.

Along with this complex, content-based charge, the space is also a site that is difficult to work with due to its idiosyncratic and compact proportions: without boundaries, it connects immediately to a bright staircase and features two more large openings within it – an extremely difficult starting-point for creating a concentrated spatial structure for a video sculpture. Furthermore, a visible and palpable caesura from the usual museum operations needs to be produced. The space is supposed to resemble a "time tunnel," which initially irritates visitors, removes them from their usual viewing habits, and circumvents their expectations on their way to the Old Masters. Even if at first this task appeared difficult to resolve, Seidel's art proves to intervene precisely upon this point. Its strengths are the movements and fluid transitions, the connection of the immaterial and material, which arise out of the formal and content-based creation of the works and exhibit references to the transience and contingency of the modern. Yet precisely this contingent flux, so exemplary for the modern, has been found since time immemorial in other epochs, albeit represented by other formal means. Seidel's installation condenses these artistic expressive possibilities and propositions of the Old Masters in terms of color, form and space. In a kind of journey through the centuries, he sets them into motion and makes their intrinsic impulse come to life. In the Museum Wiesbaden, he works with the essence of old art by selectively concentrating on color densities, textures, folds and gestures. He thus sets free the abstract and timeless qualities of art and represents their mental, as well as technical affiliation. In Goethe's sense, they make *Elective Affinities,* although without the tragic ending.

If the Old Masters' pictorial world already surpassed the imaginative power of their contemporaries, Seidel adds a new chapter to our imaginative power and visual habits with the quite individual pictorial cosmos of his film sequences. Yet, at core, one finds forms of the past, only briefly verifiable, particularly fold-formations that spread out in cascades in order to irrevocably liquefy in the next moment. The art-historical models of these works can be located in painterly terms in the works of Rogier van der Weyden and Giovanni Bellini. These masters filled their entire pictorial space and achieved an intensification of perspective through the fall of drapery folds and casts of paint, which continuously extend the field of vision onto the space and figures. However, it is above all Greek Classicism that exercises a certain exemplary function, as represented, for instance, by the *Moirai*, a sculptural group from the east pediment of the Parthenon. Seidel already approached this figurative group in the 2011 work *folds*.

folds (2011), p. 118–121

In examining the details of these repeatedly damaged and re-copied sculptures, a degree of abstraction is inherent, which matures into complete abstraction in the transformation achieved by Seidel's projection. Seidel metaphorically compresses time and its consequences in a filmic manner. In his work, the real degree of deformation of the surface structure due to corrosion and weathering turns, in a figurative sense, into a continuous natural flux of changes: an ineluctable and consecutive process that feeds on becoming and passing.

Although Seidel's works frequently do not generate any real pictorial recognizability, they contain his personal "sum of all pictures" of the Old Masters. In doing do, Seidel capitalizes less on pure pictoriality than on the power of association, in which the character of previous art is reflected. A prerequisite to this is an understanding of this art and the capability for empathy with its techniques and histories of creation. In this regard, the basis is drawing – both for Seidel as well as for the Old Masters. While the "old ones" drew on the substrate of paper, in accordance with their time, and manifested their ideas in this medium, Seidel's drawings move in the present and are created, alongside classical materials such as lead pencil, principally with modern technological means. On and with the computer, Seidel's singular pictorial transformations arise on the basis of these graphic findings. They are difficult to describe because something amorphous or even calligraphic adheres to them, as though one were present at something hardening in a curing process. In multiple layers, the scenes are ranked on top of one another, flow and meander together into previously unimagined form-worlds, only to dissolve in the next moment into delicate gossamer webs.

The most recognizable affinity to the Old Masters can be found here, because it is a matter of "mental constructs" that open new horizons and are released from illustrating the real. For the Old Masters, it was also not simply a question of representing the world as they perceived it. Rather, they wanted to expand upon new symbolic and religious levels and in the process went beyond the purely representational. Likewise, Seidel consistently develops a timeless and spaceless mesh of animated color- and figure-constellations that work like an illusionistic carrying-forward of previous art. His palette is the computer; here, mixtures of all techniques and genres take place. Where the Old Masters applied layer on layer in their glazing technique, Seidel projects color on color, movement on stillness, relief on surface. In quasi-Baroque overloads, a luxury of color arises, in part dramatically signed. It recalls, for example, Caravaggio's scenes of beheading, in which the deep-red blood appears to spray observers formally in the face. Seidel's "digital drippings" also appear to take up the eruptive gestures of Jackson Pollock and extend the painterly movement frozen under the spell of the canvas into images continually reconstituting themselves. The dynamization of the congealed flow of paint is a continuation of painting by other means. While van Gogh maintained that "the painter of the future is, however, a colorist such as there hasn't been before," Seidel is that artist of the future. This is not because he works with contemporary media, but because he understands that he must redefine art itself and with the knowledge of the past lead on into the present.

Filme und Installationen/ Movies and Installations

E3
82–83

_grau
84–89

futures
90–91

appearing
disappearance
92–93

dive
painting #1
94–95

processes:
living paintings
96–99

chiral
100–105

meander
106–109

scrape
110–113

black mirror
114–117

folds
118–121

erratic
122–123

tearing
shadows
124–127

advection
128–131

grapheme
132–137

ligature
138–141

stains
142–145

recoil
146–149

magnitude
150–153

lux aeterna
154–155

suturae #2
156–157

mold
158–159

vitreous
160–165

E3
—
Experimentalfilm
2002

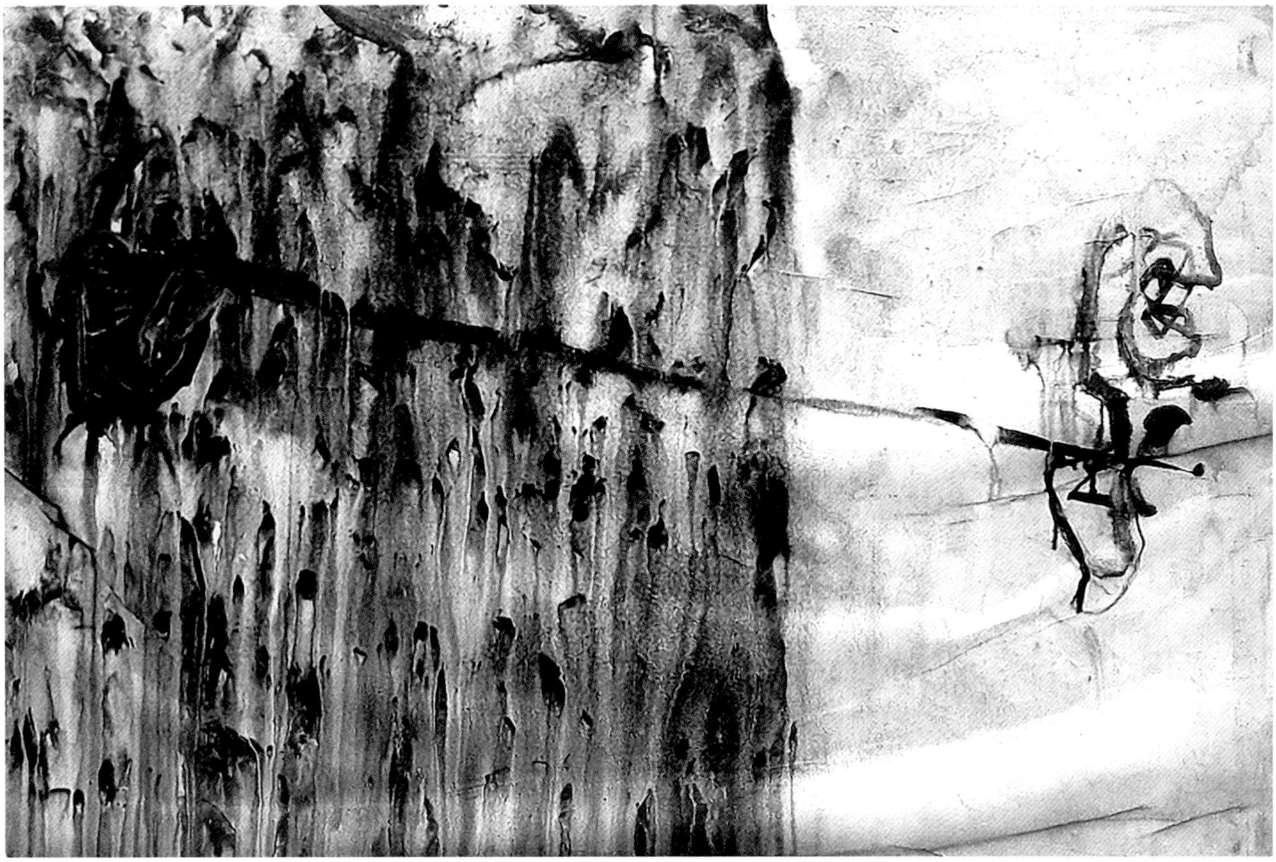

_grau

—

Experimentalfilm
2004

84–89

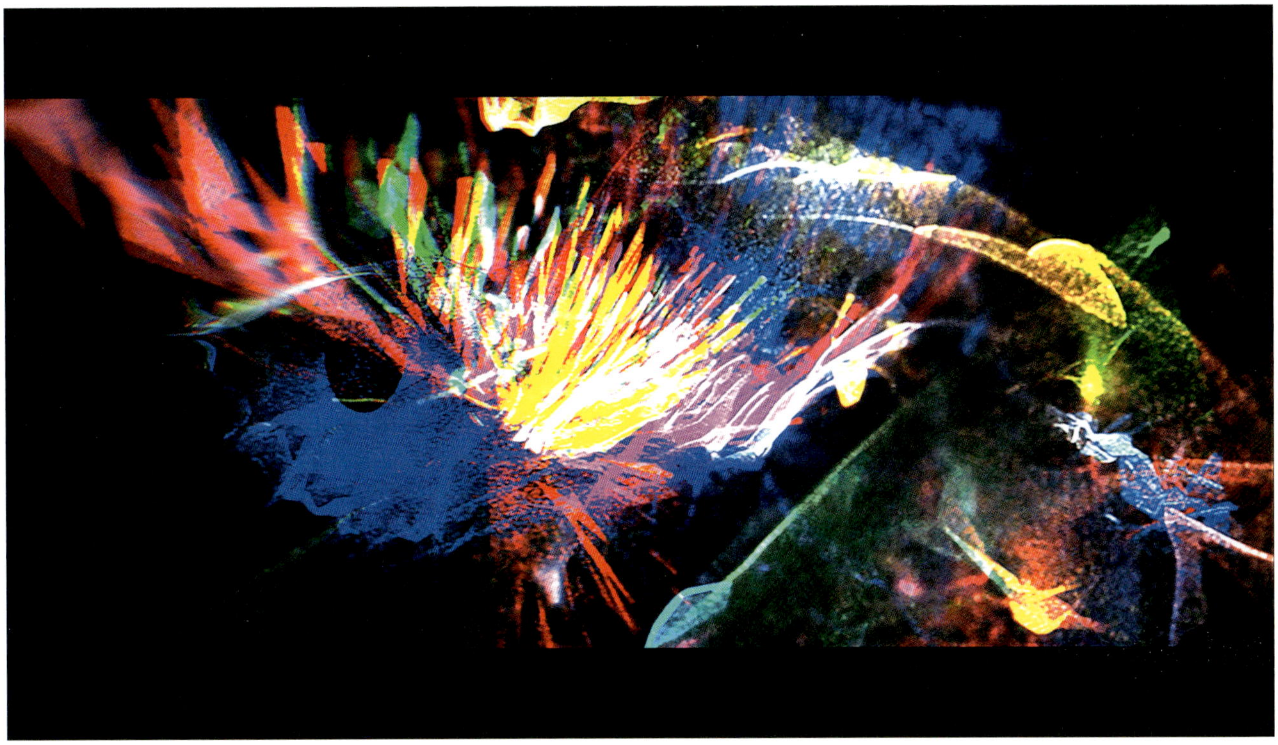

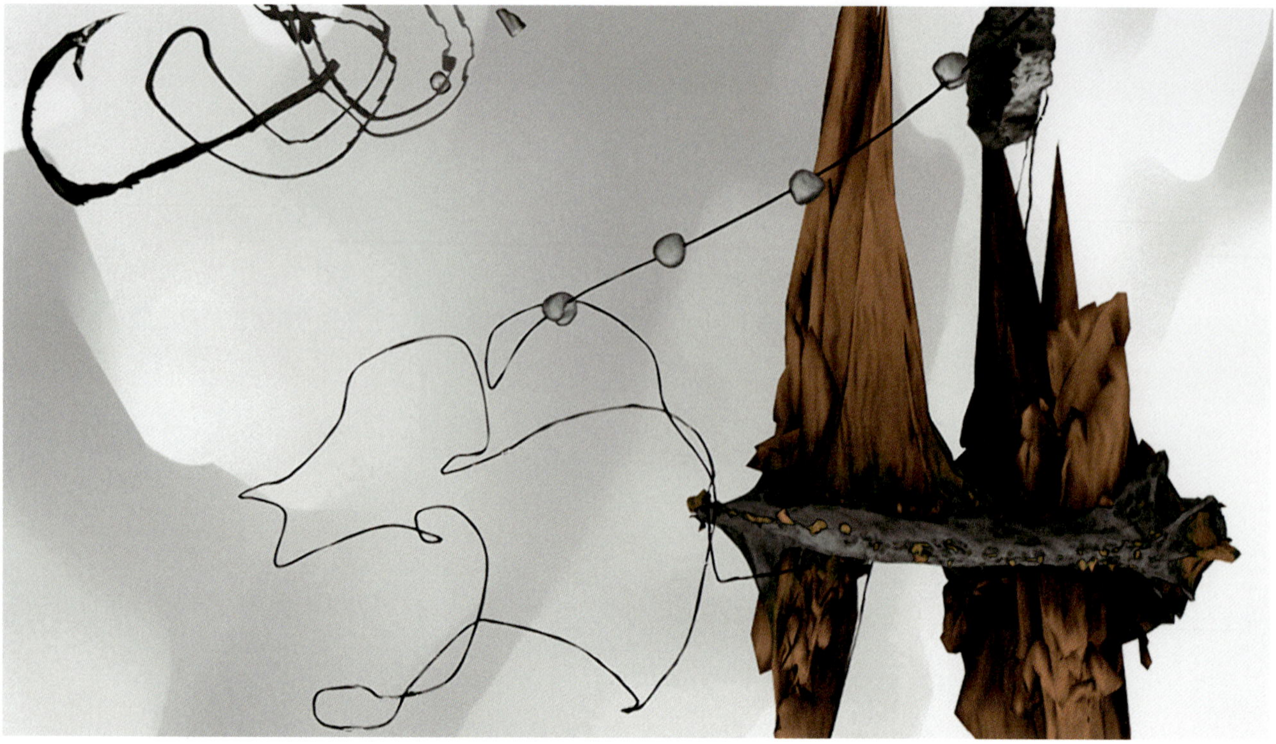

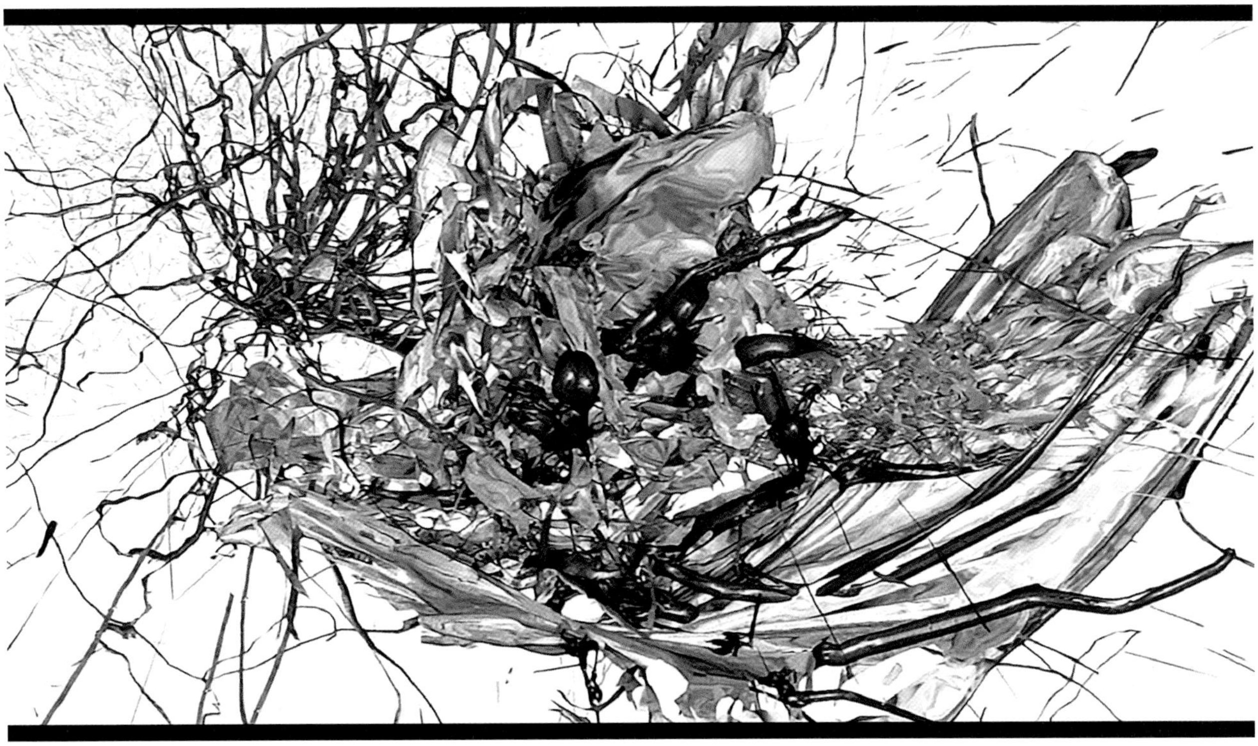

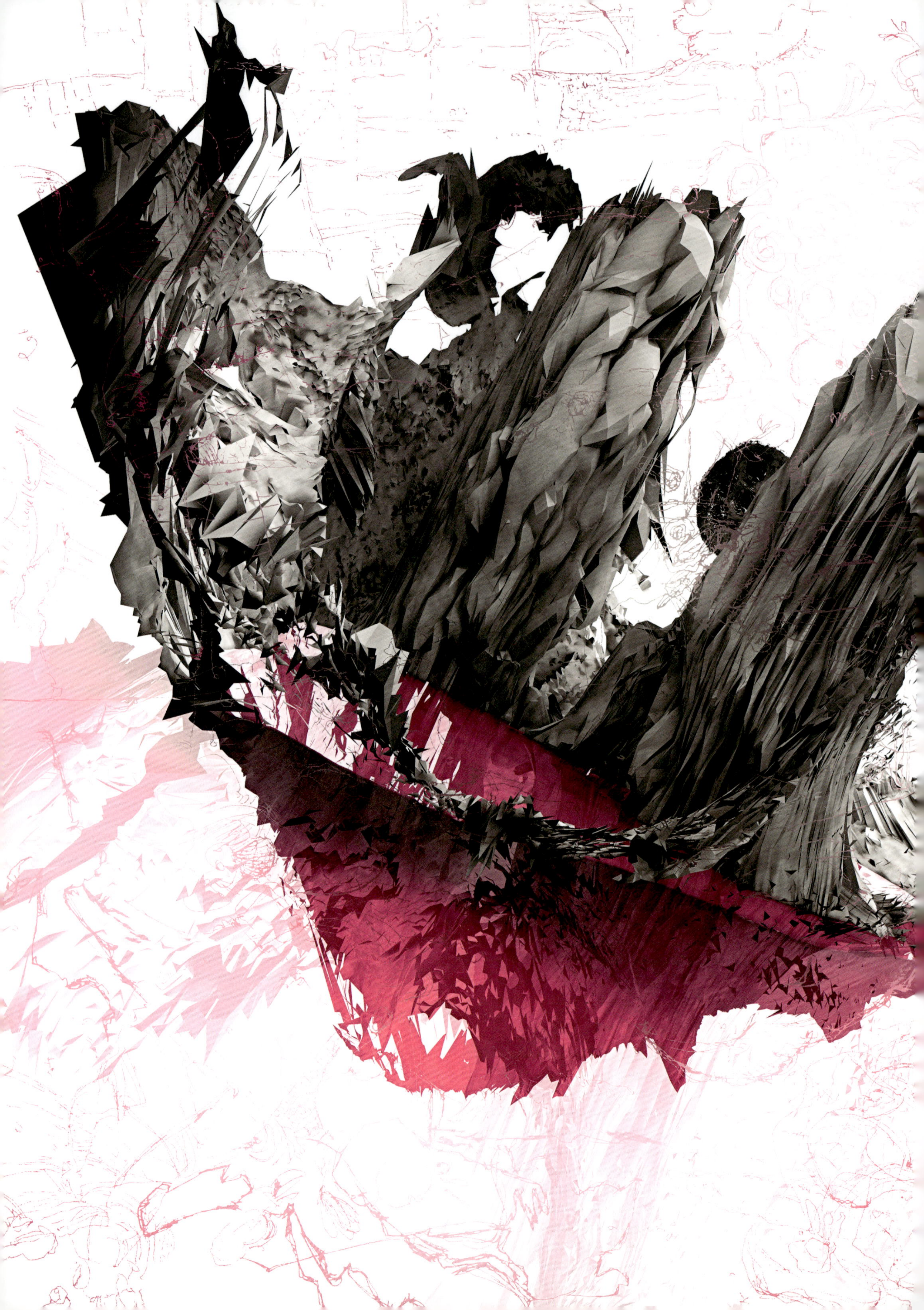

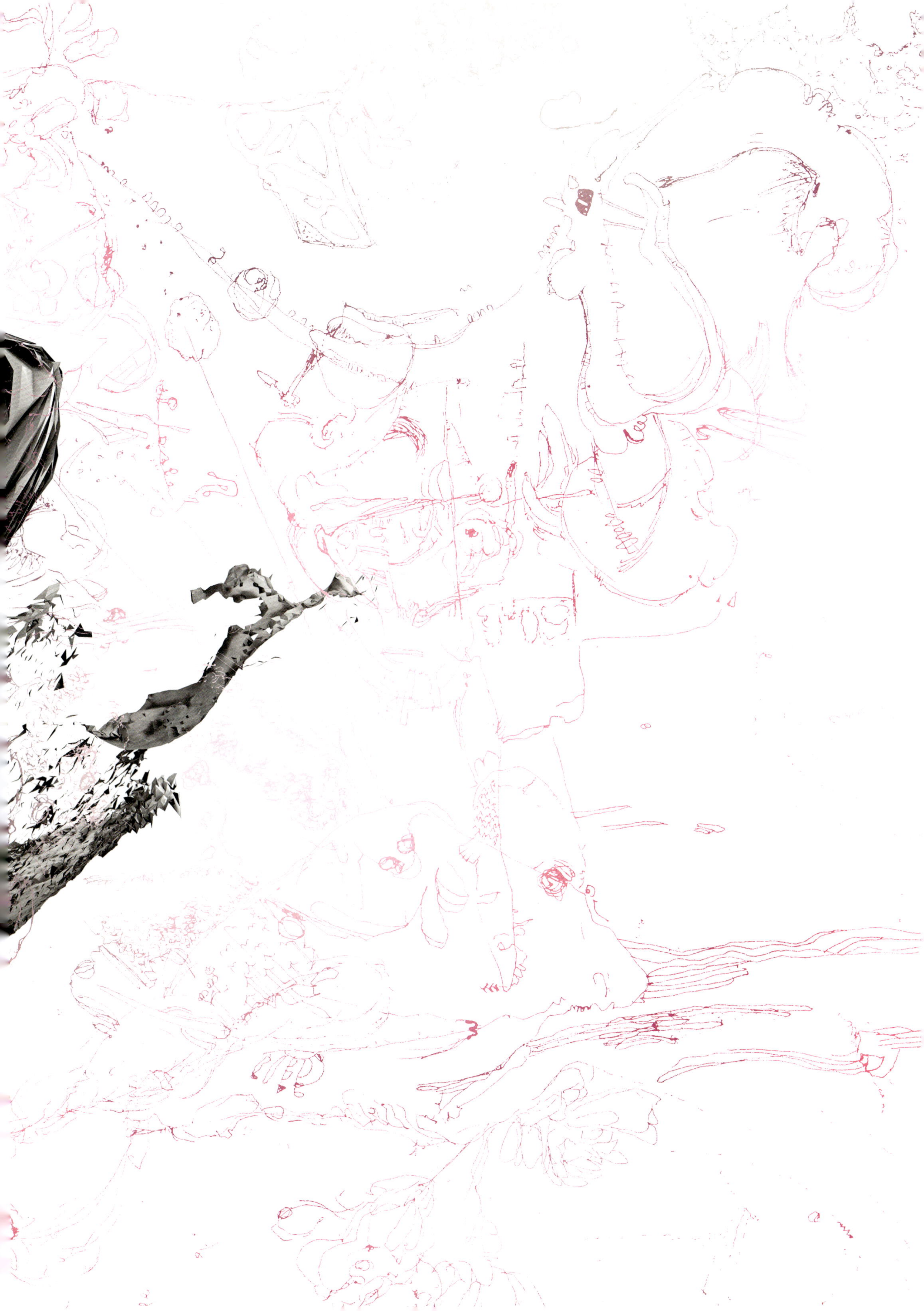

futures

—
Experimentalfilm
2006

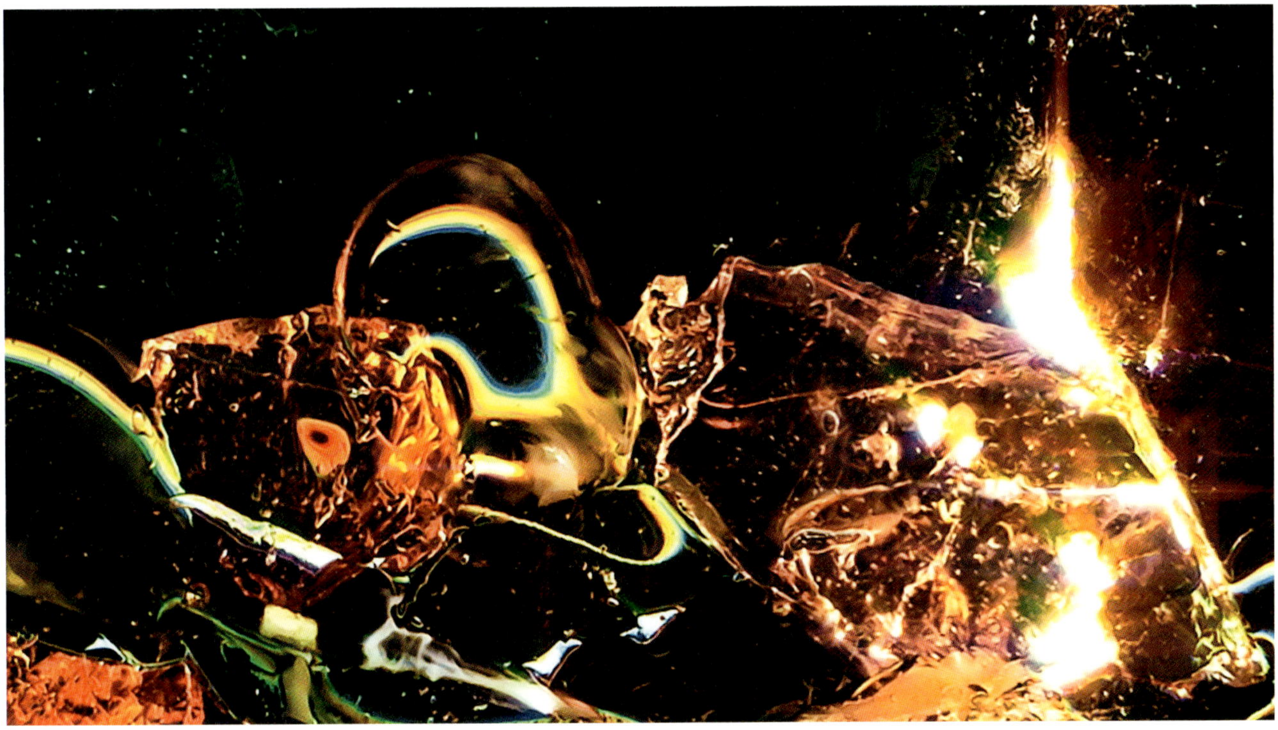

appearing disappearance
—
Experimentalfilm
2007

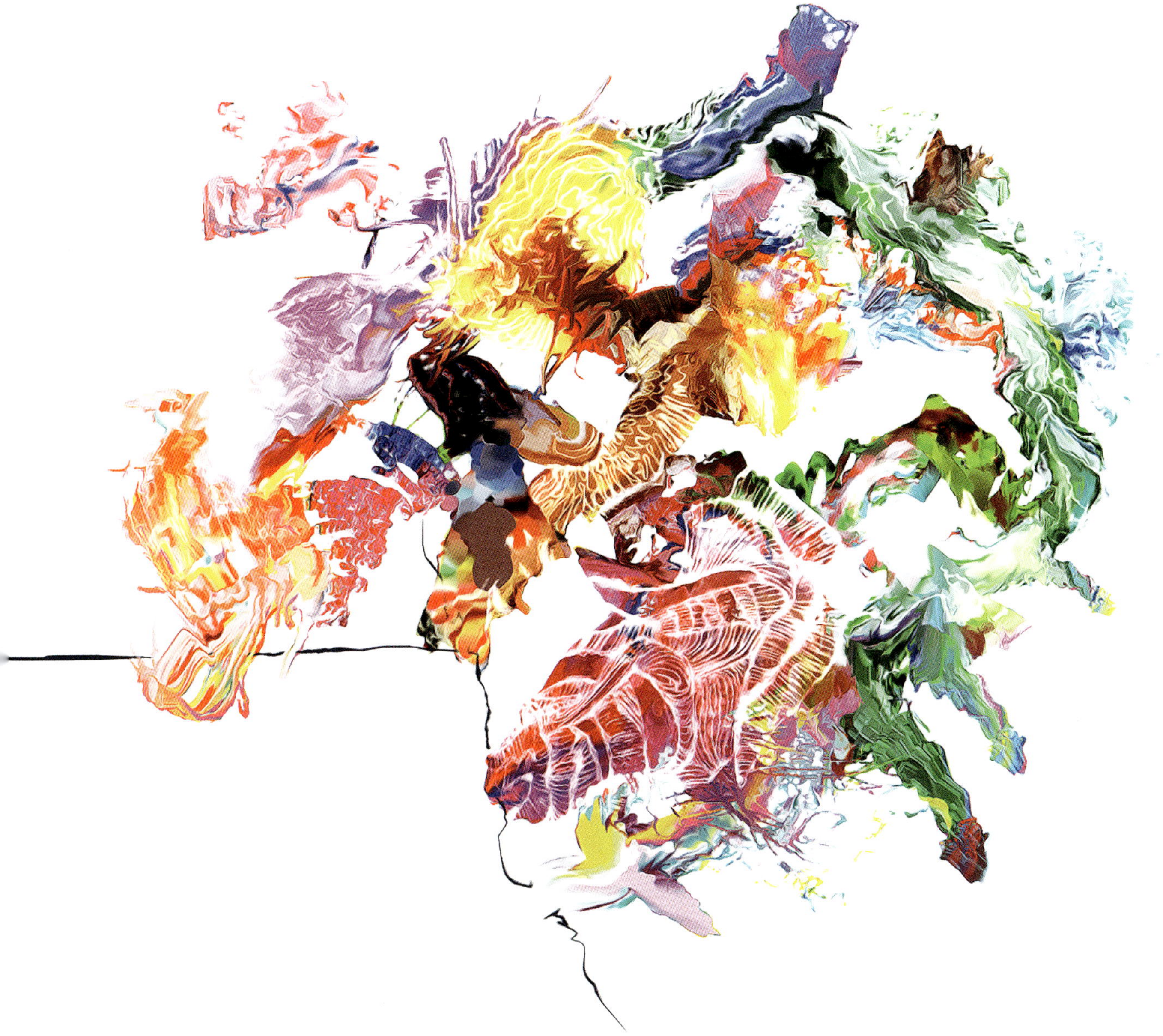

dive painting #1
—
LED-Fassade
2007

processes: living paintings
—
Fassadenprojektion
2009

96–99

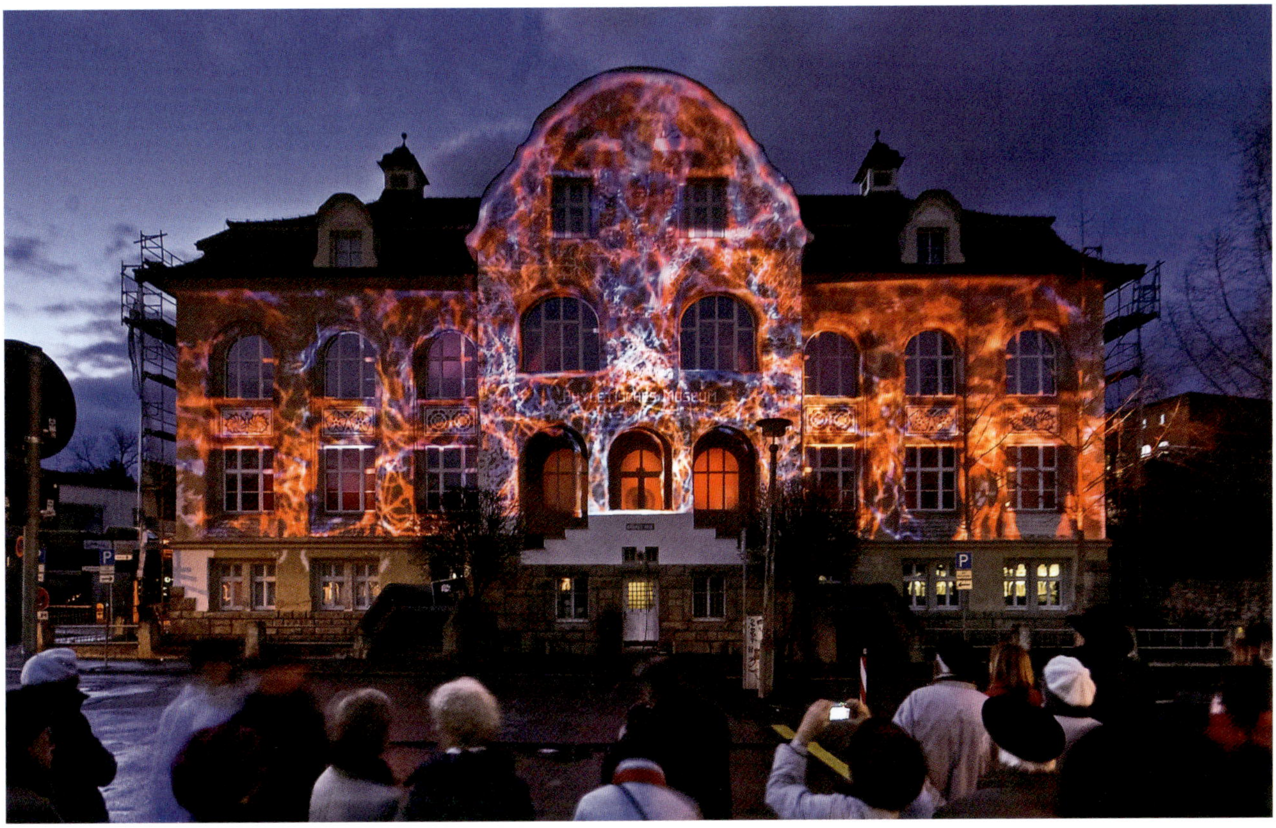

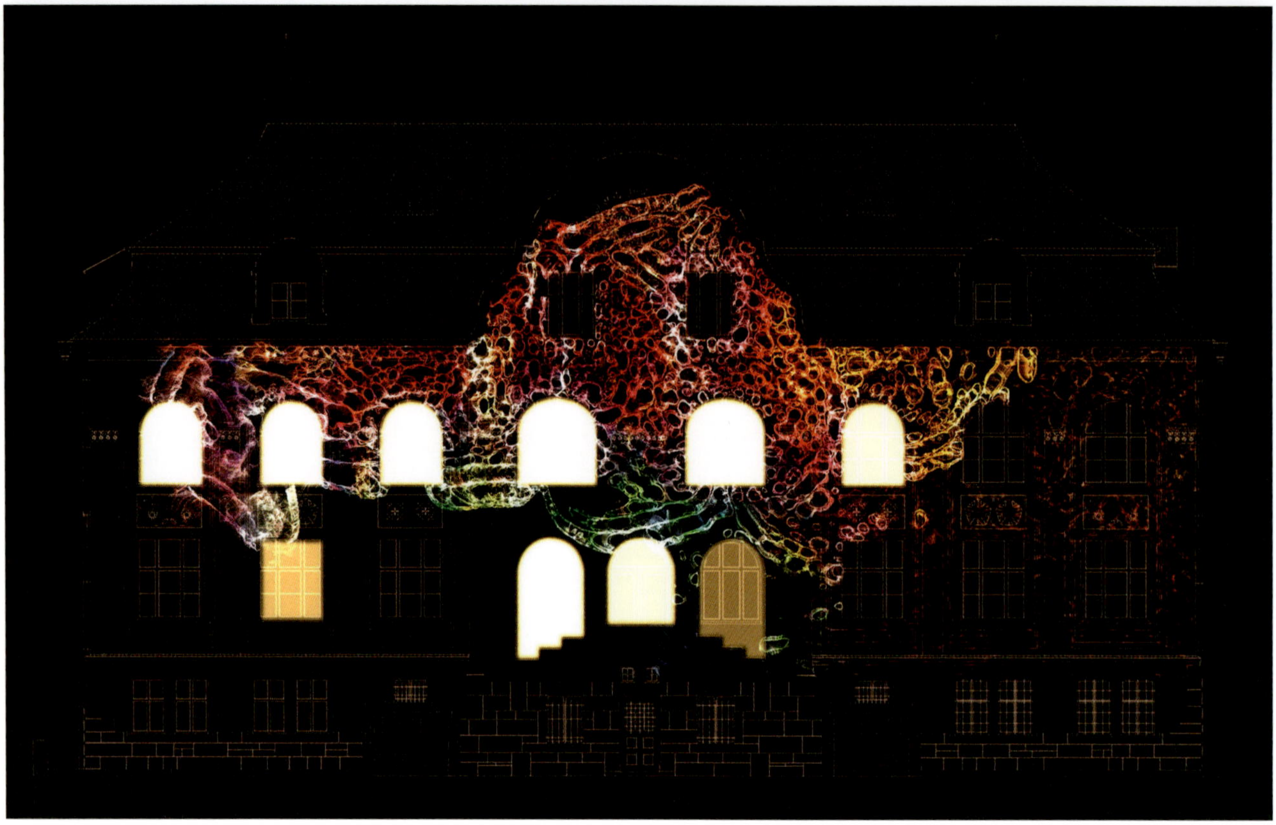

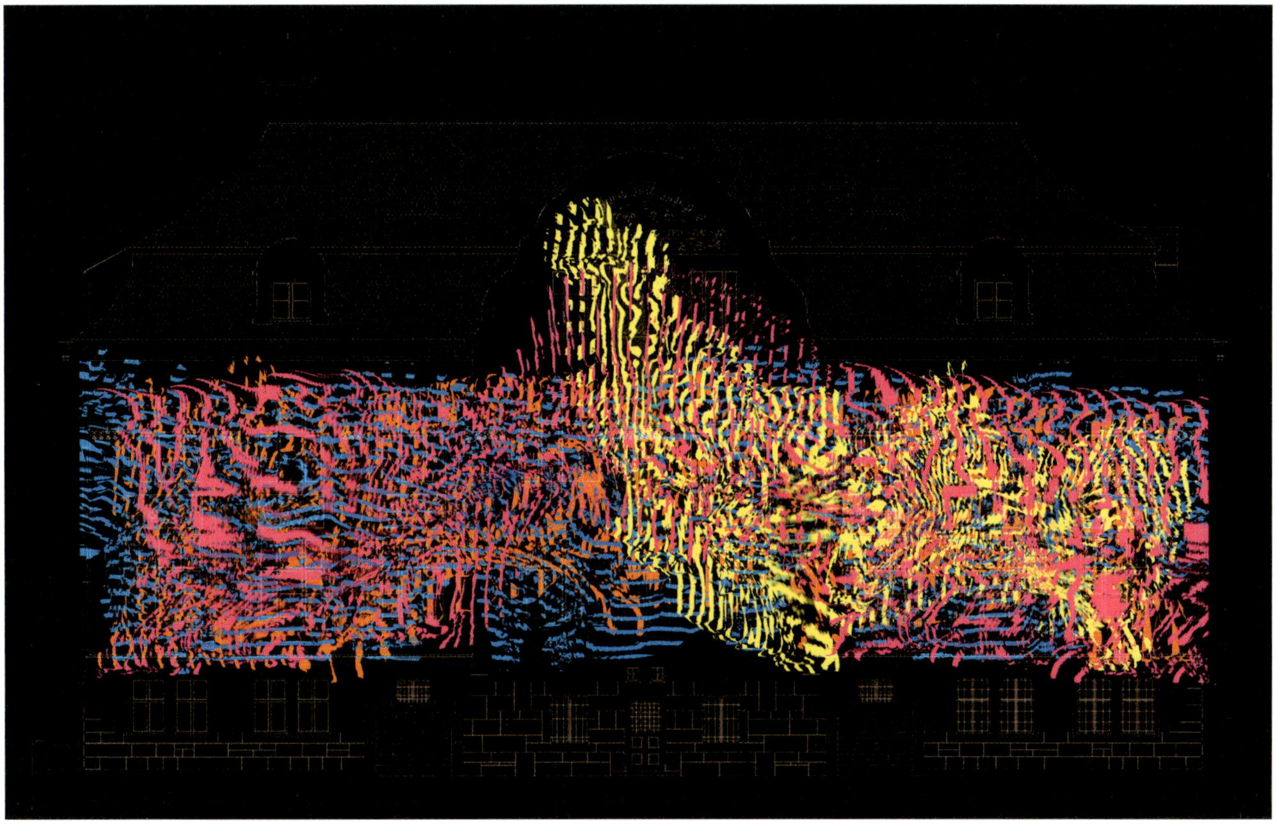

chiral

—

Projektionsskulptur
2010–2015

100–105

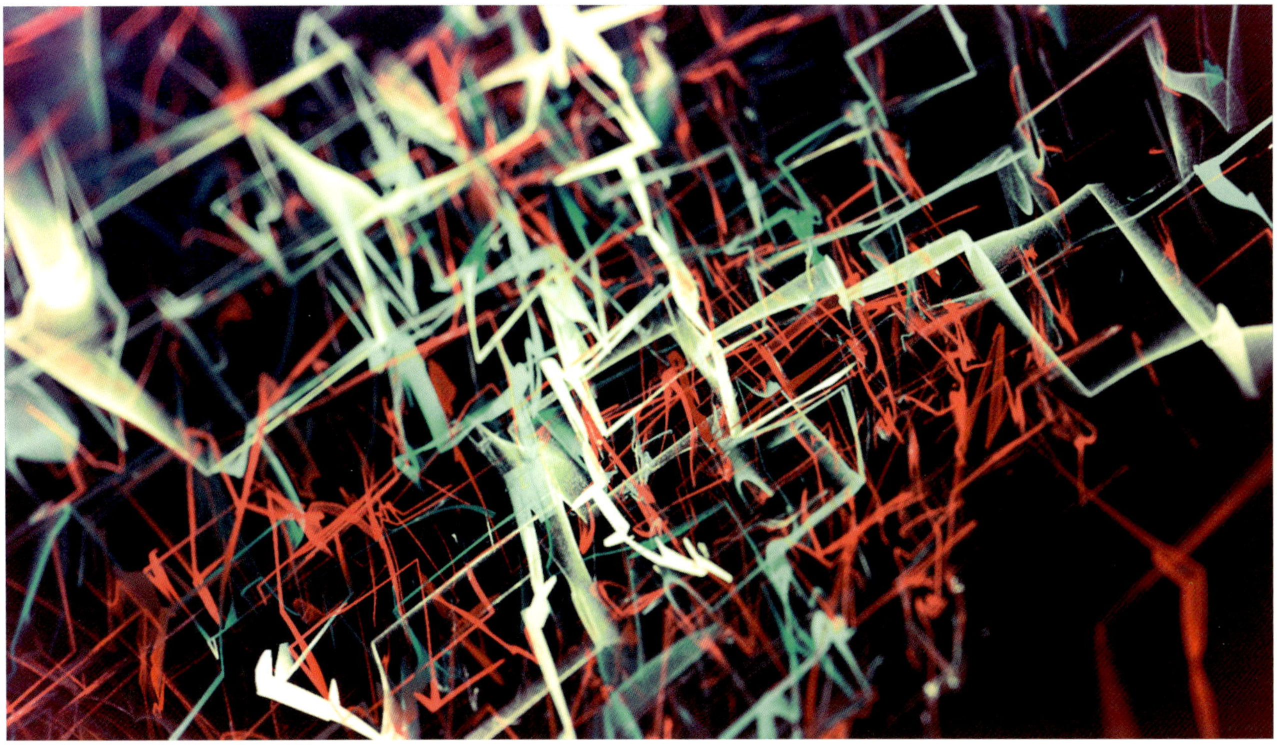

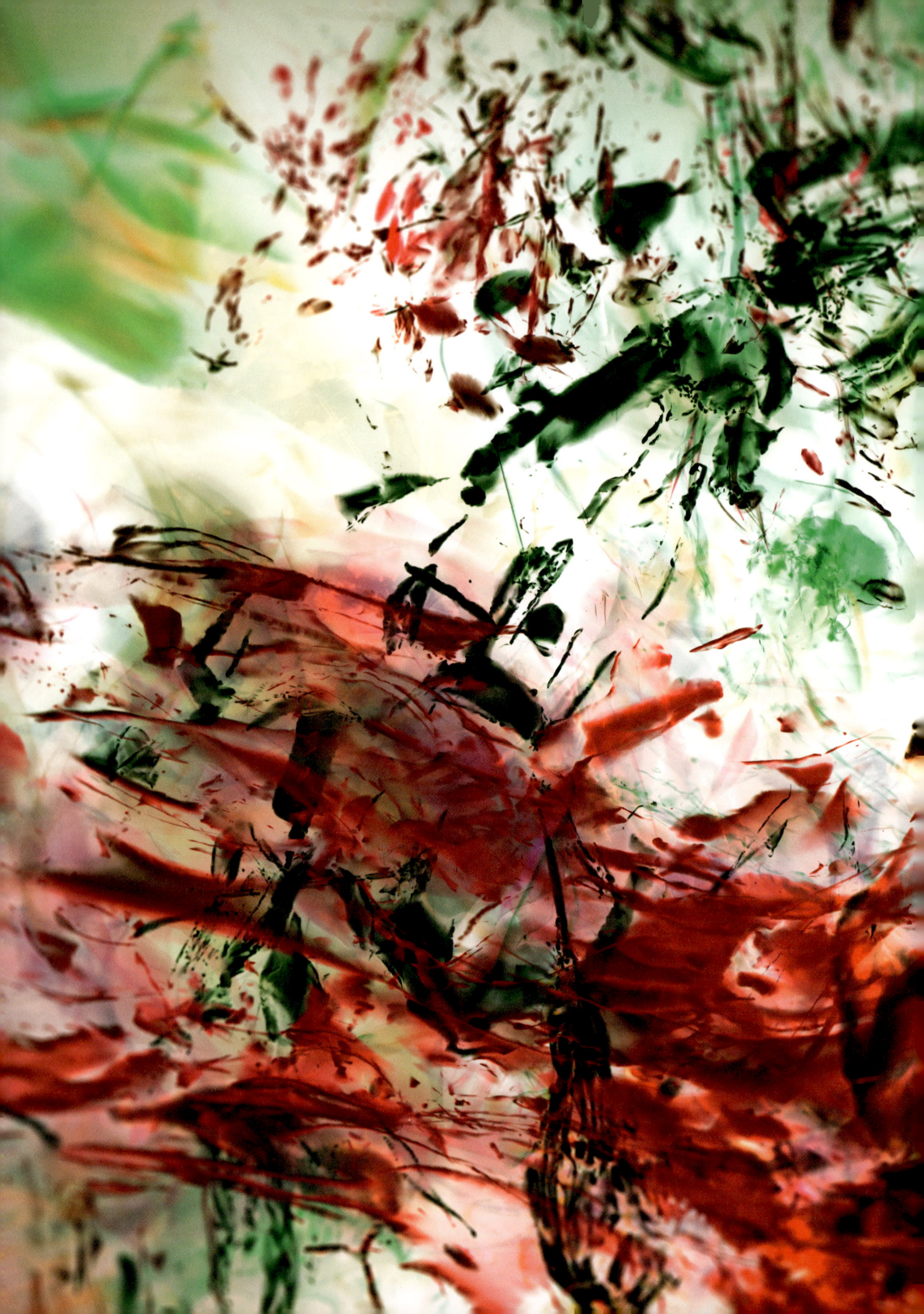

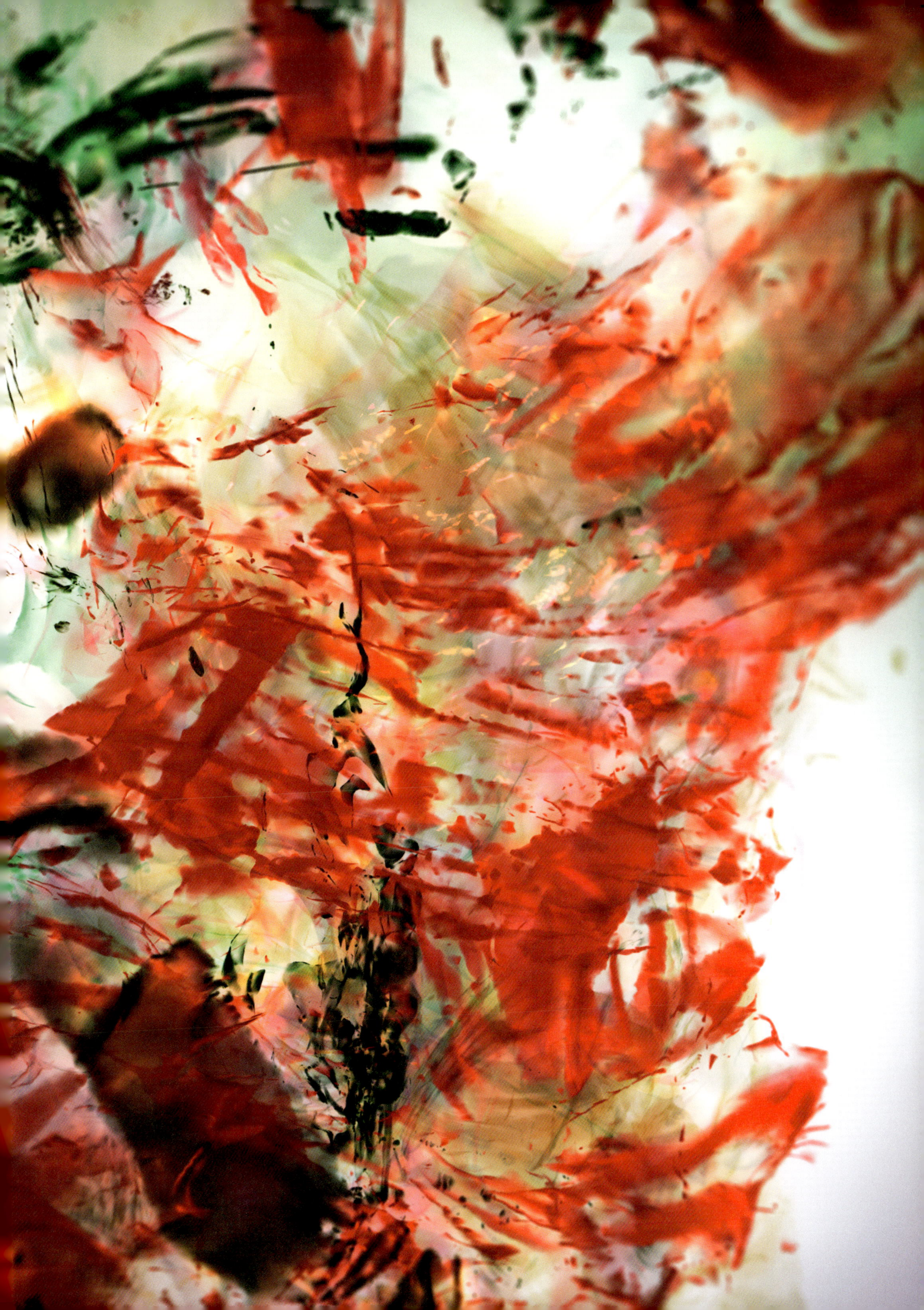

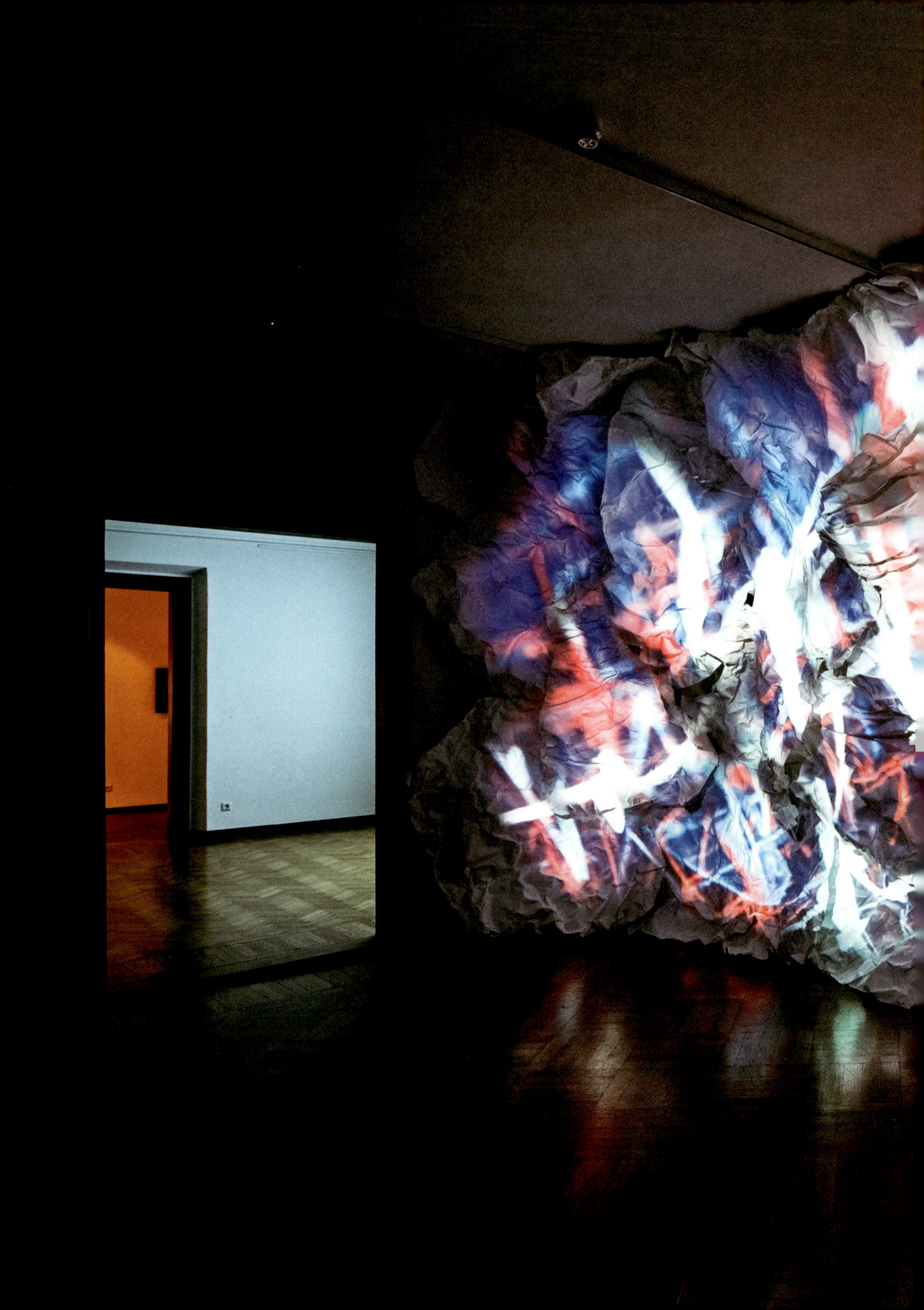

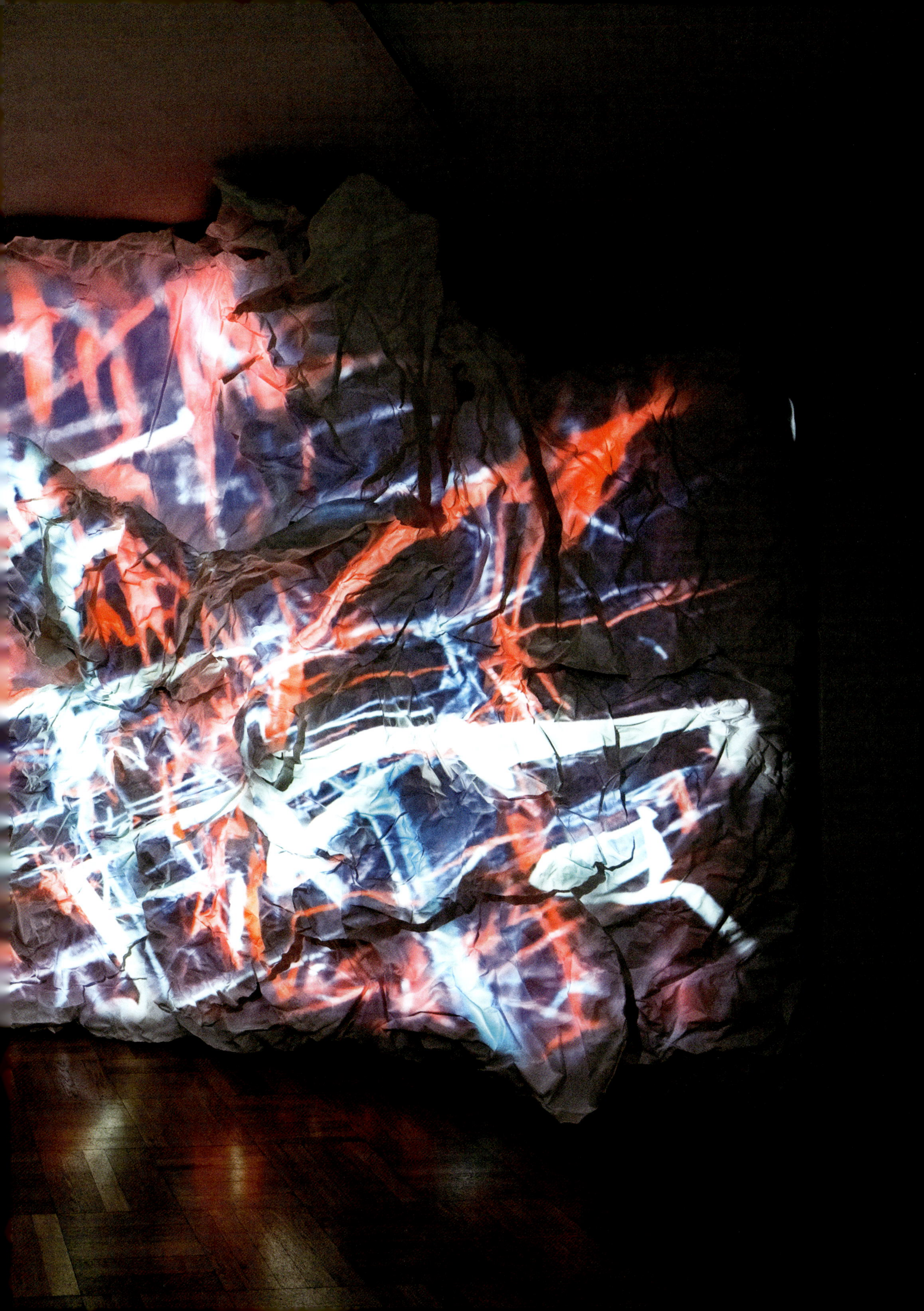

meander

—

Video-Performance
2010

106–109

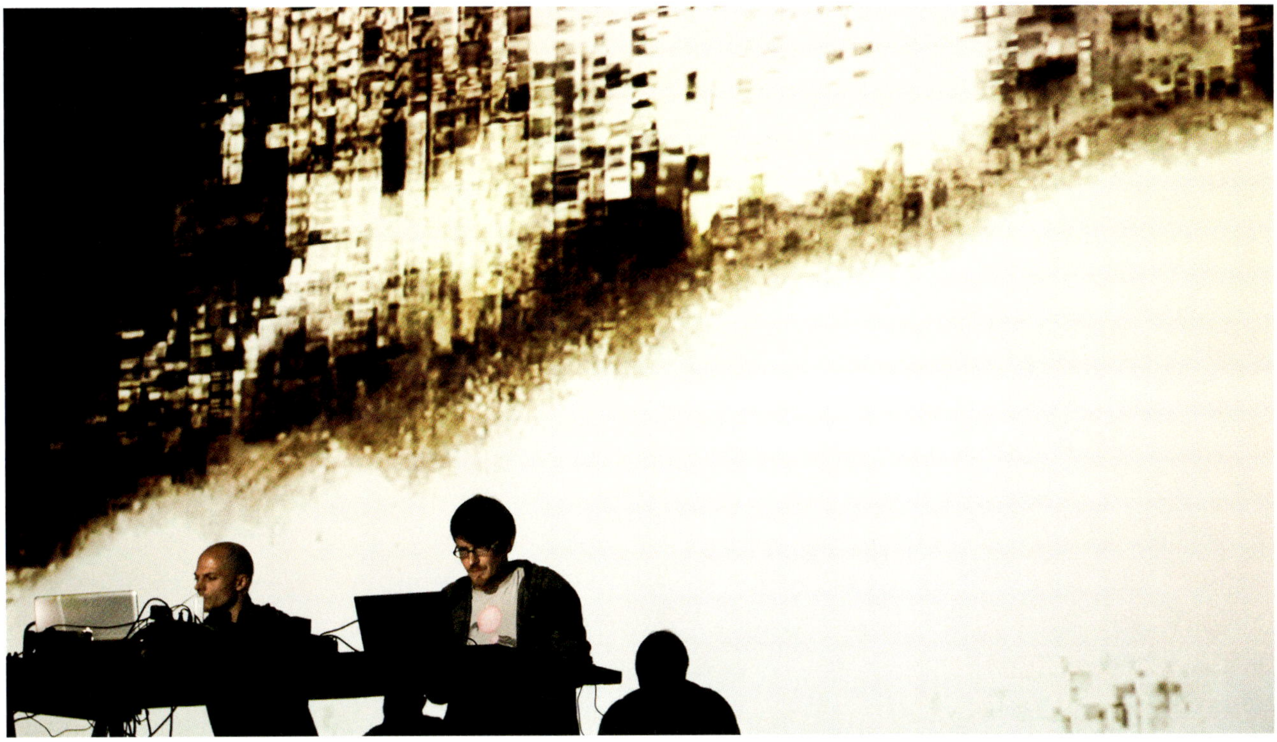

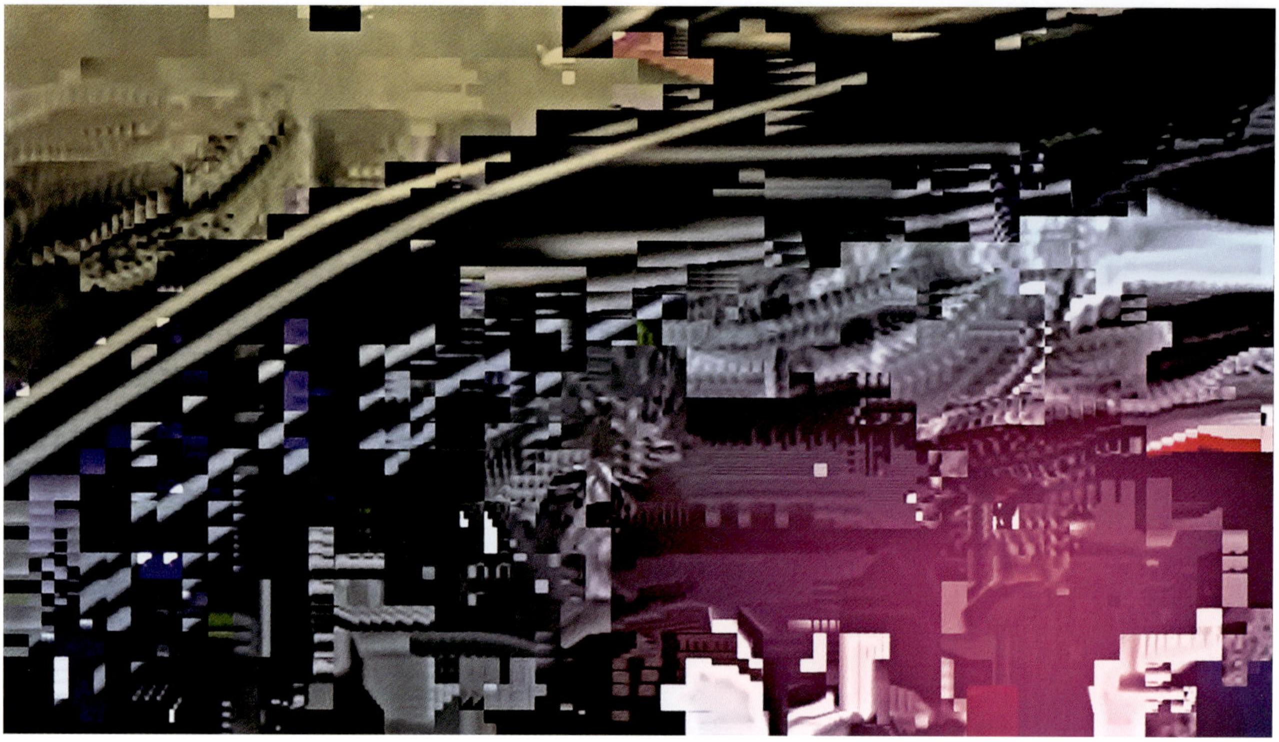

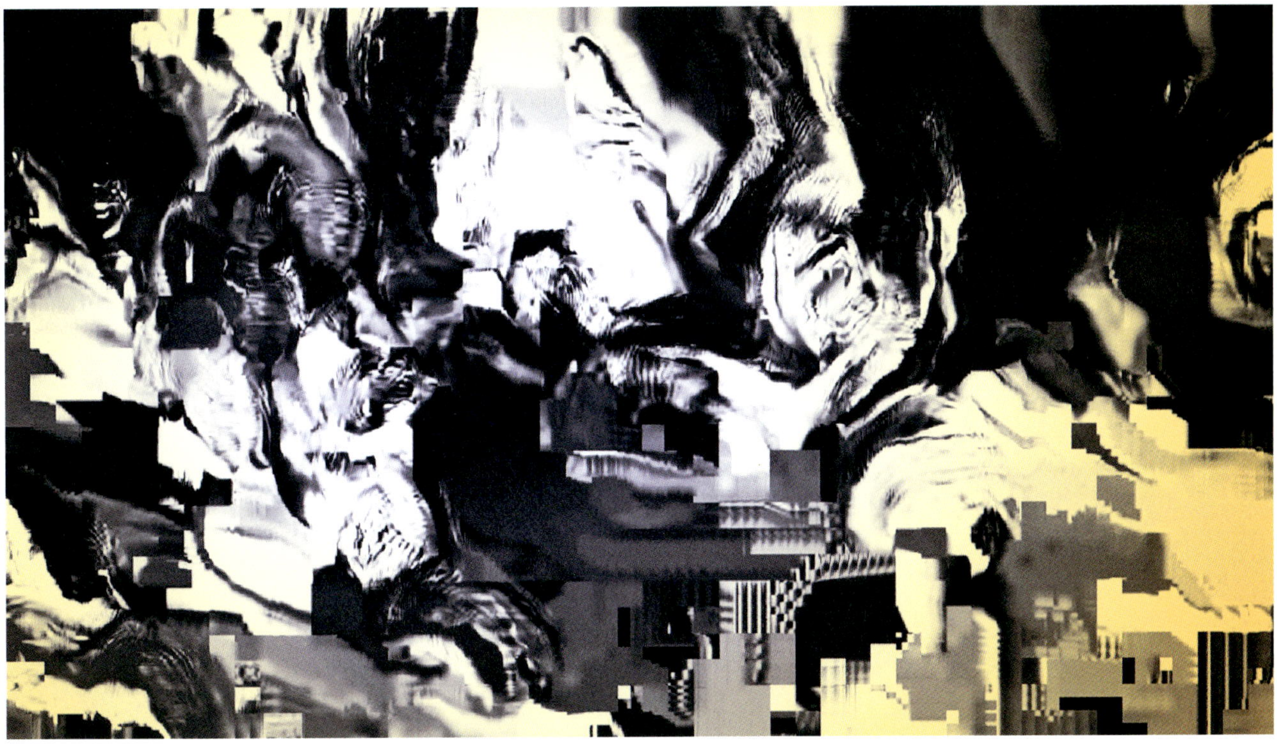

scrape

—

Experimentalfilm
2011

110–113

111

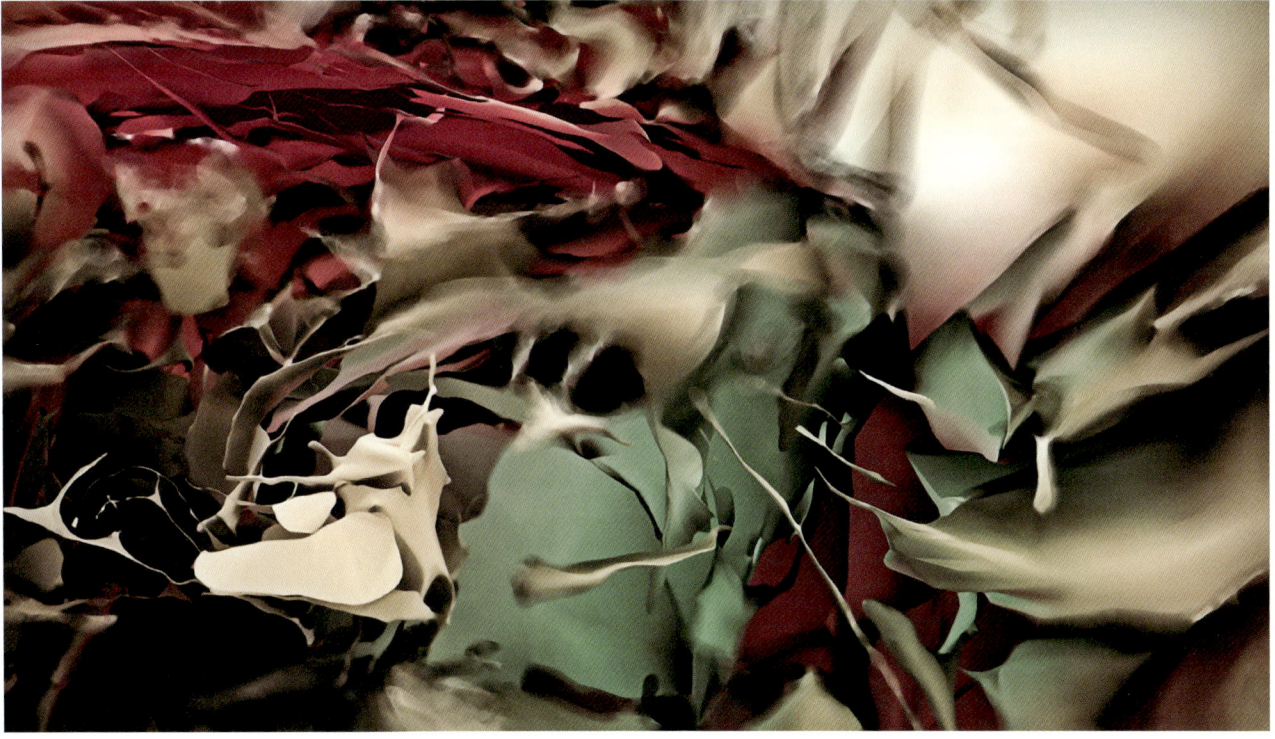

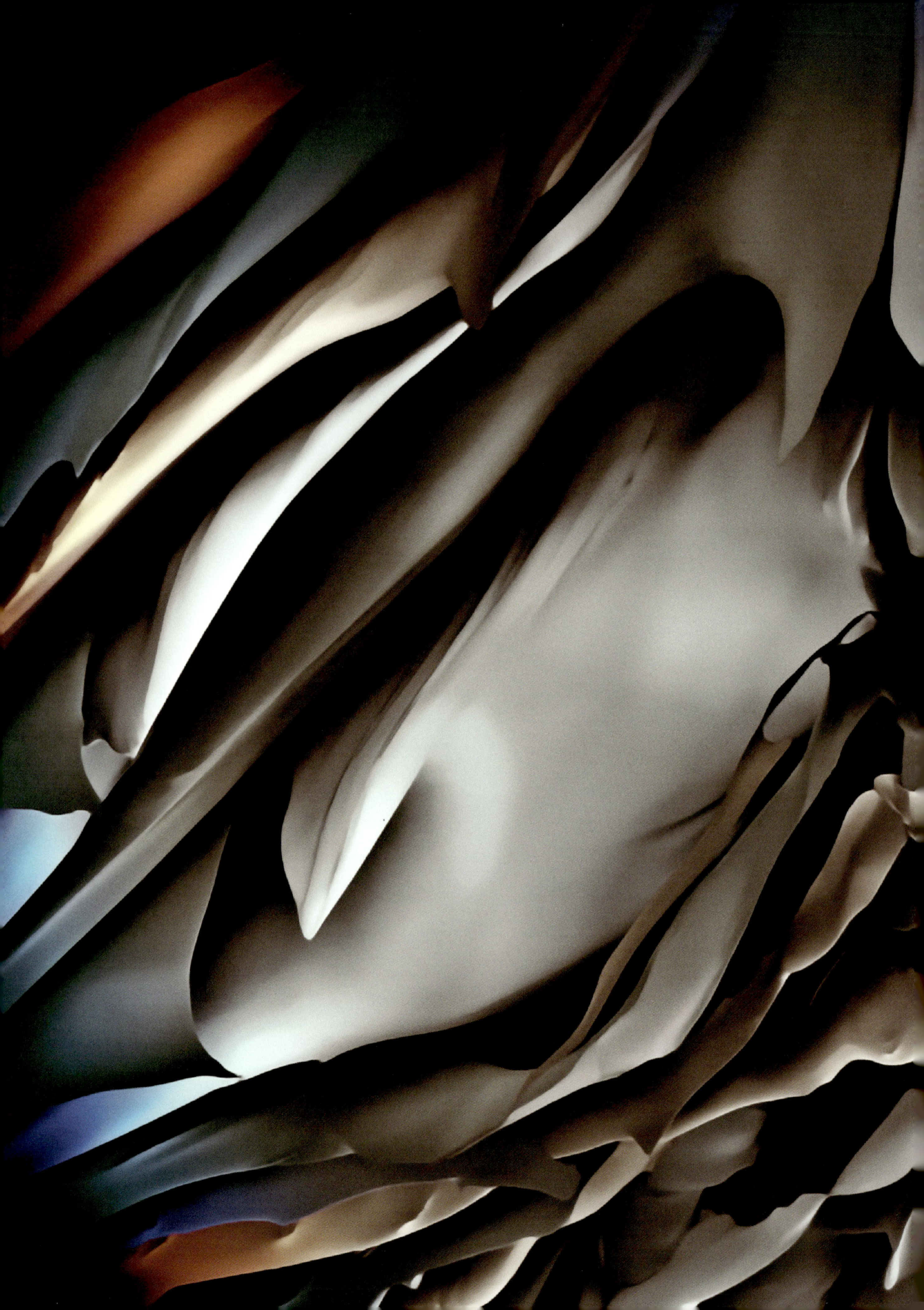

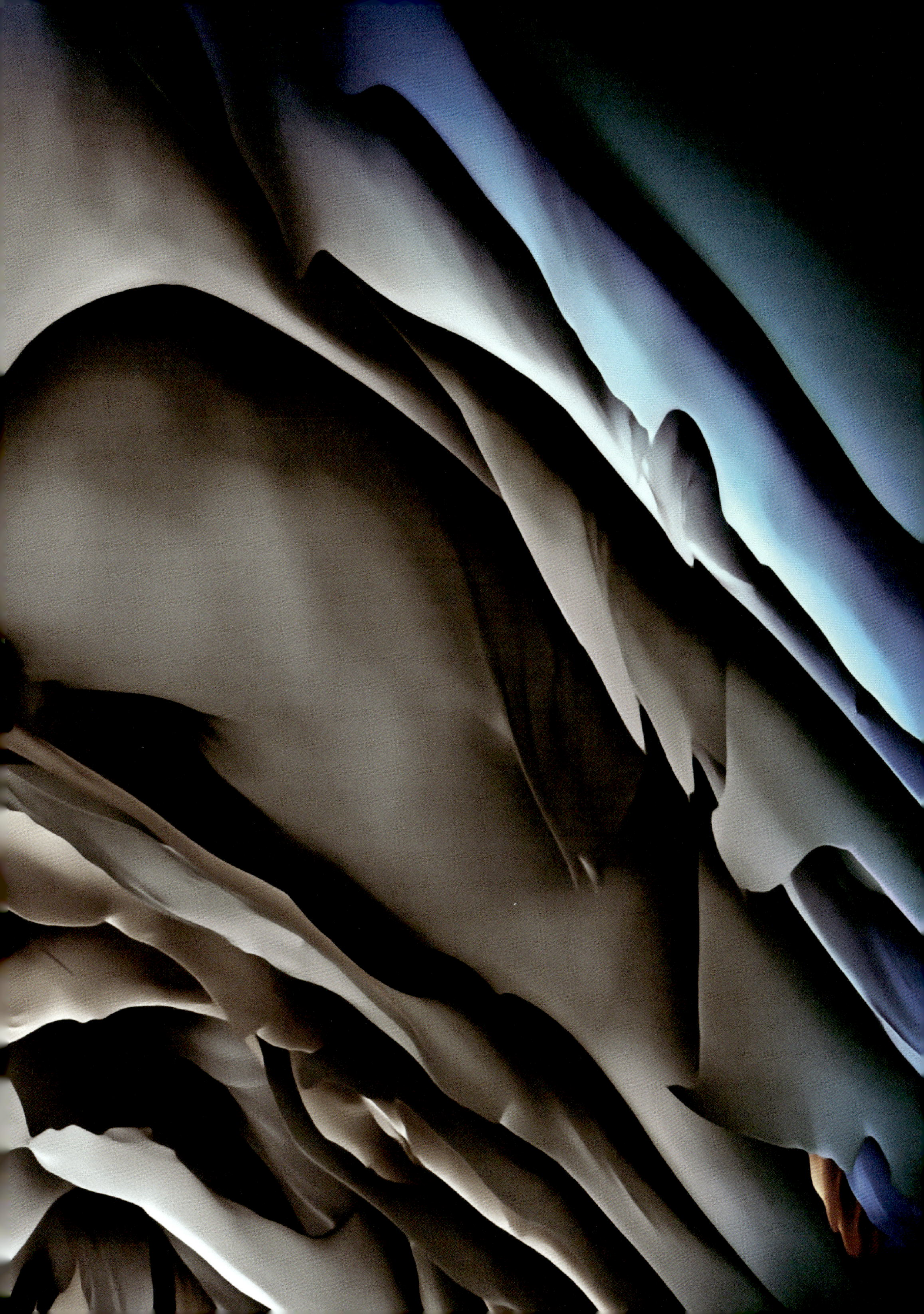

black mirror
—
Projektionsskulptur
2011

114–117

115

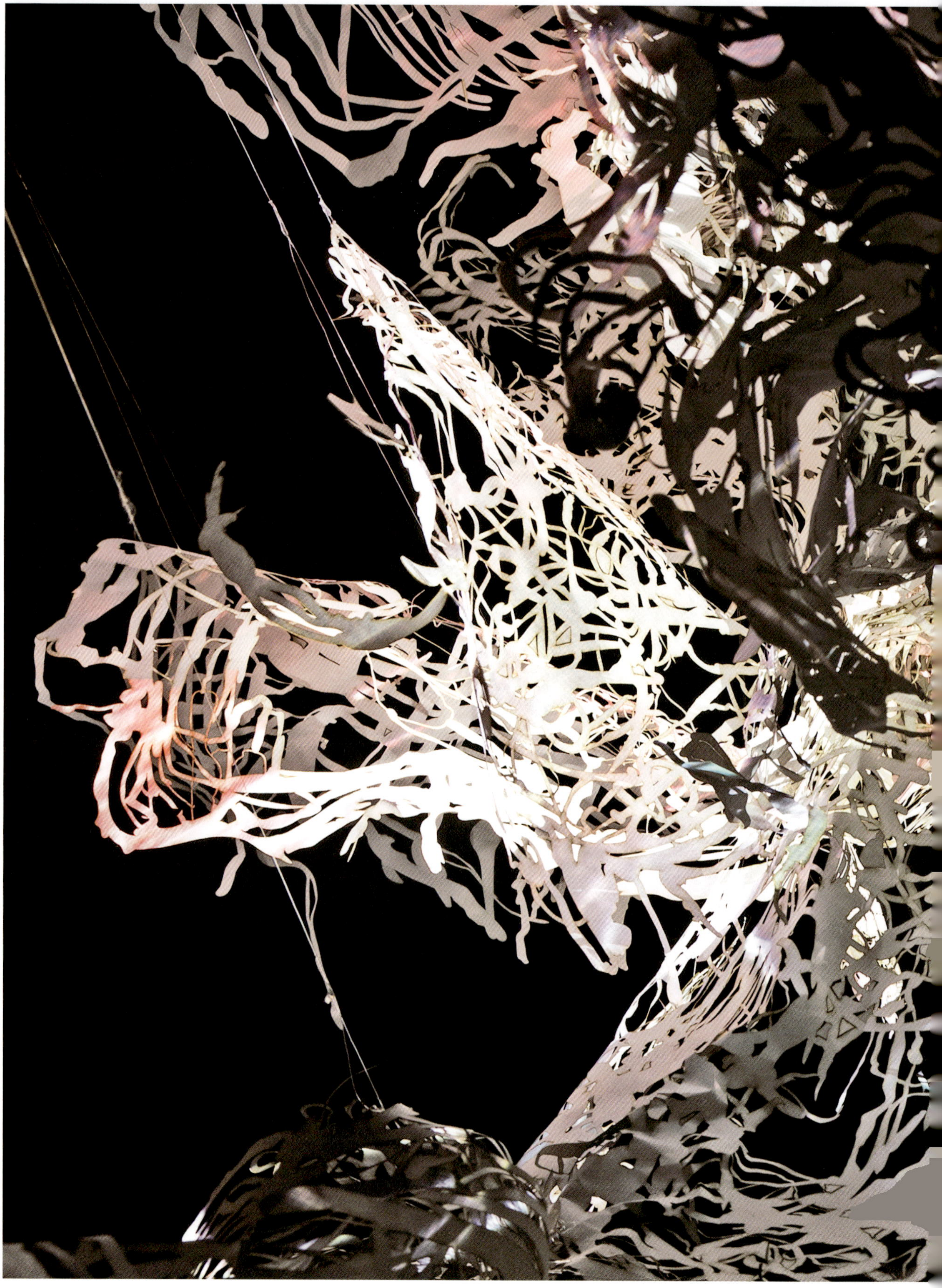

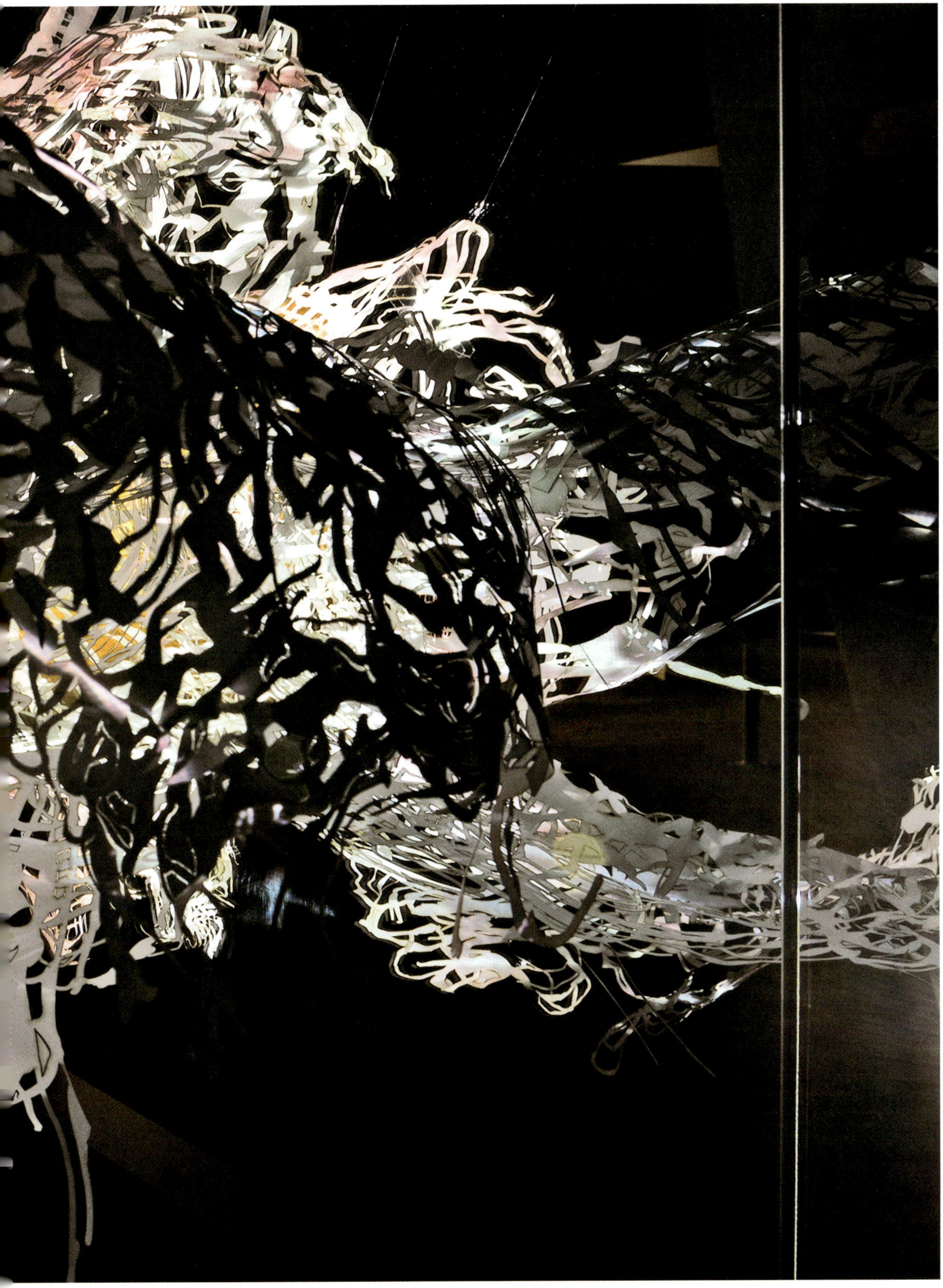

folds
—
Videoprojektion
2011

118–121

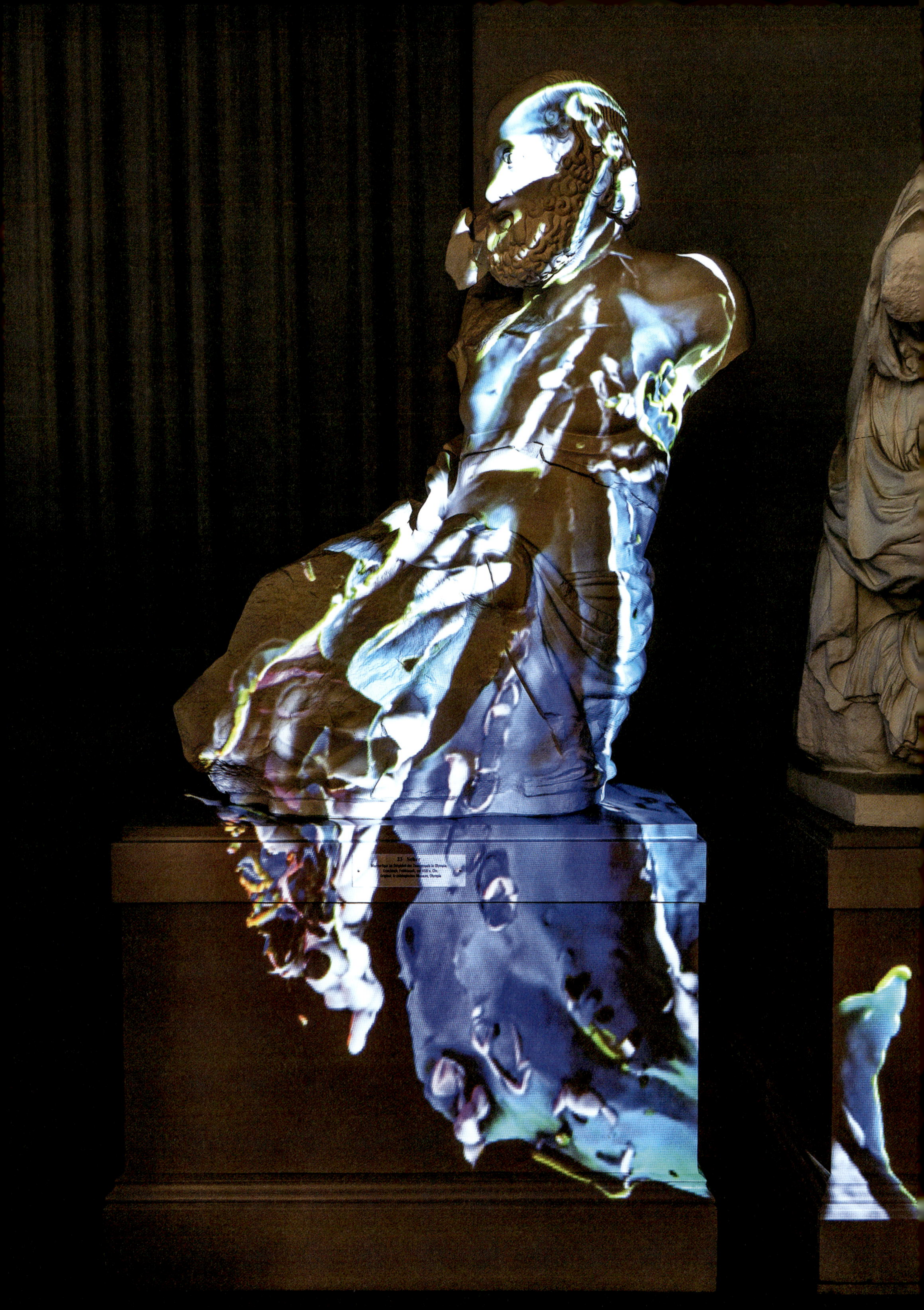
23 Seher

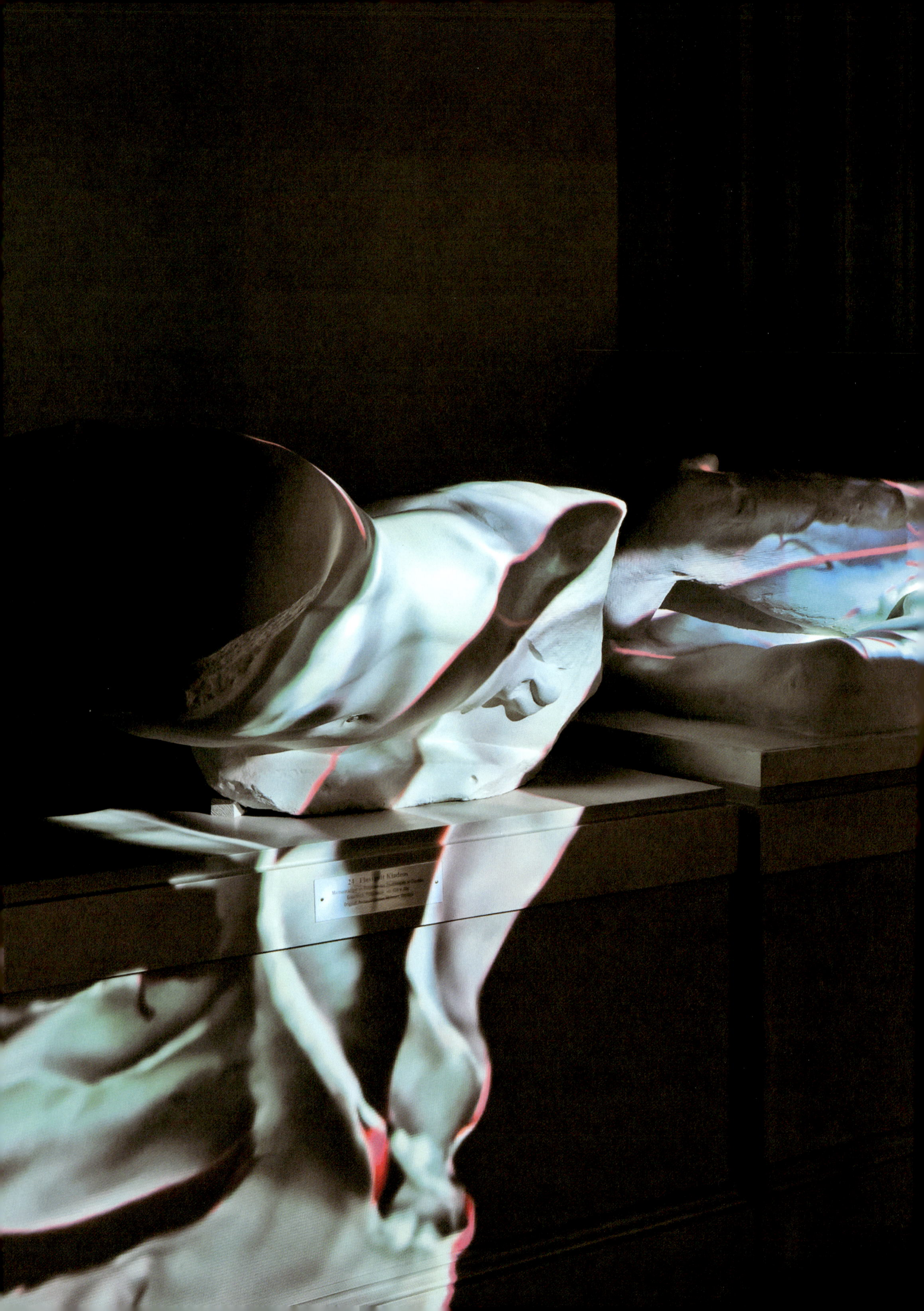

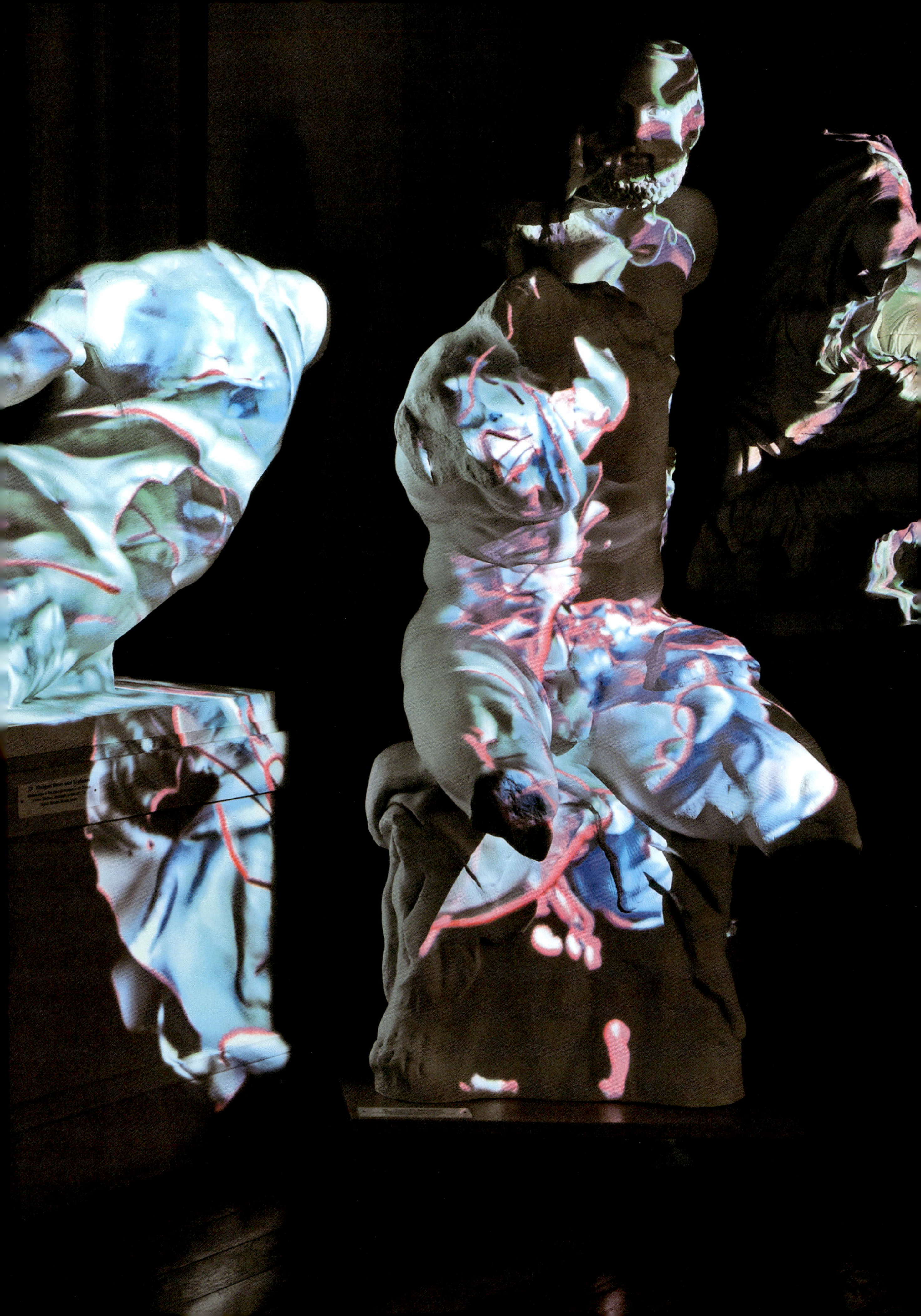

erratic
—
Video-Performance
2012

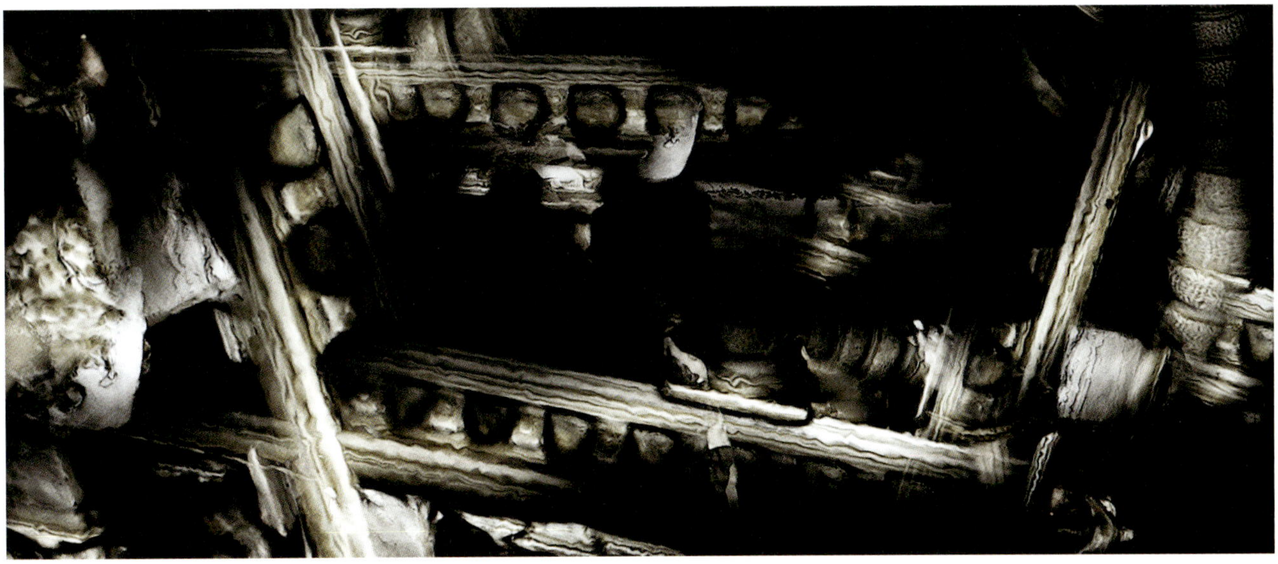

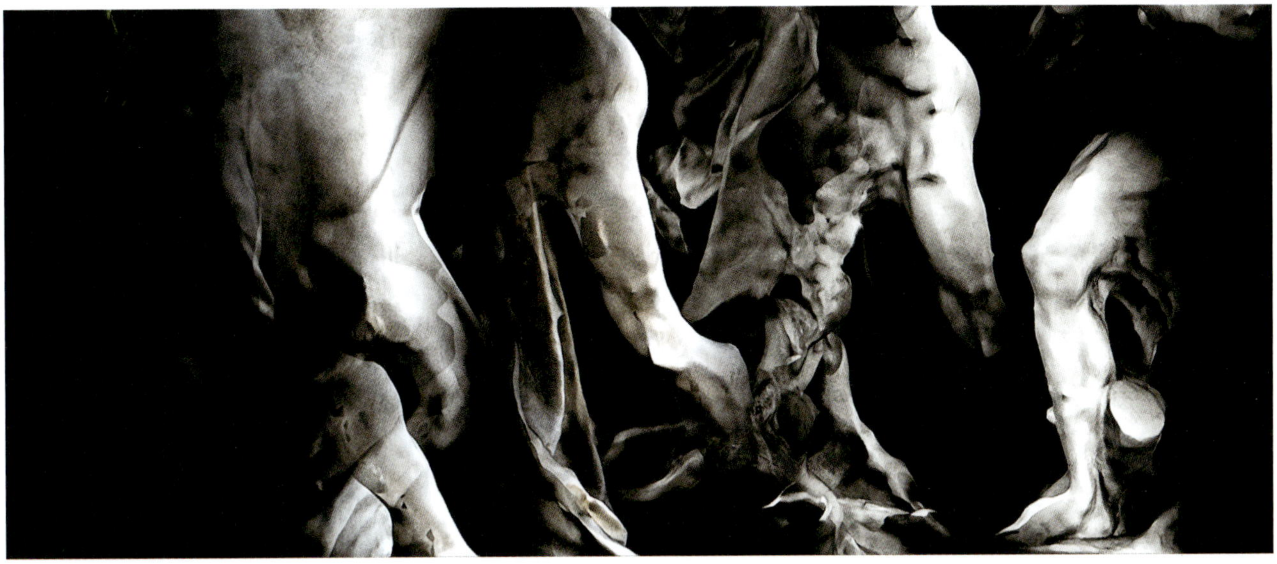

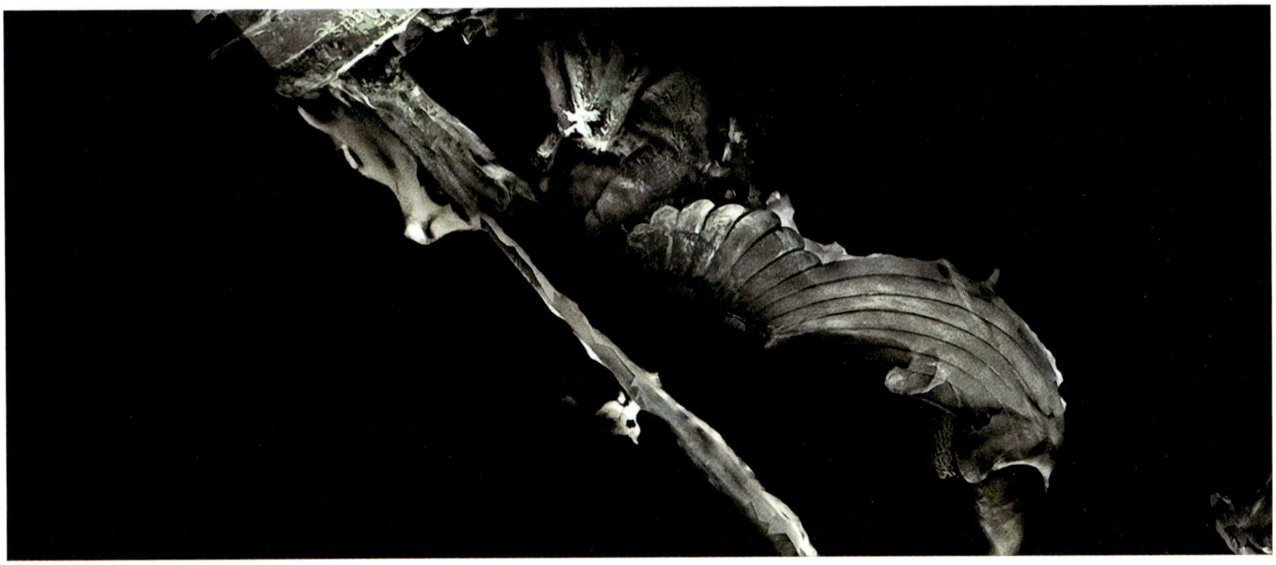

tearing shadows
—
Projektionsskulptur
2013–2015

124–127

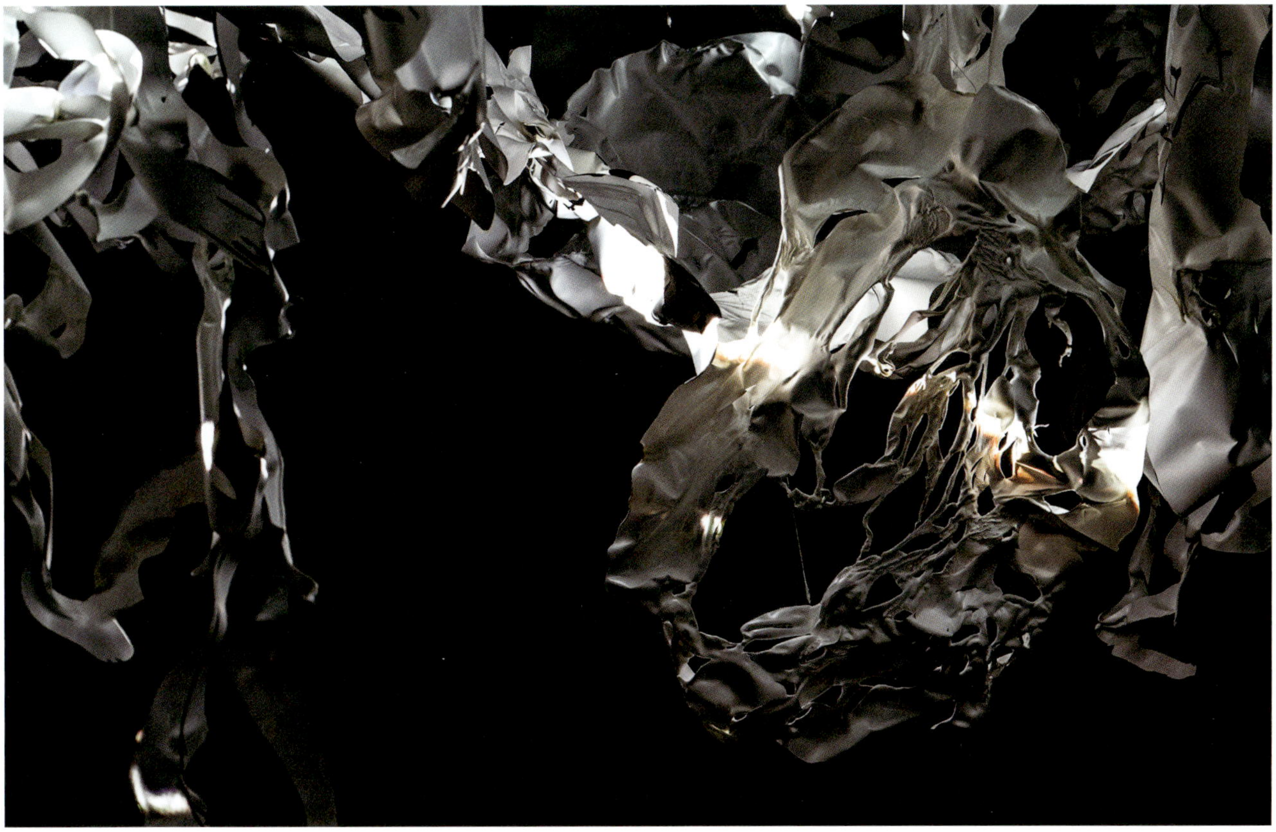

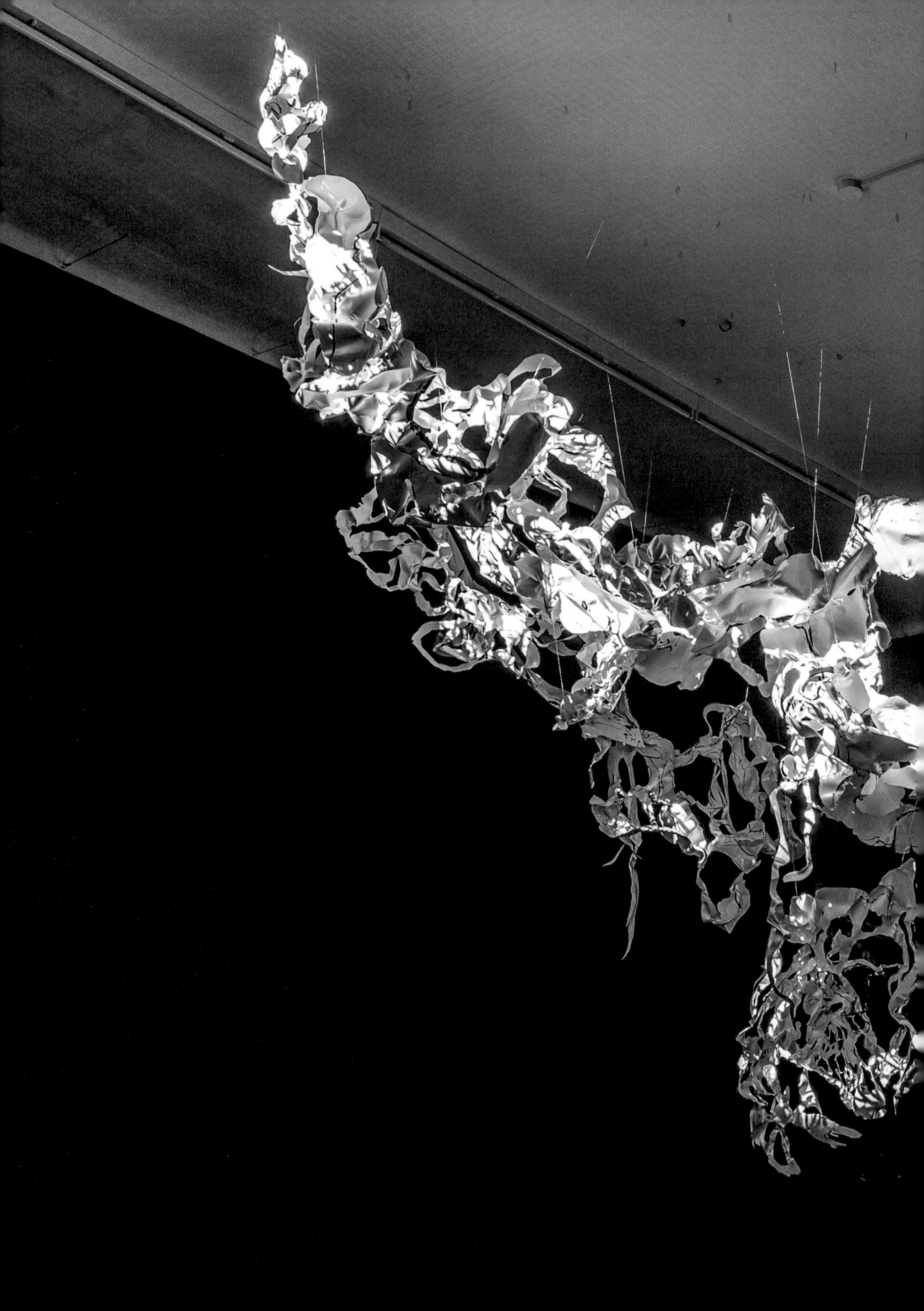

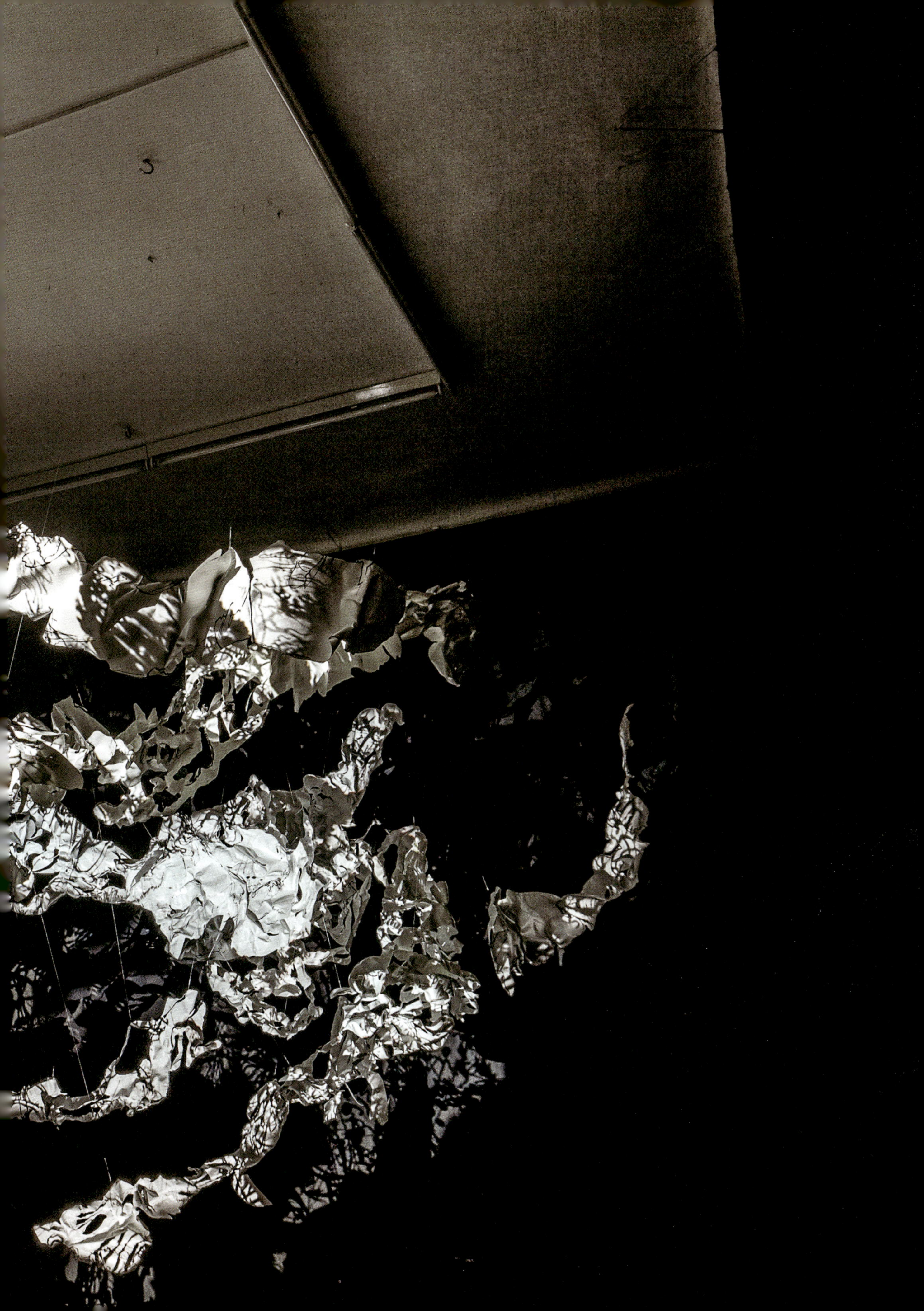

advection
—
Wasserfontänenprojektion
2013

128–131

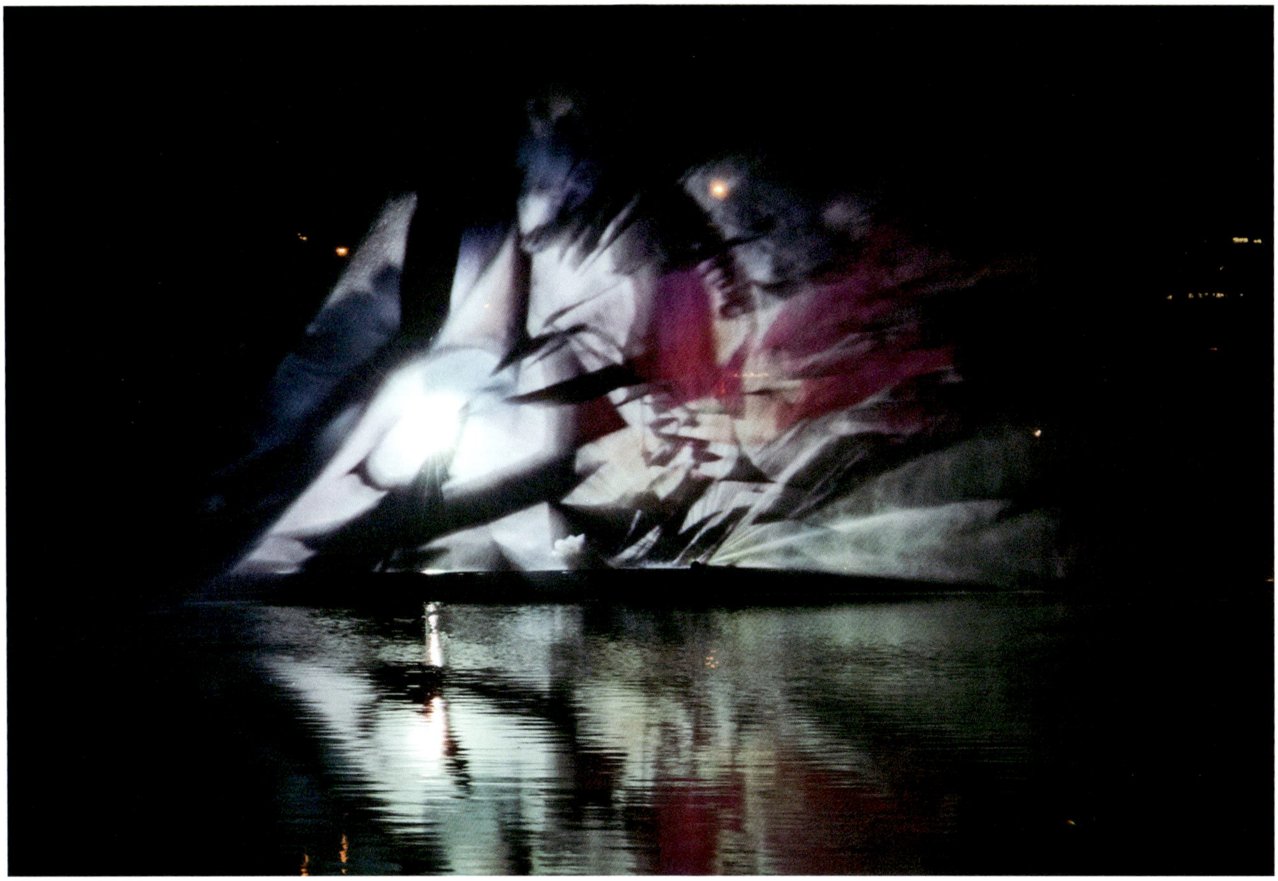

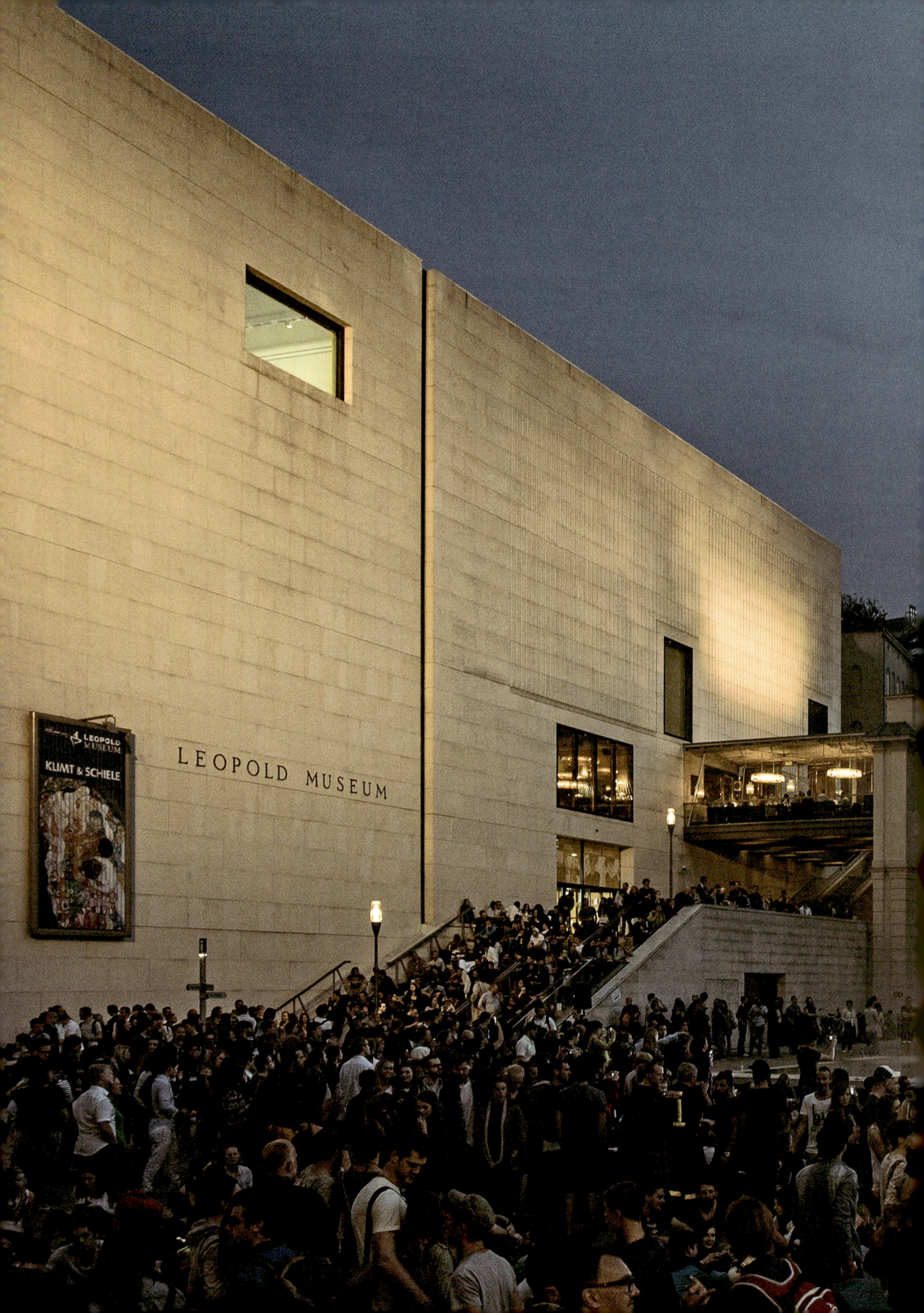

LEOPOLD MUSEUM
KLIMT & SCHIELE
LEOPOLD MUSEUM

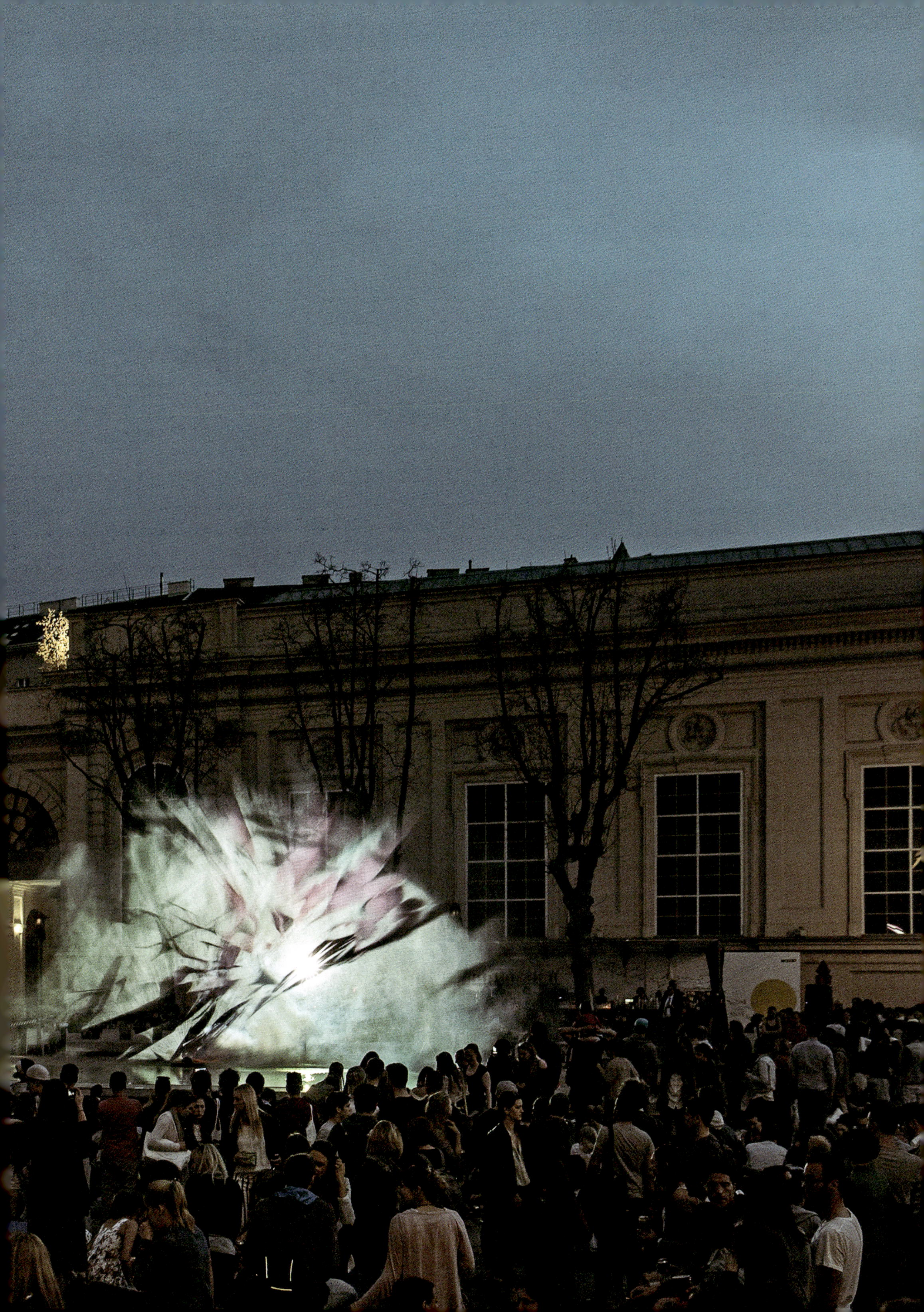

grapheme
—
Projektionsskulptur
2013

132–137

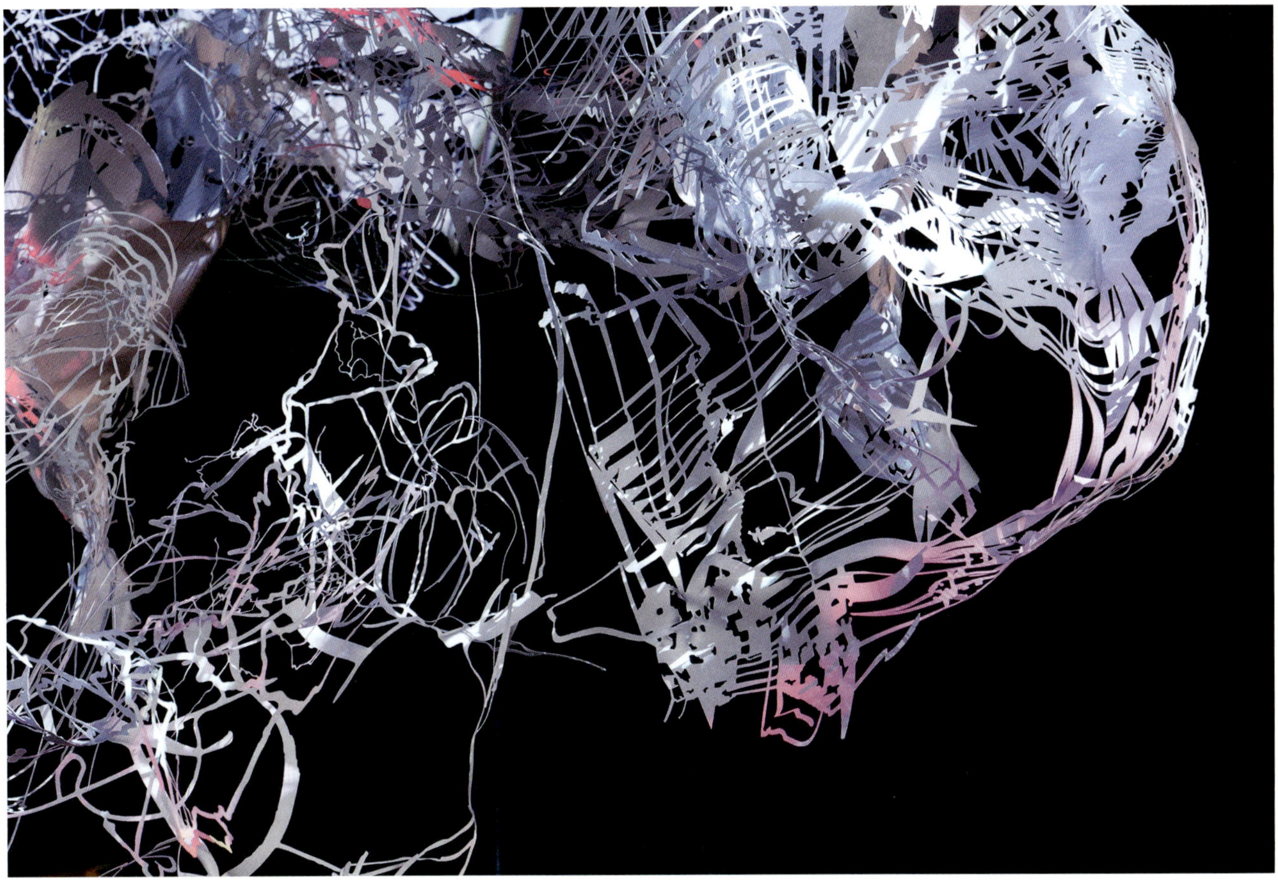

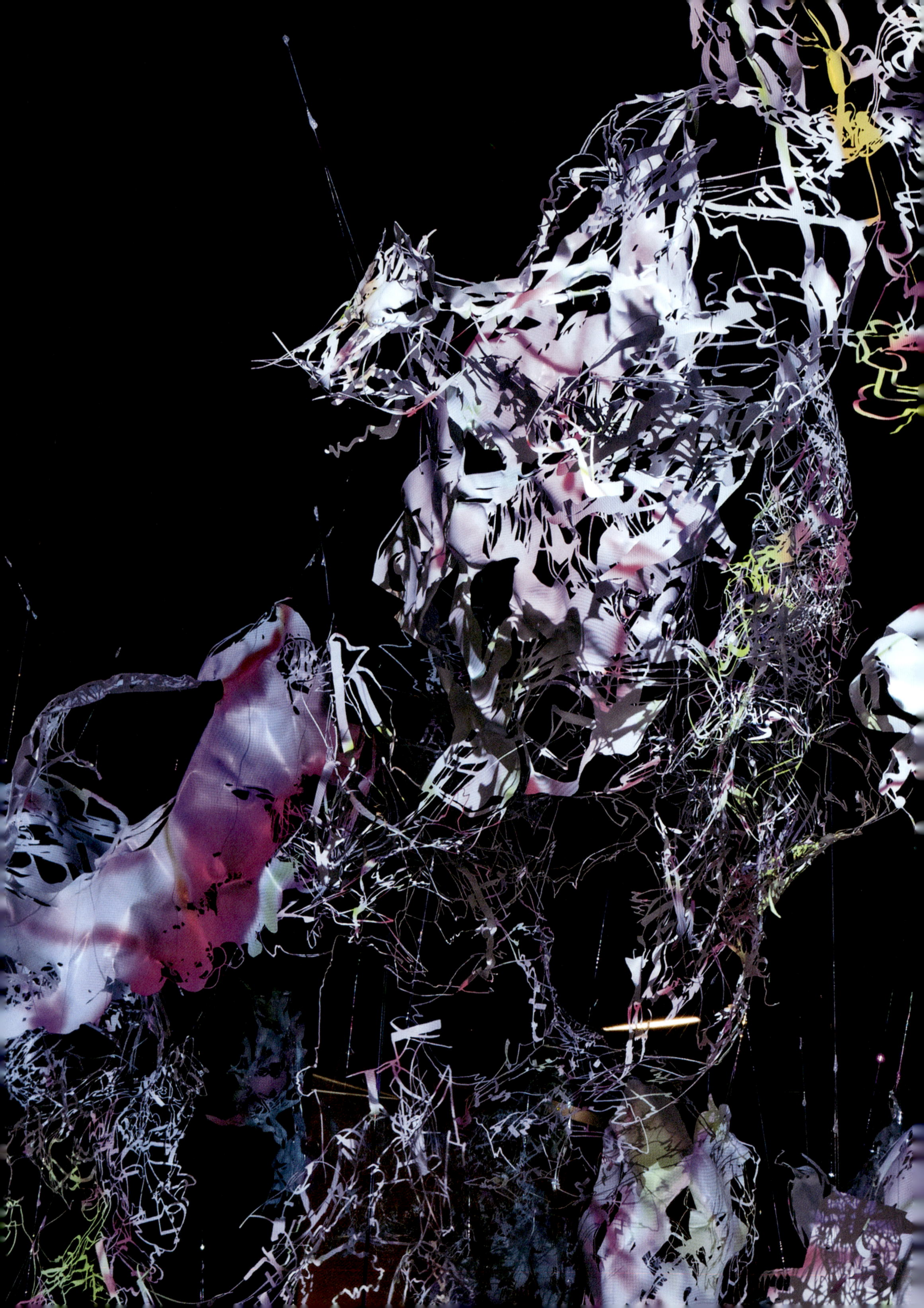

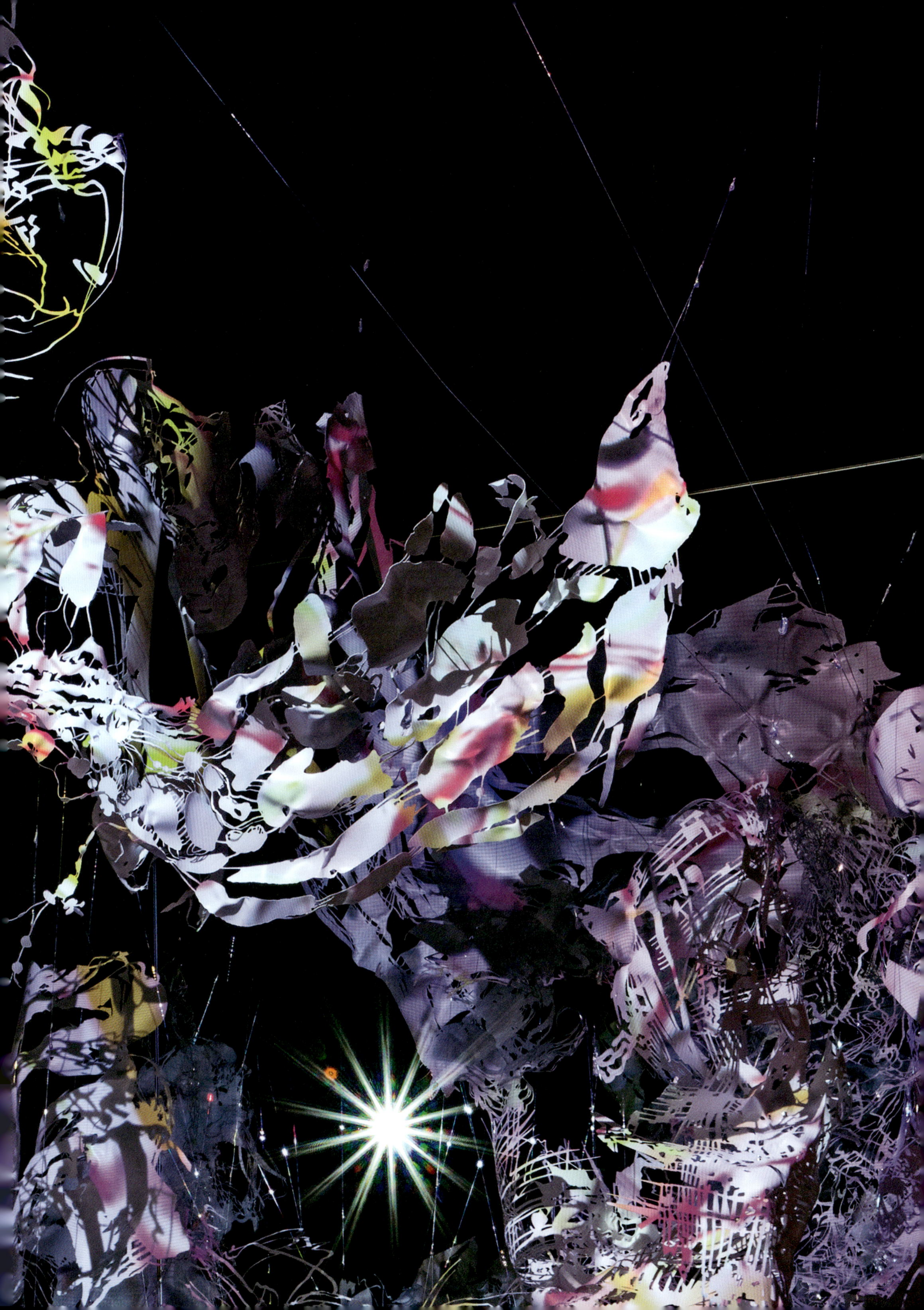

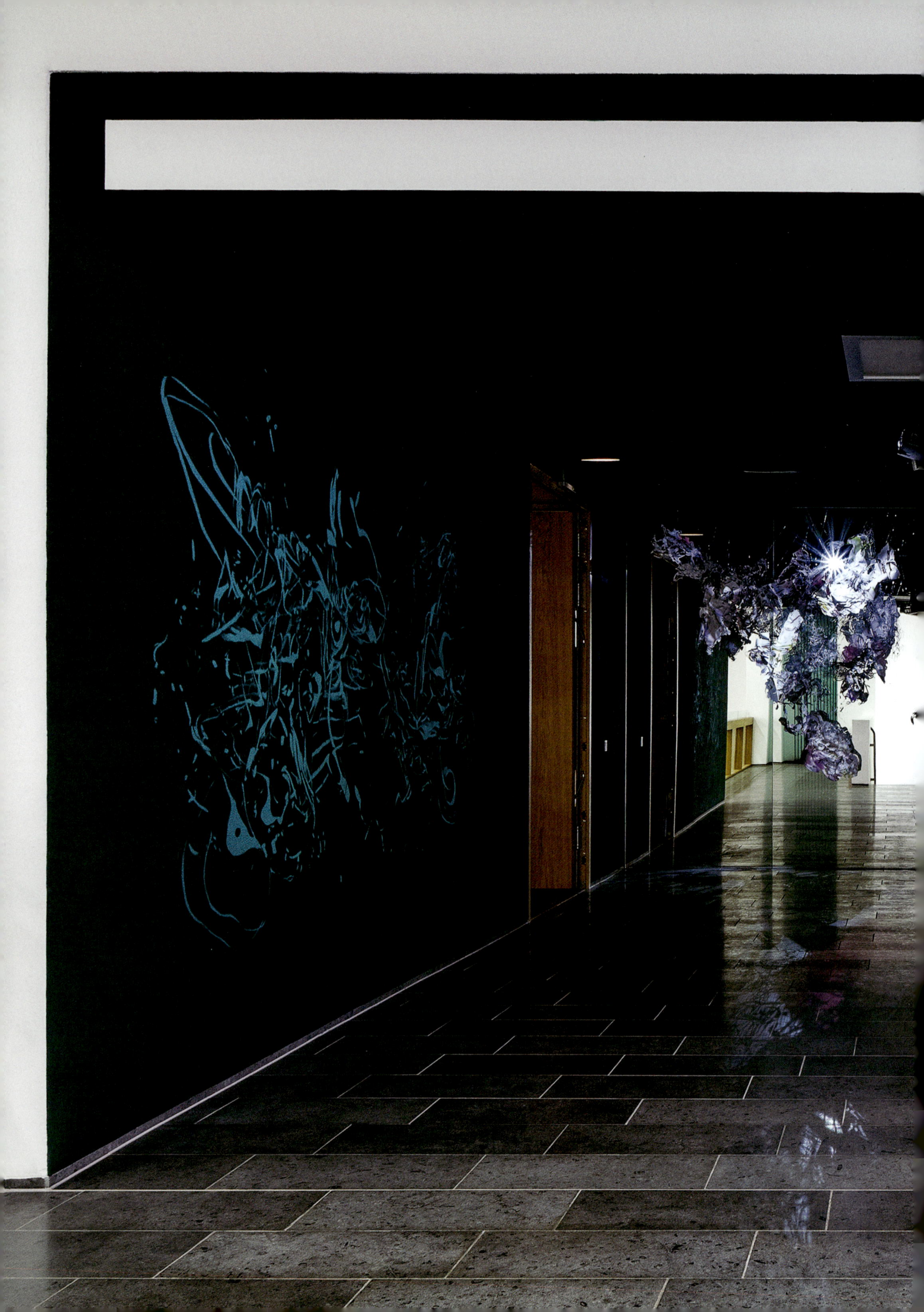

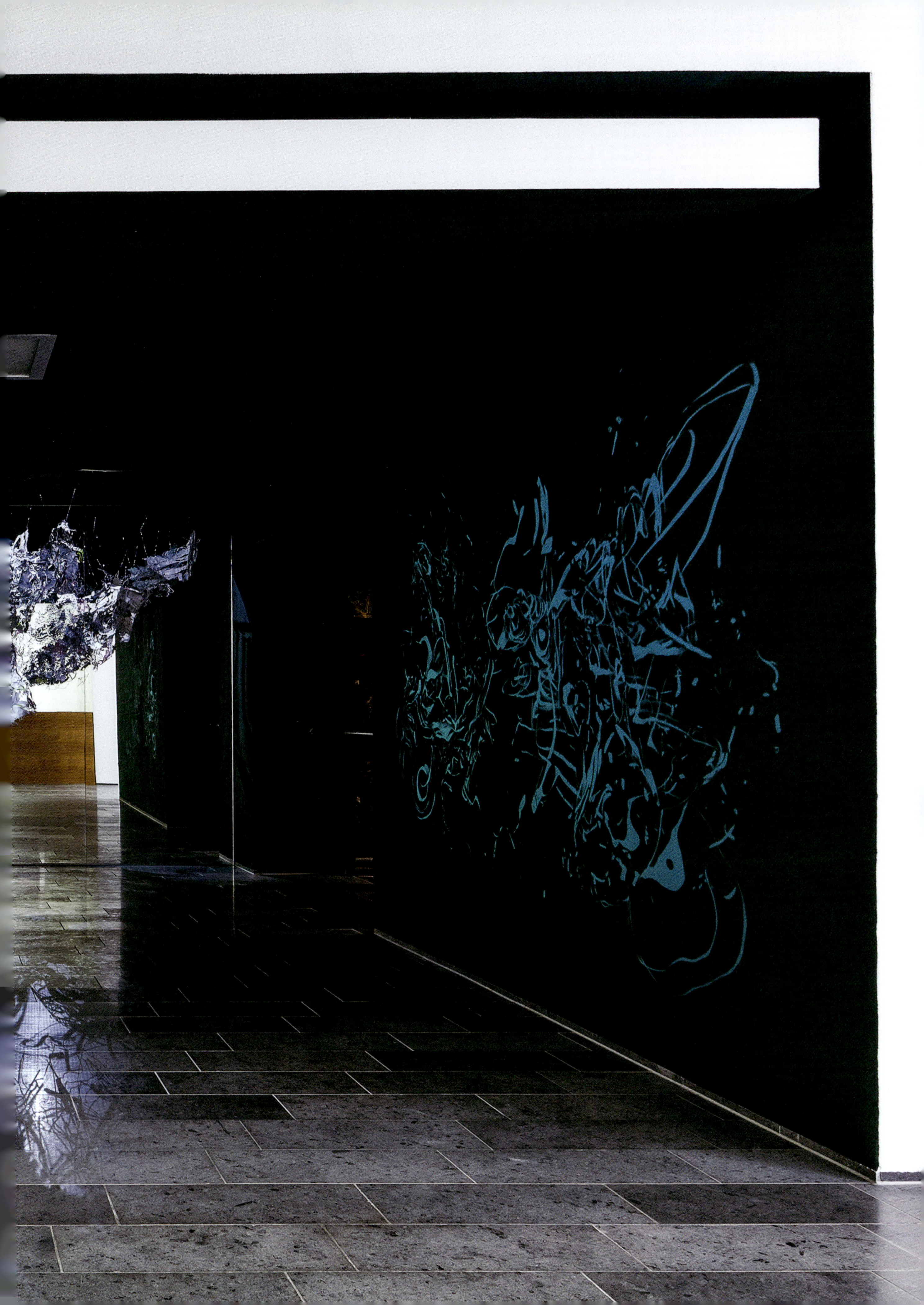

… # ligature

—

Fassadenprojektion
2014

138–141

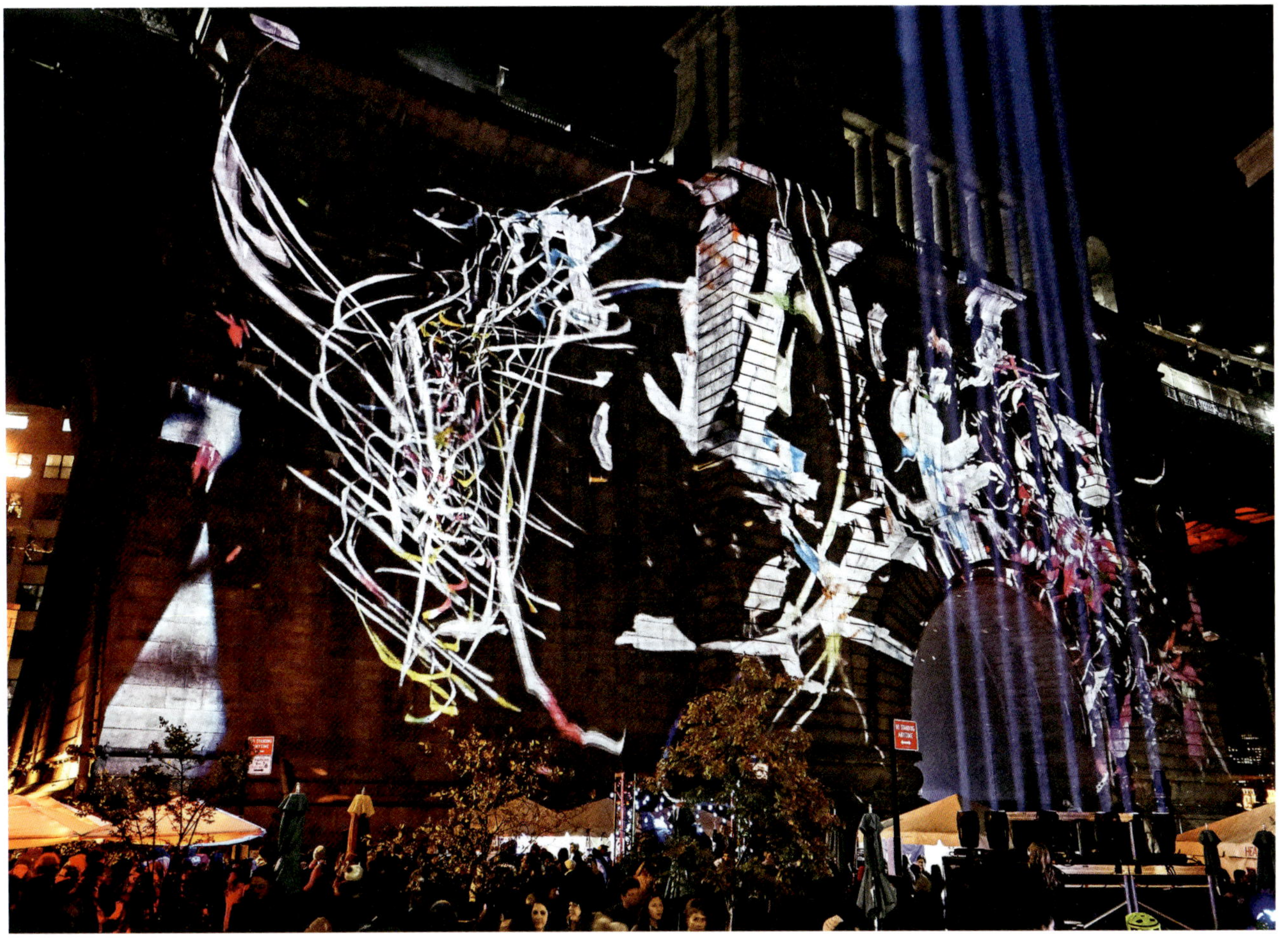

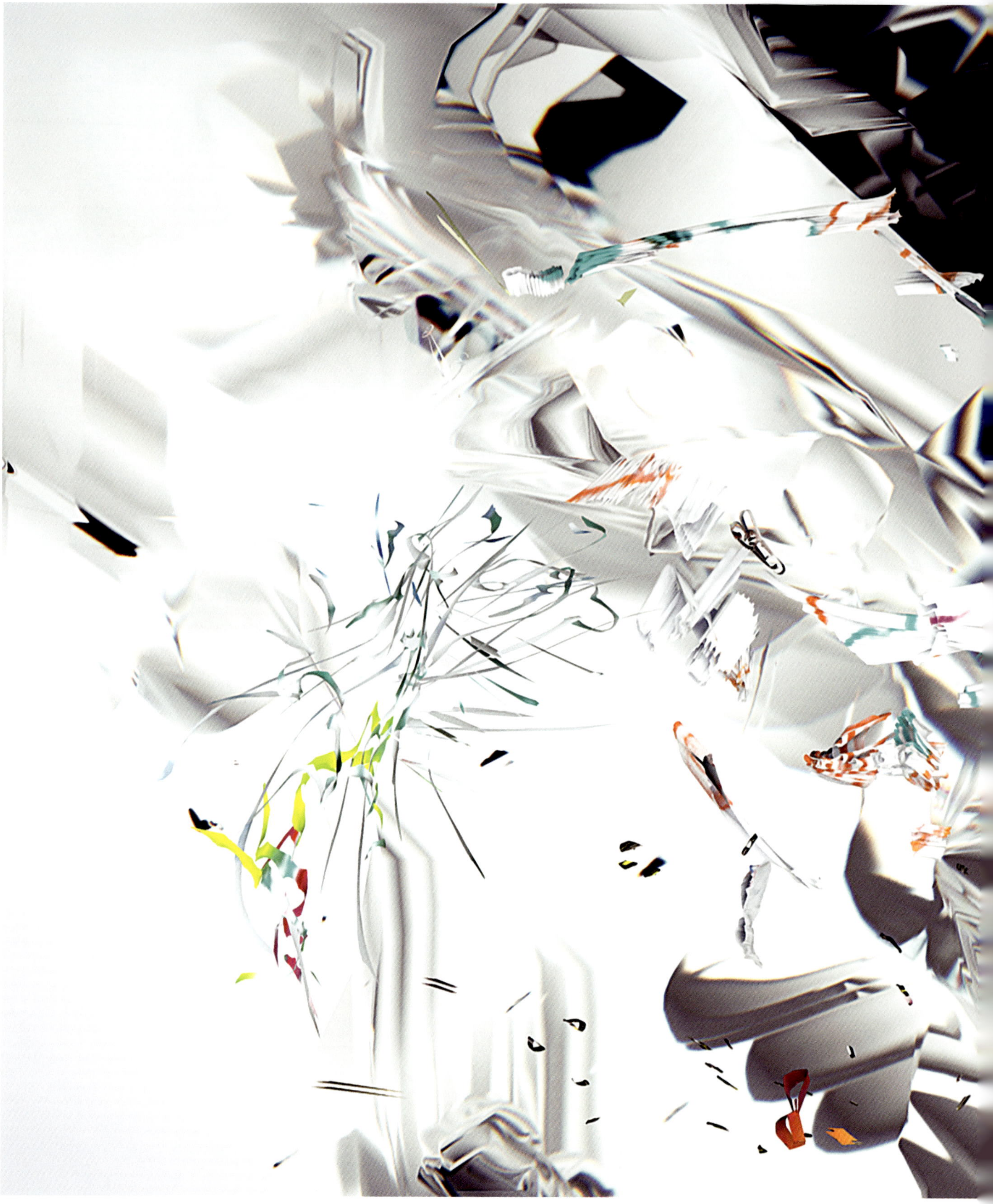

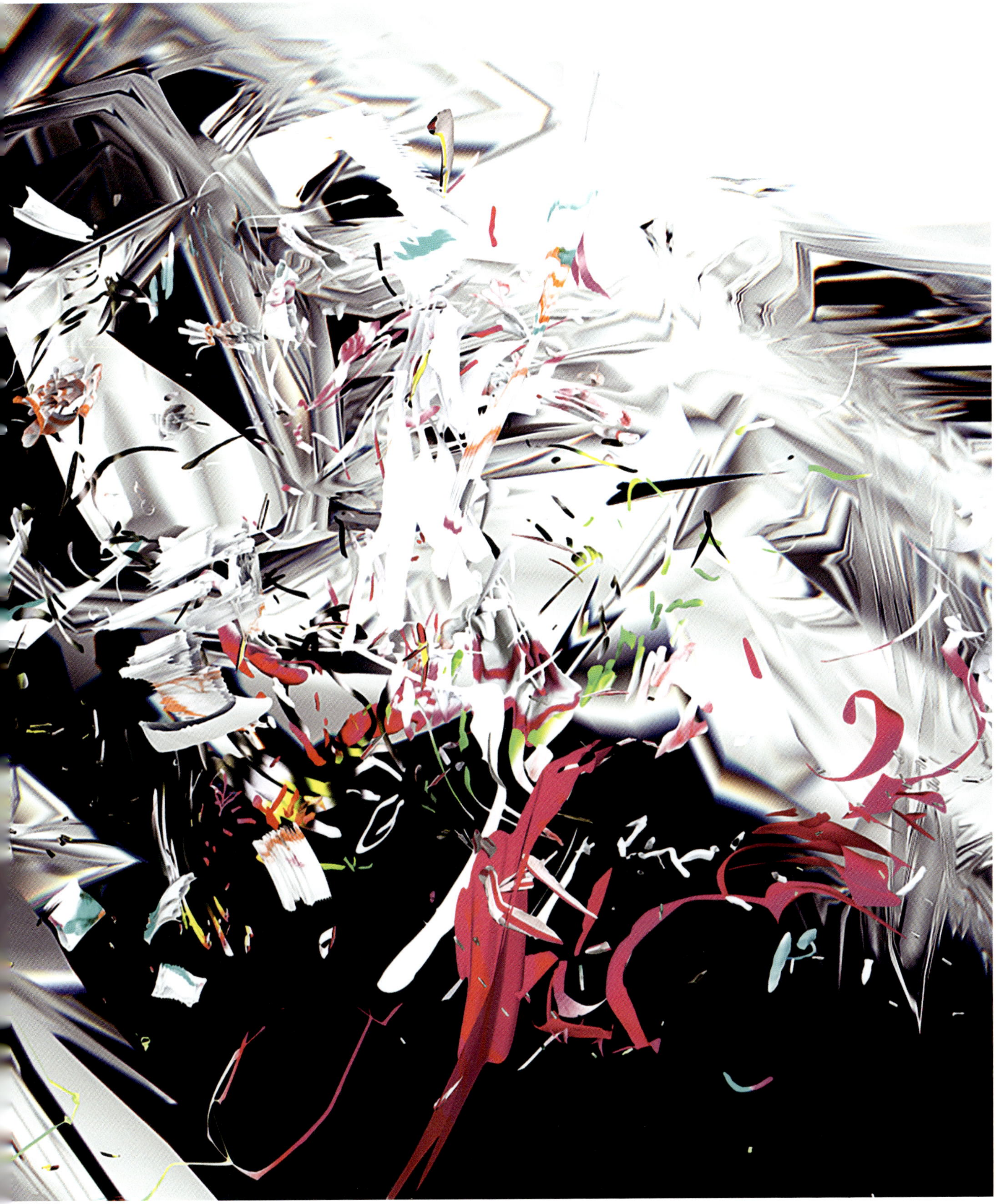

stains
–
Videoprojektion
2015

142–145

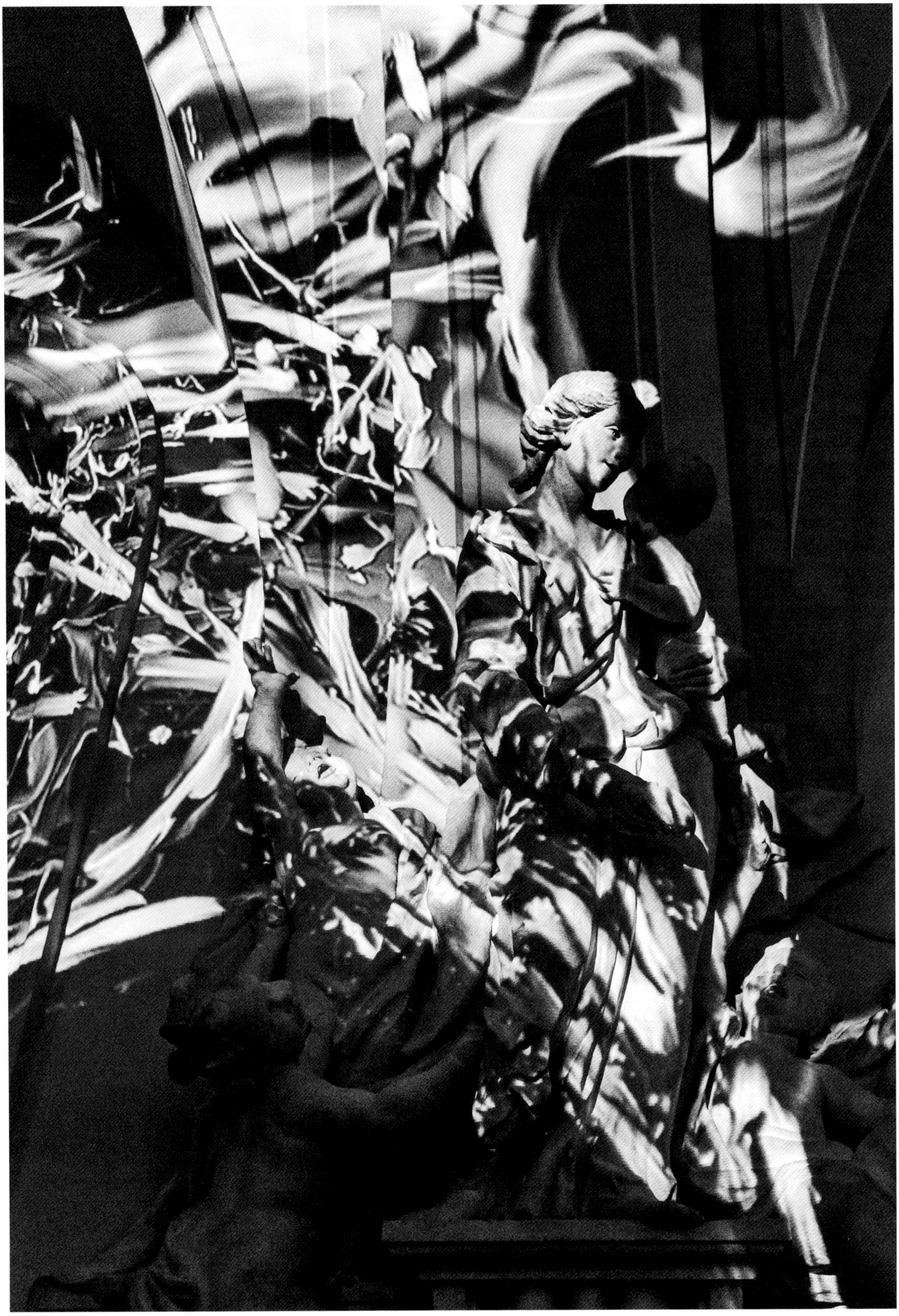

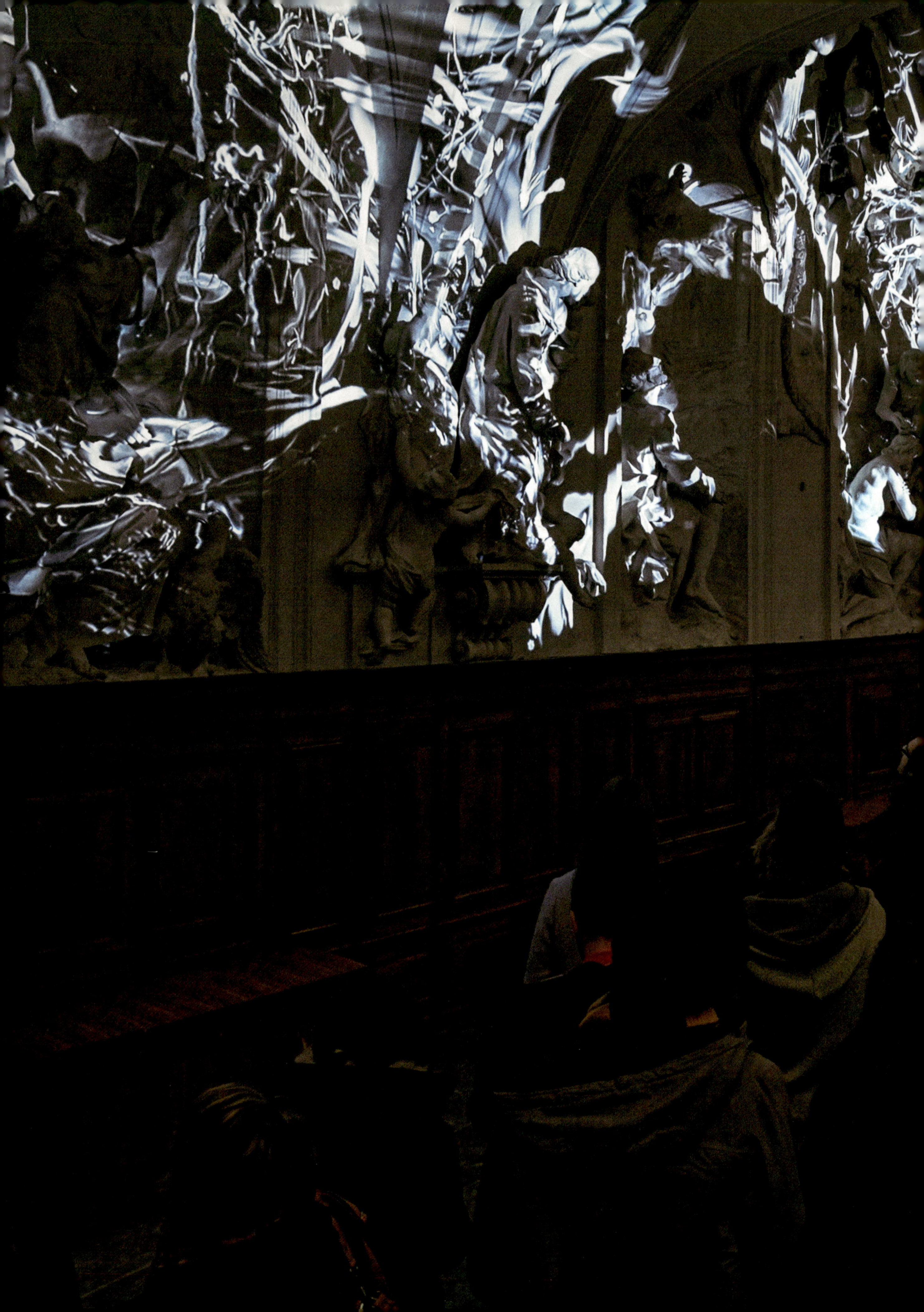

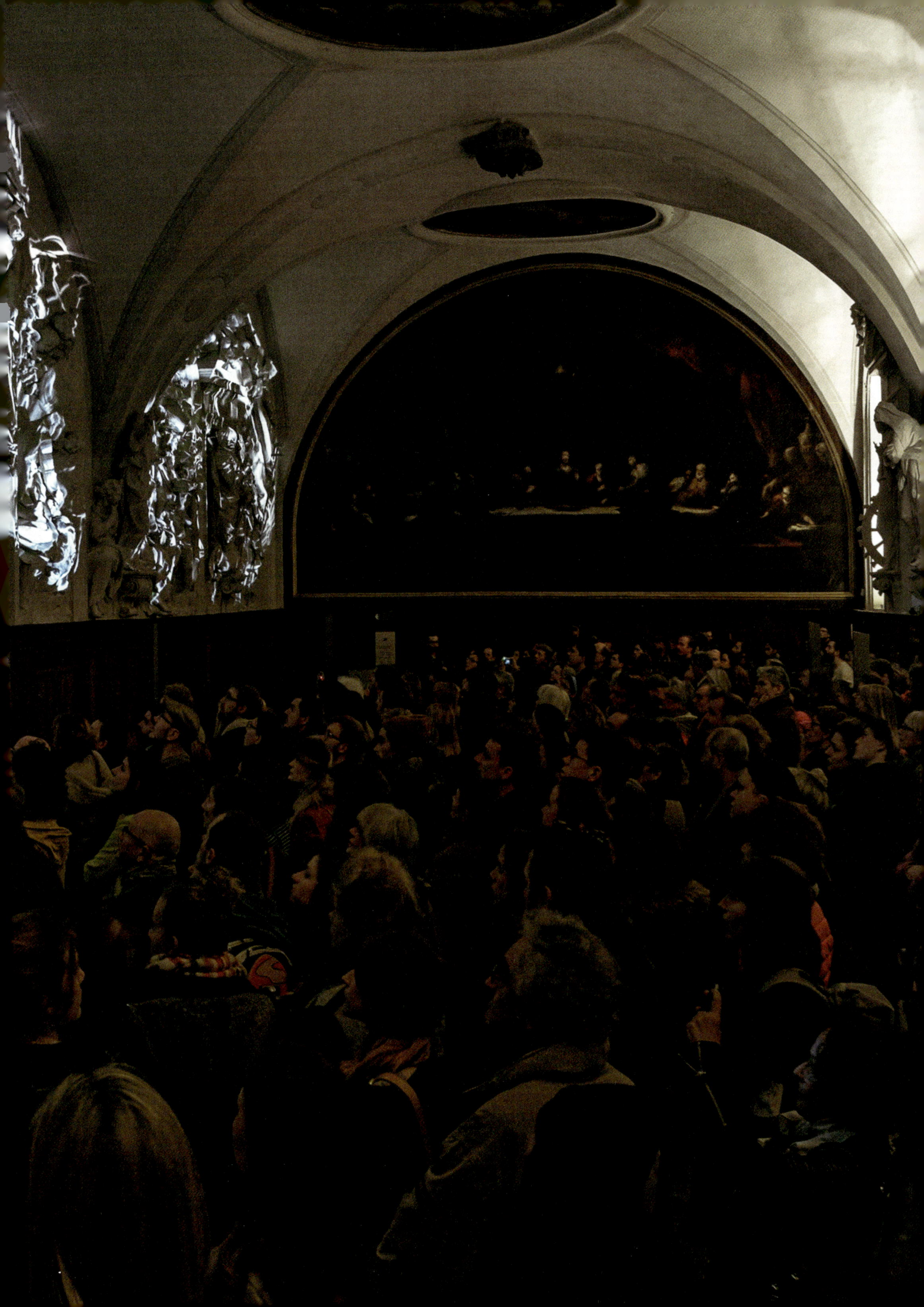

recoil
—
Fassadenprojektion
2015

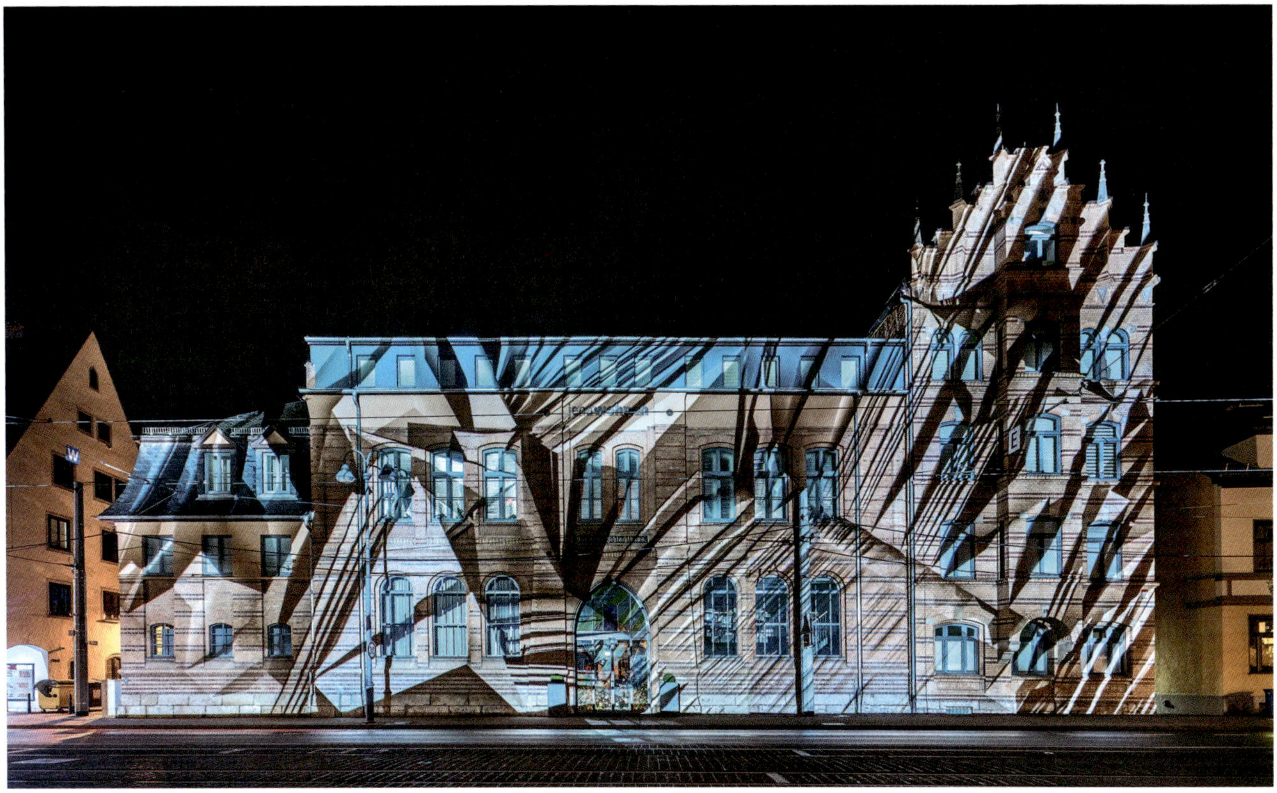

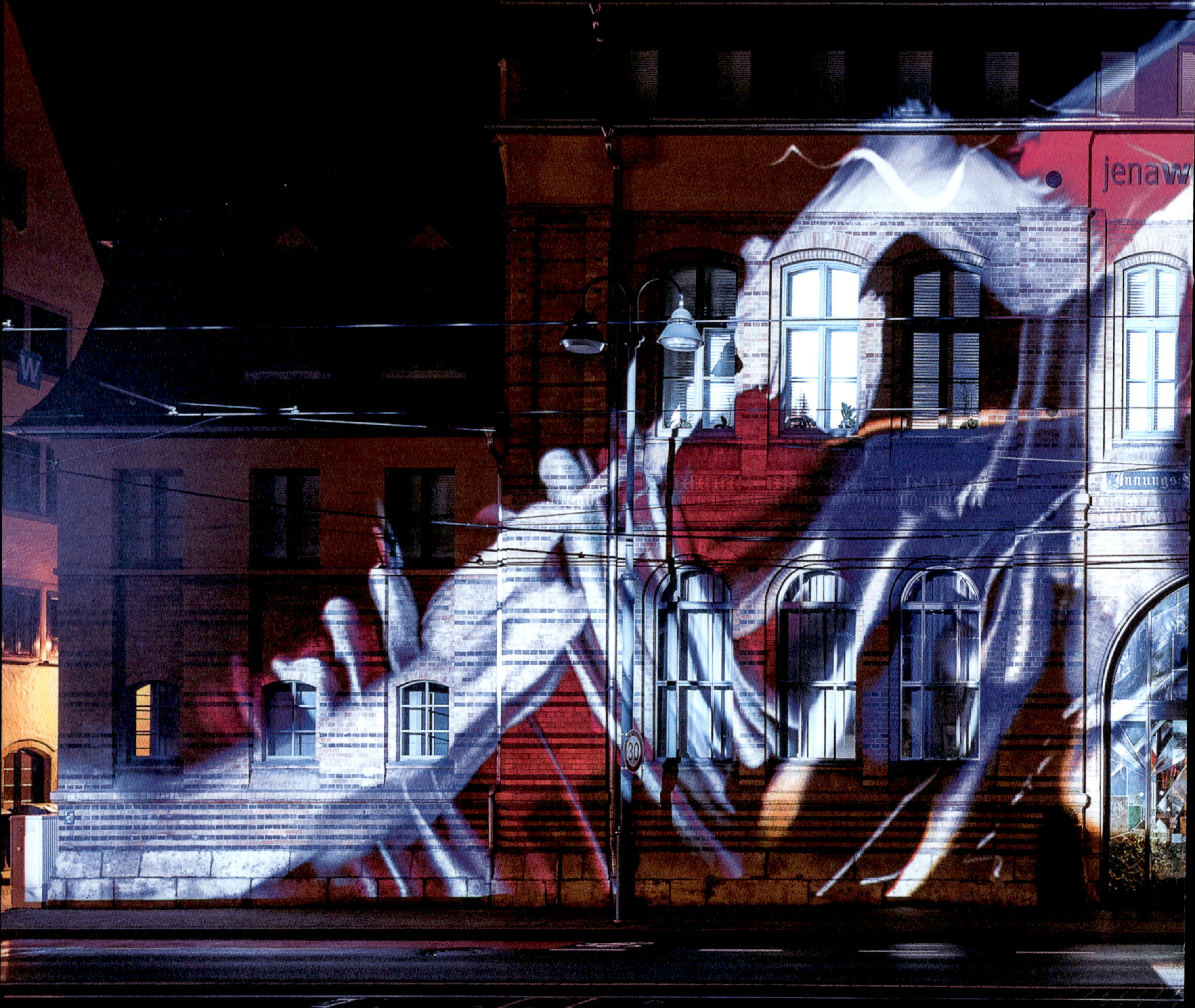
jenaw
Innungs-
30

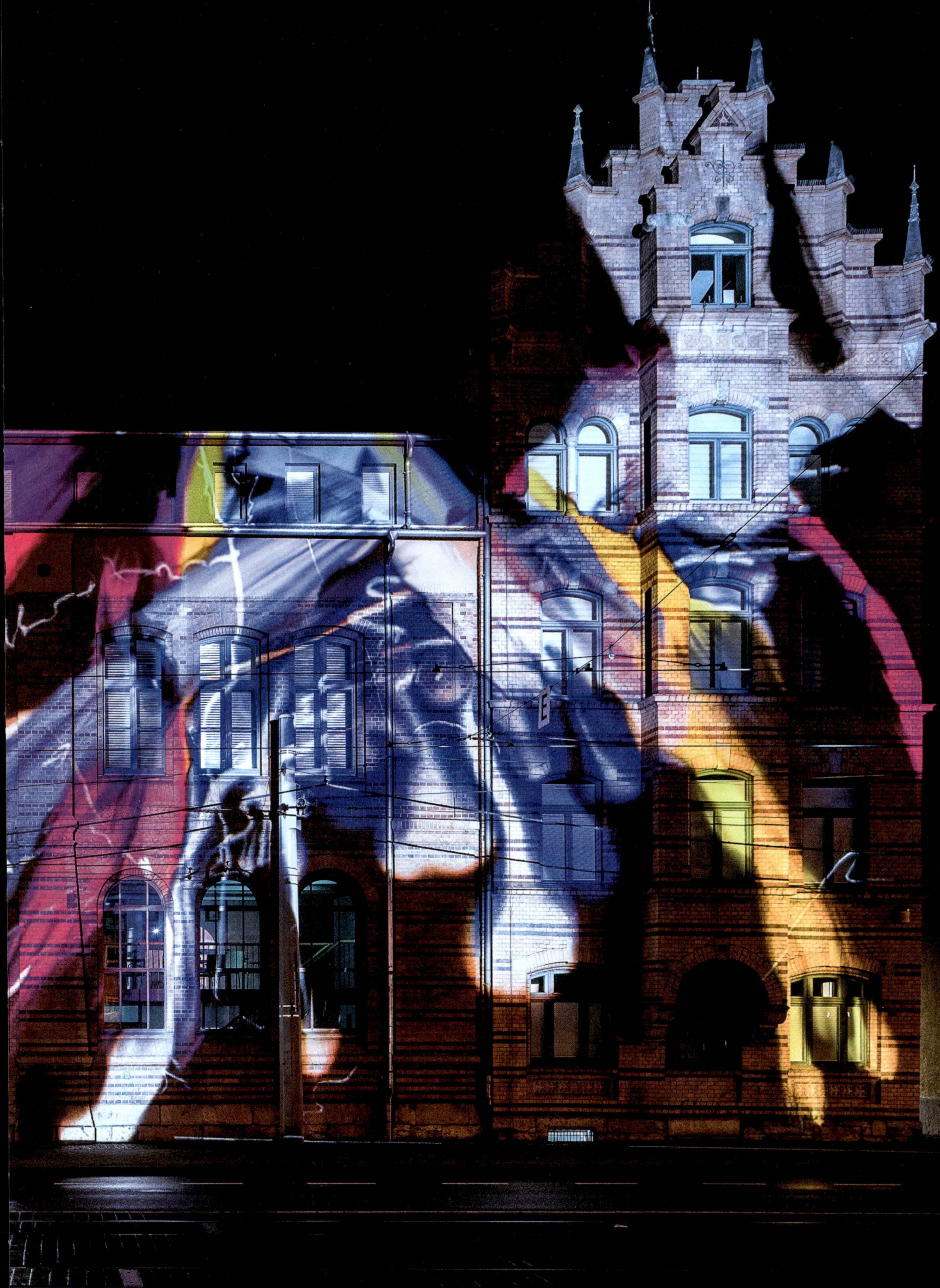

magnitude
—
Laser-Performance
2015

150–153

151

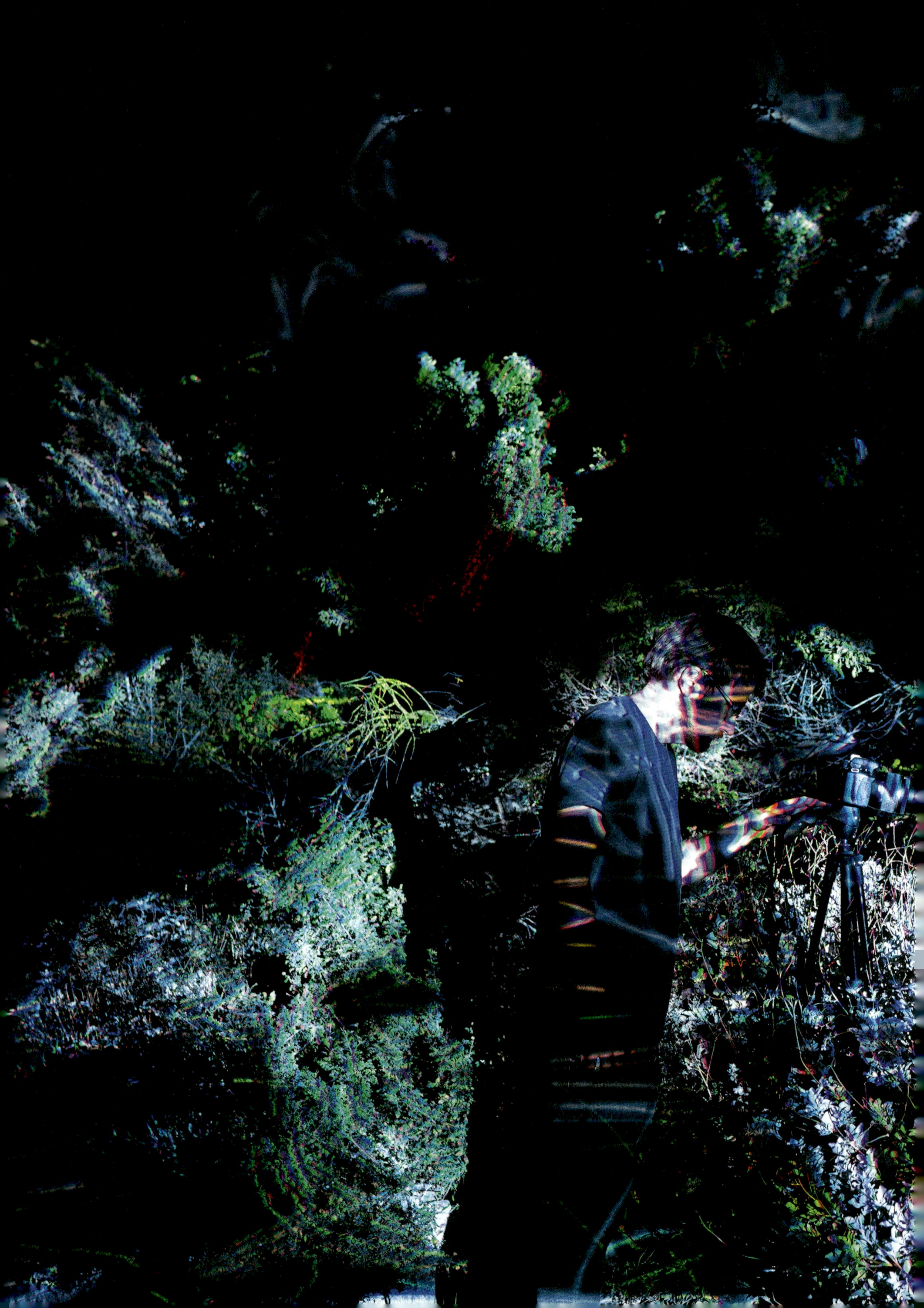

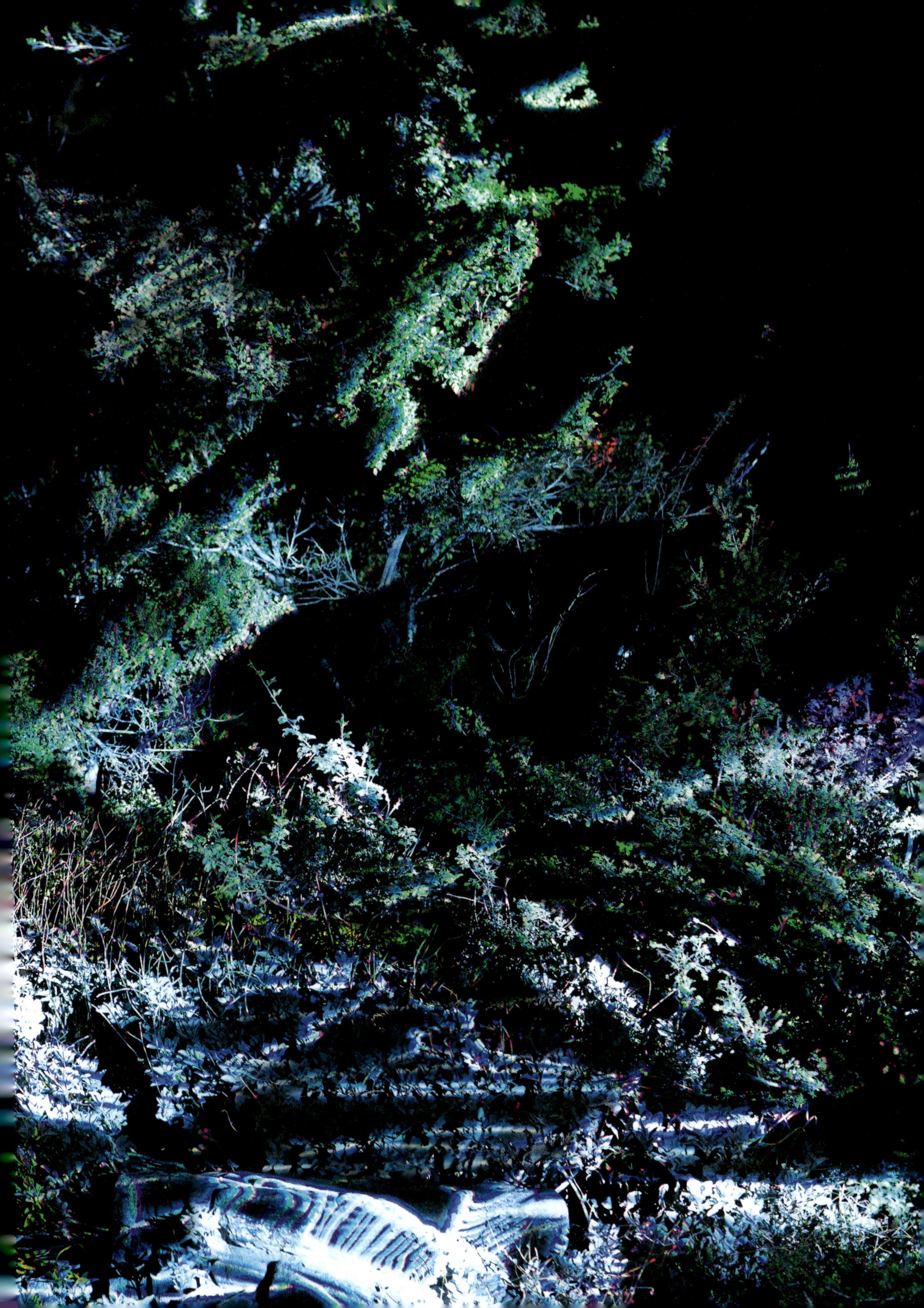

lux aeterna
–
TV-Installation
2015

155

suturae #2
—
Laserinstallation
2015

157

mold
—
Licht-Raum-Zeichnung
2015

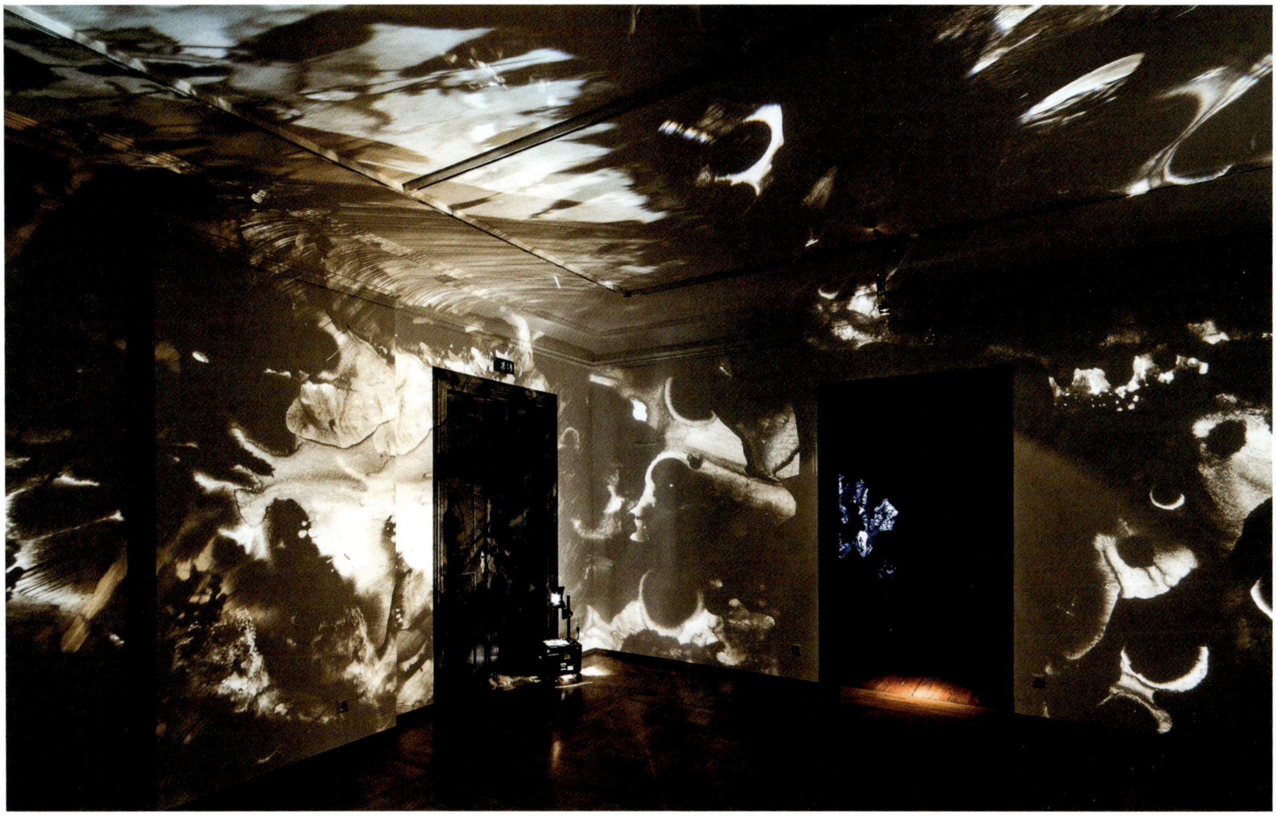

vitreous
—
Experimentalfilm
2012–2015

160–165

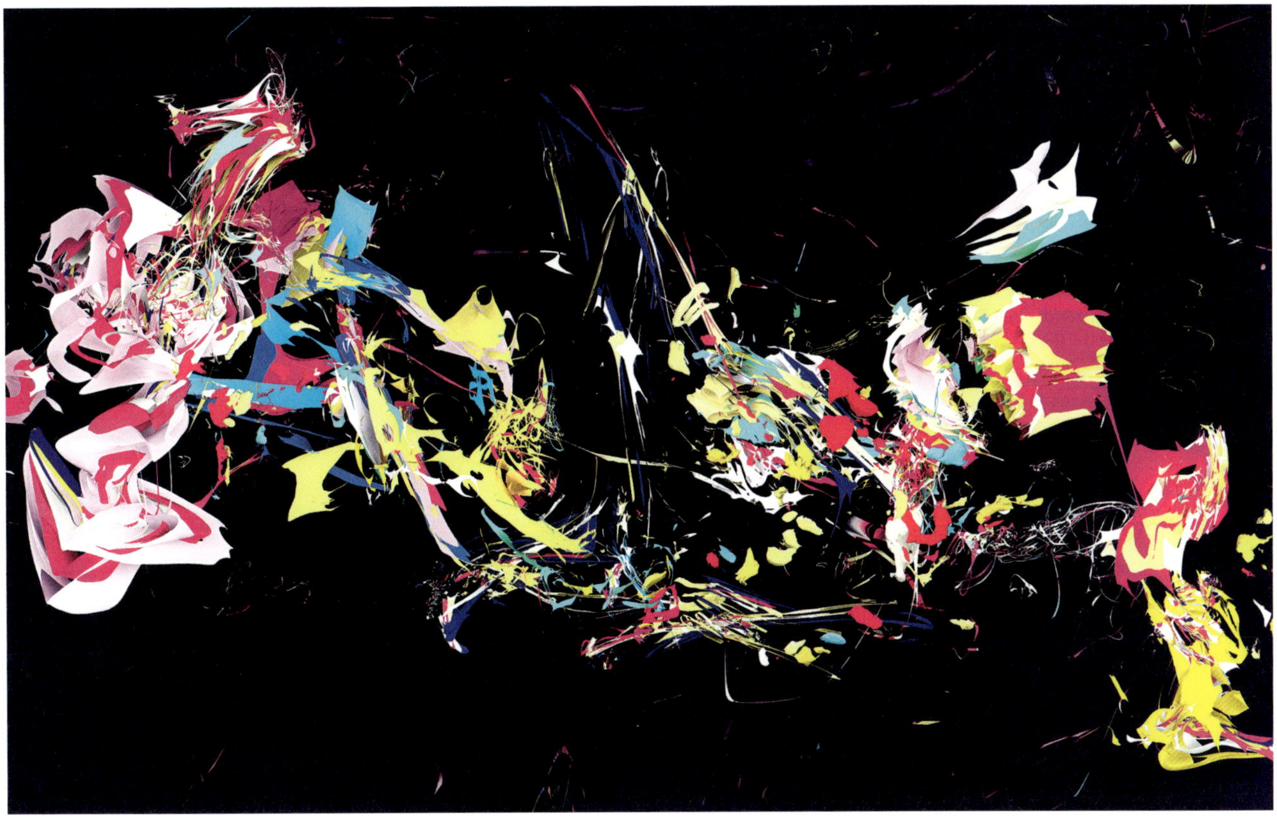

163

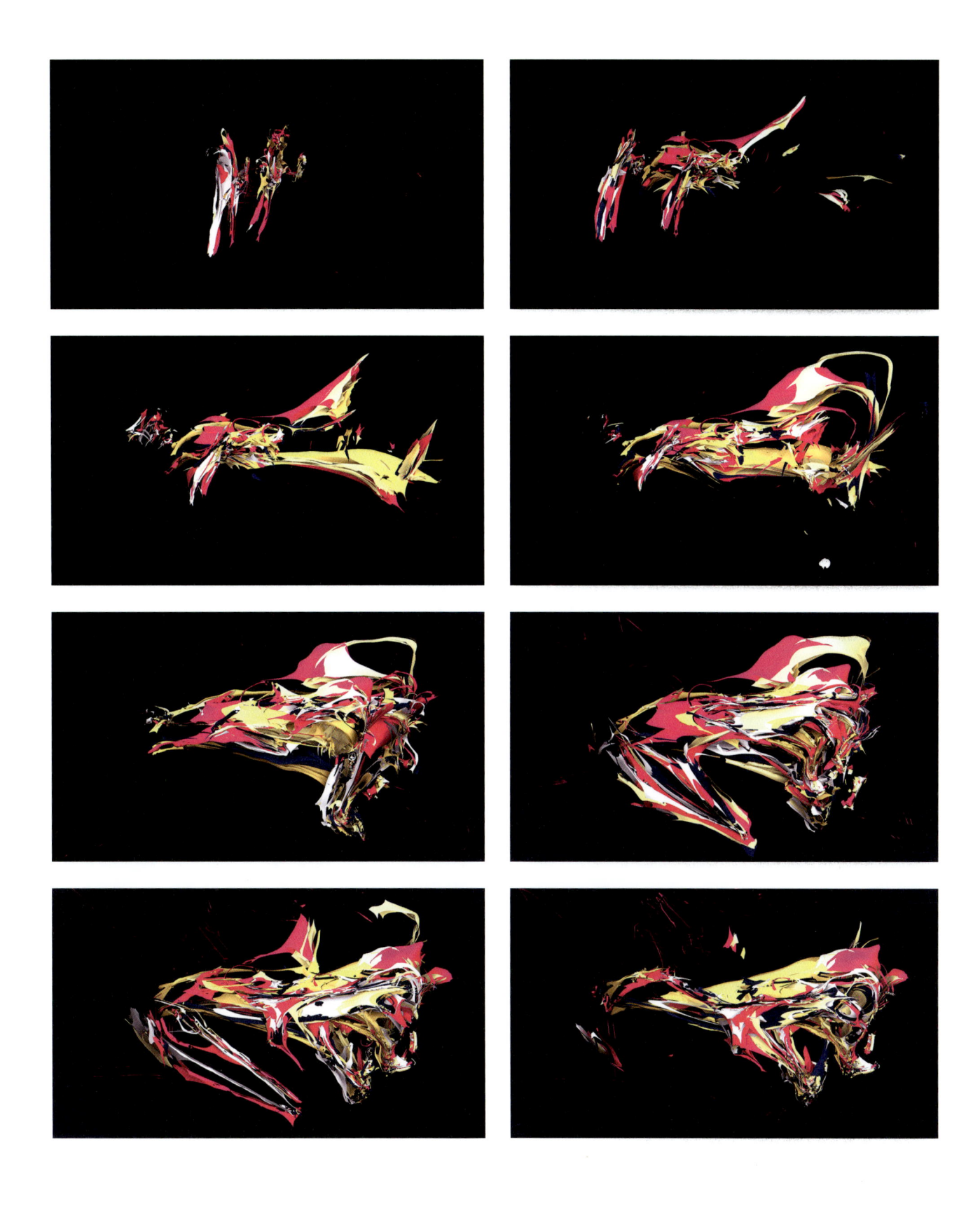

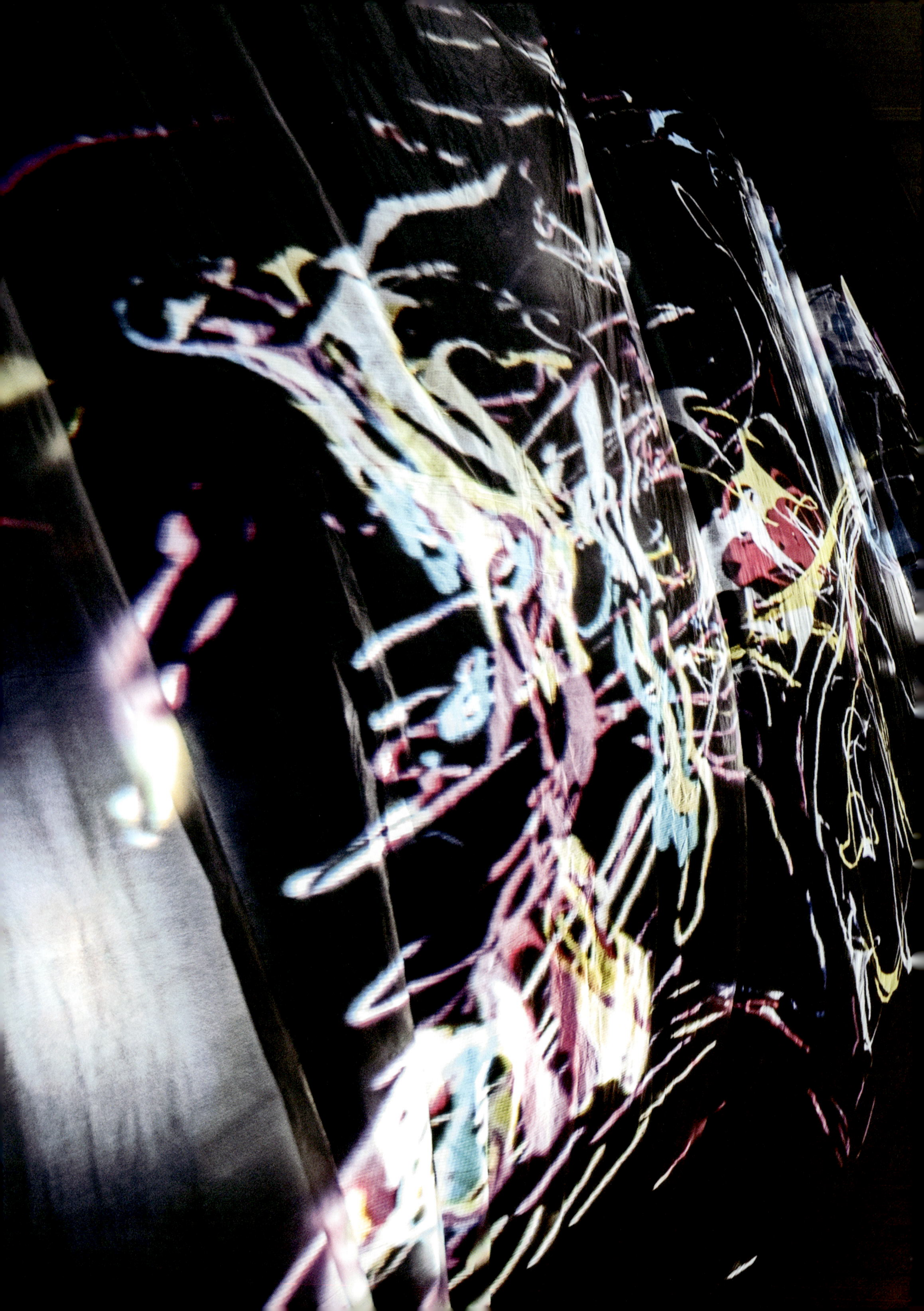

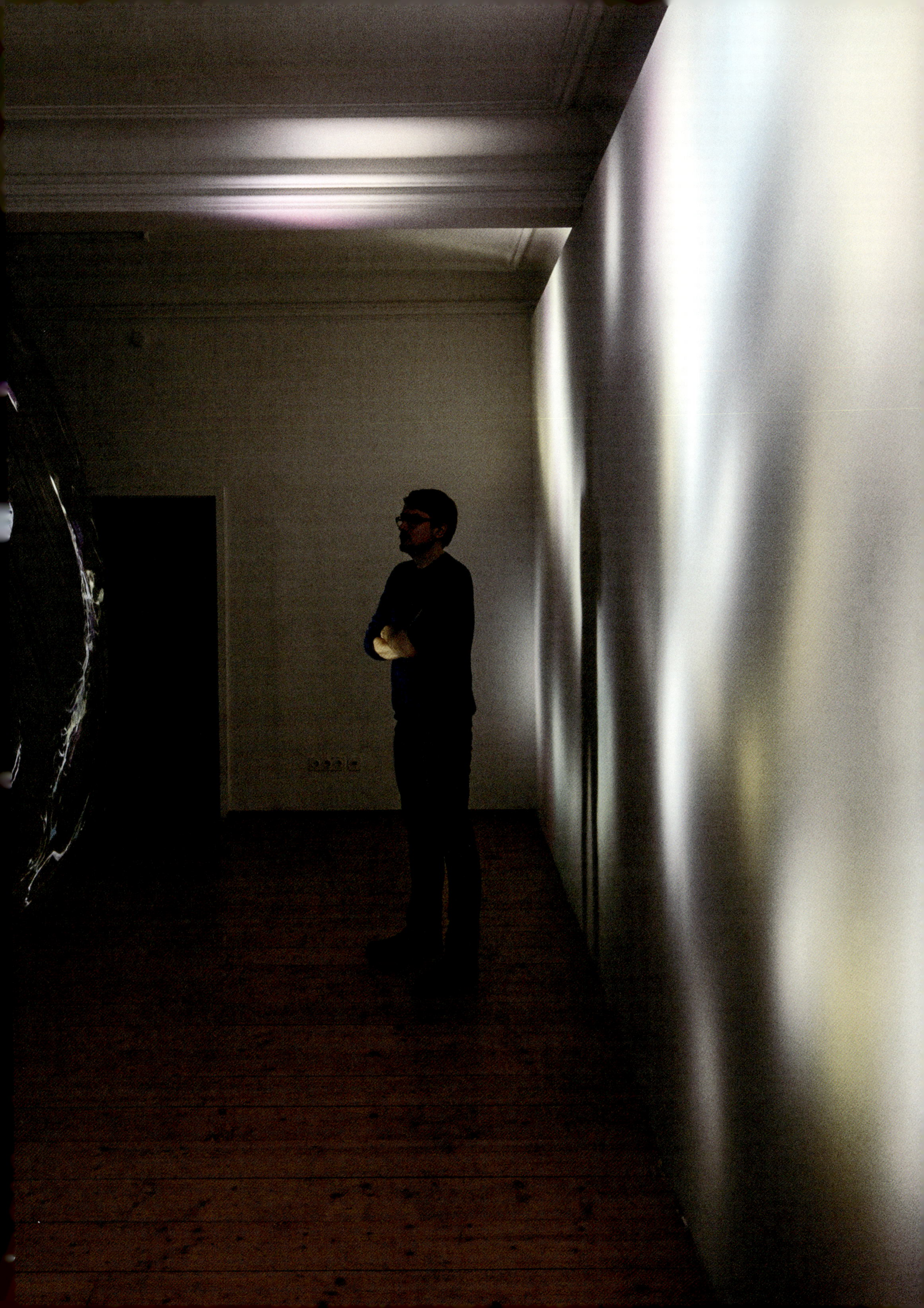

Fotografien und Zeichnungen/ Photographies and Drawings

vitreous
168–169

sputter #1–3
170–173

glimmer #1–3
174–177

fever
178–179

fulcrum #1–3
180–183

vitreous #1
—
Zeichnung
2012

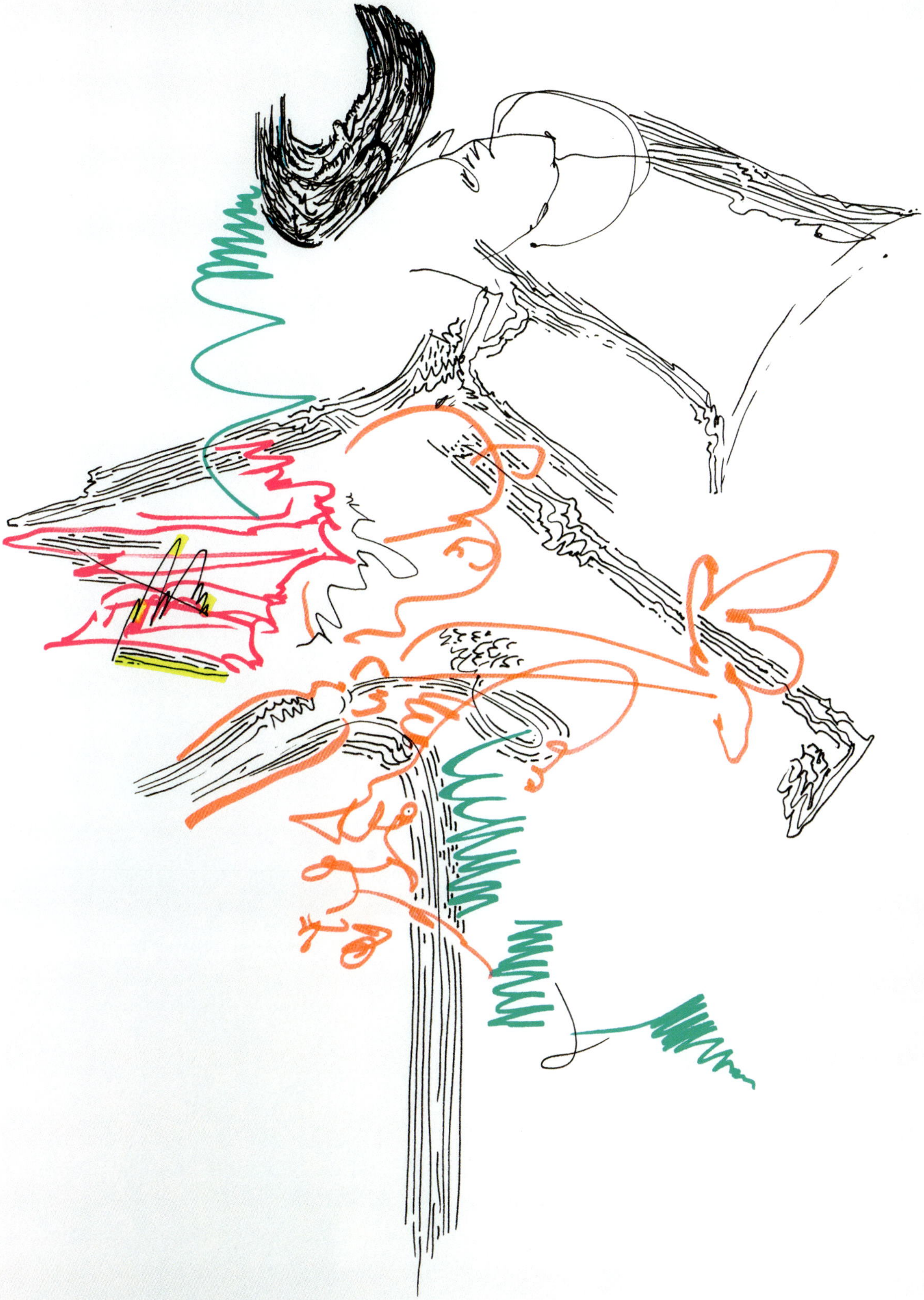

sputter #1–3
—
Rasterelektronen-
mikroskop-Aufnahme
2014

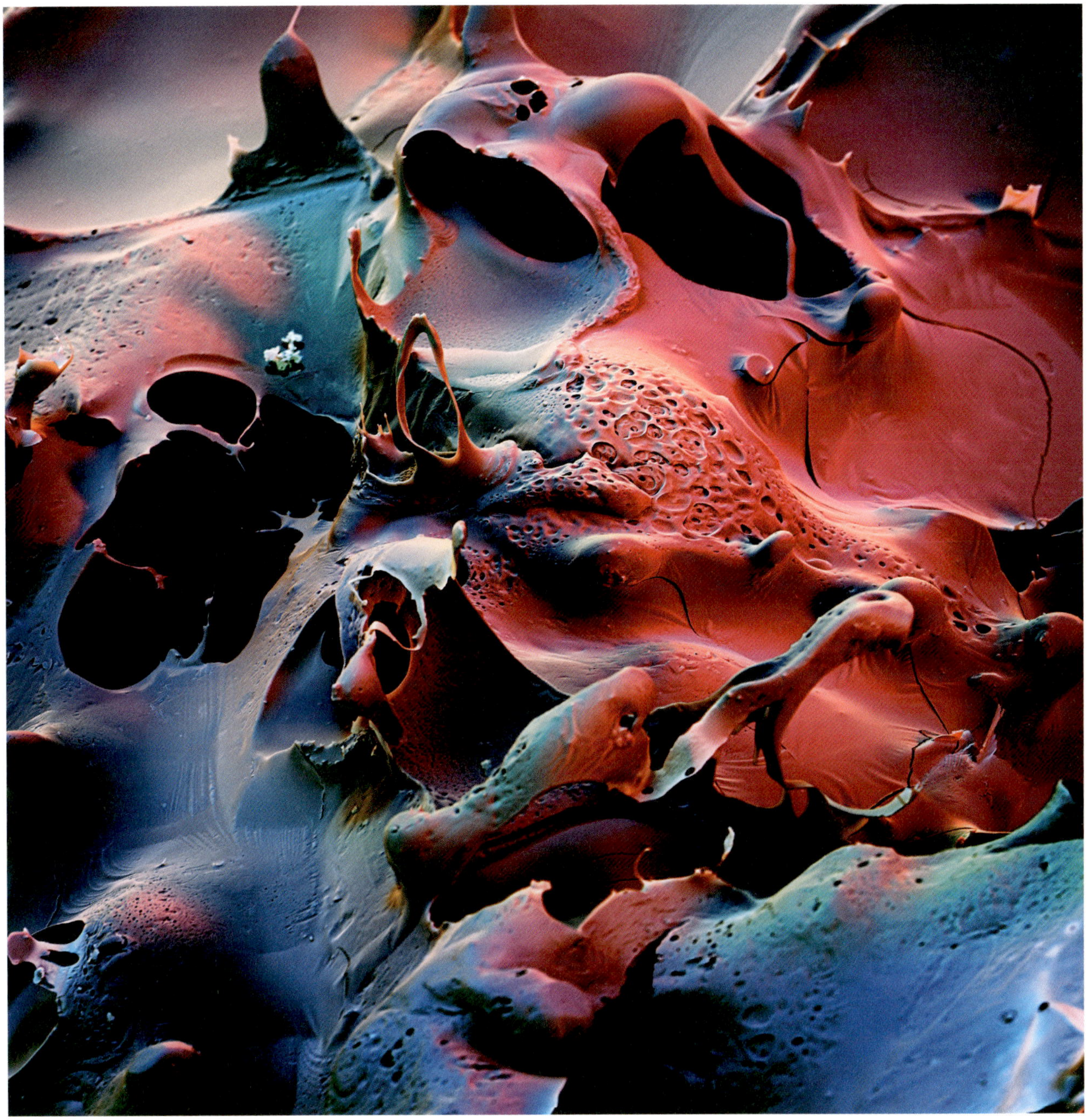

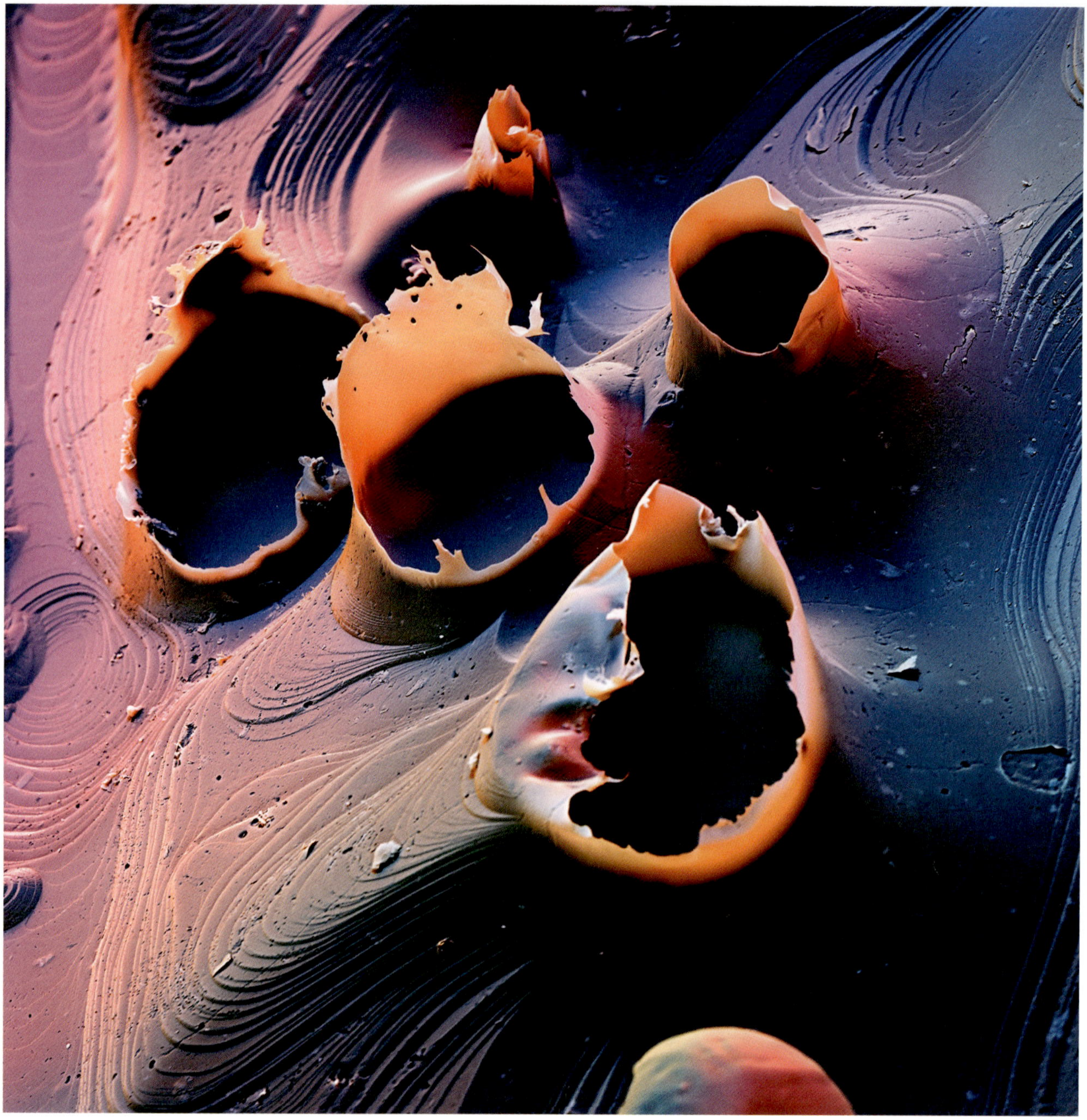

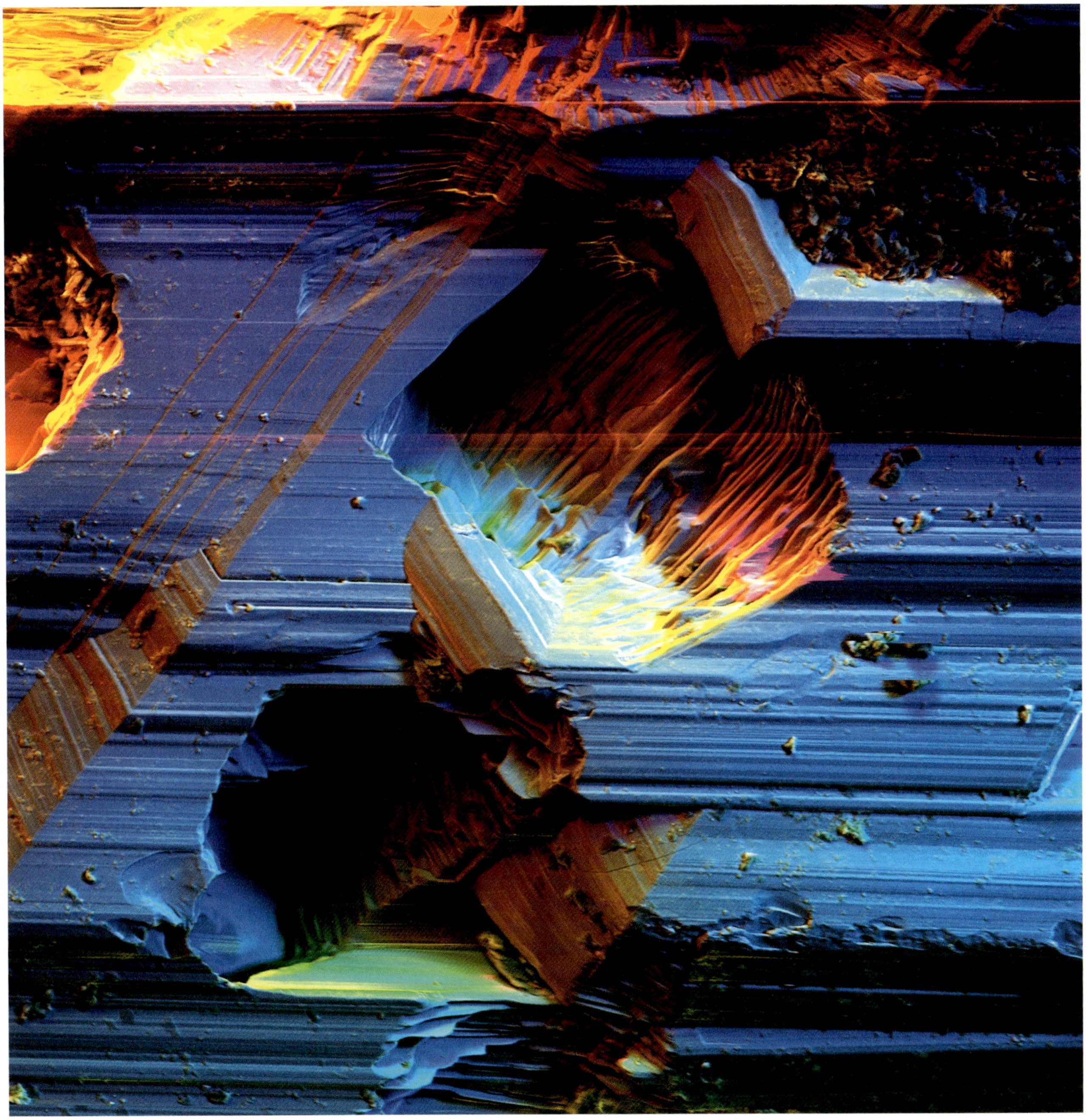

glimmer #1–3
–
Graphit und Tusche auf Papier
2015

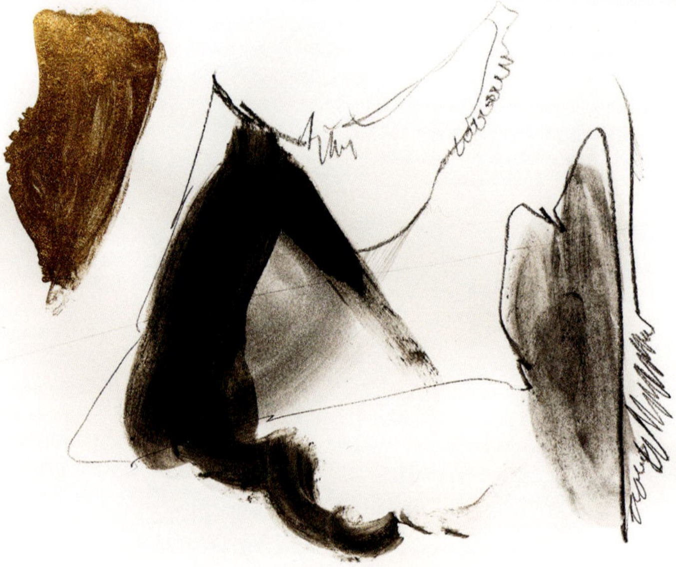

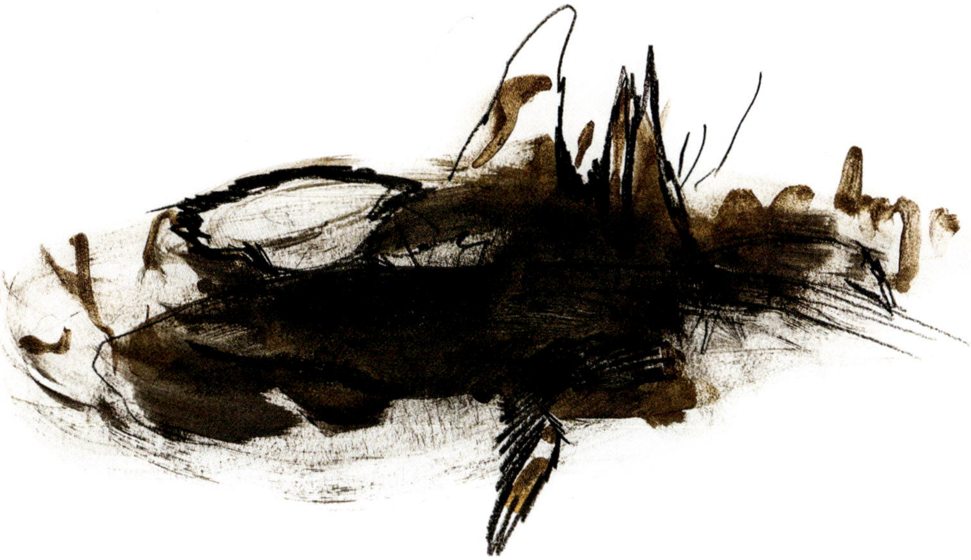

fever

—

Digitale Zeichnung
2015

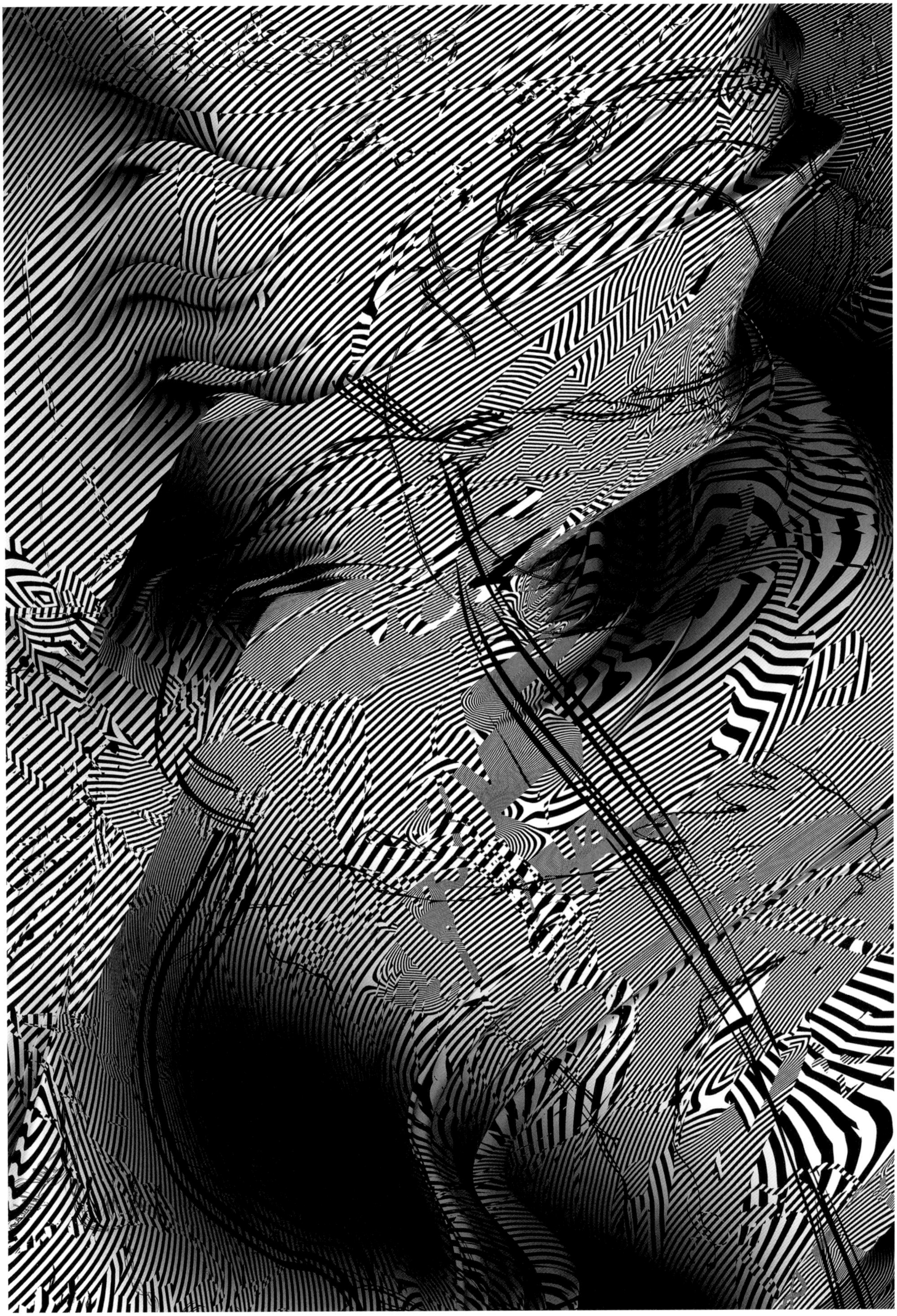

fulcrum #1–3
—
Graphitzeichnung
2015

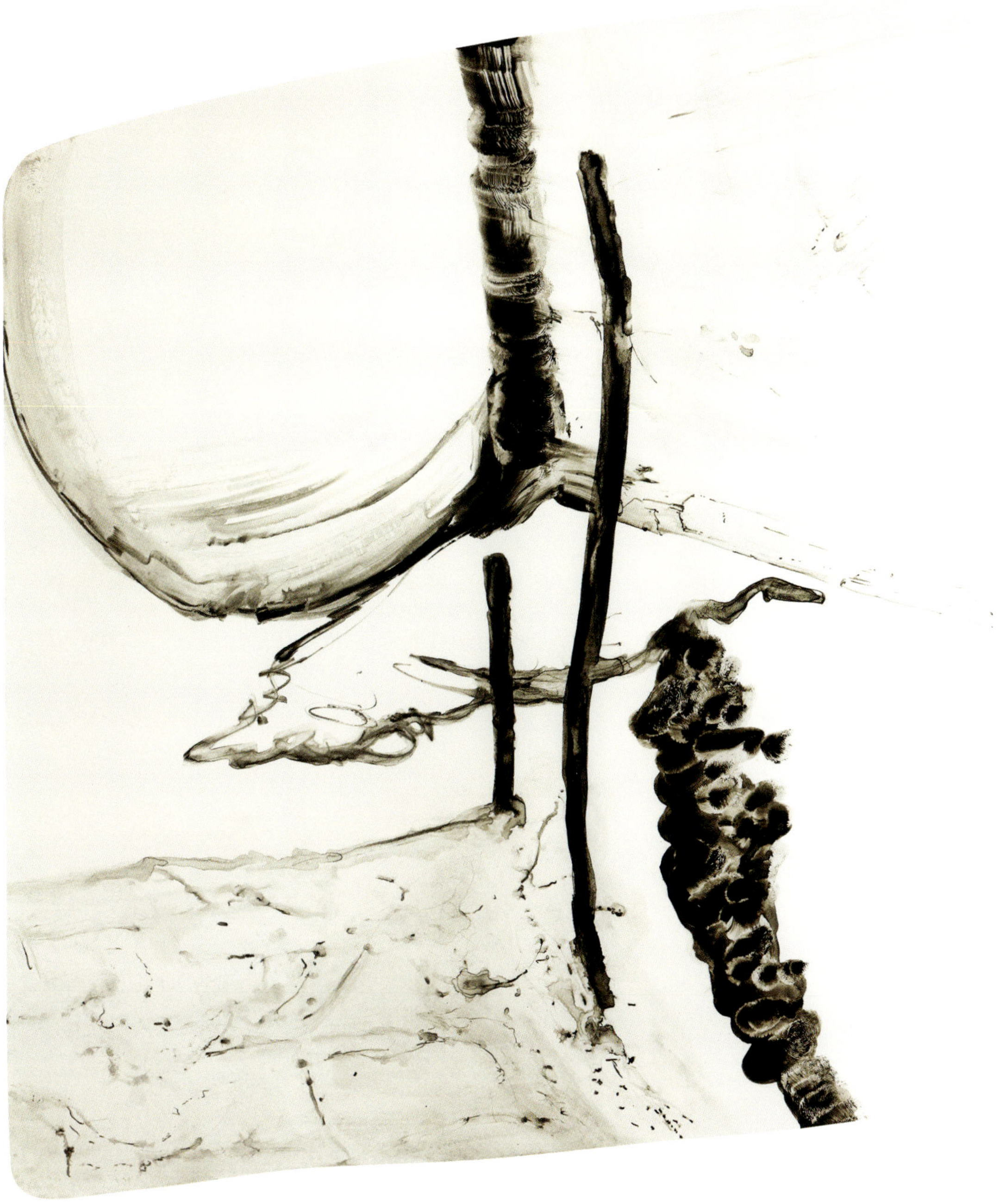

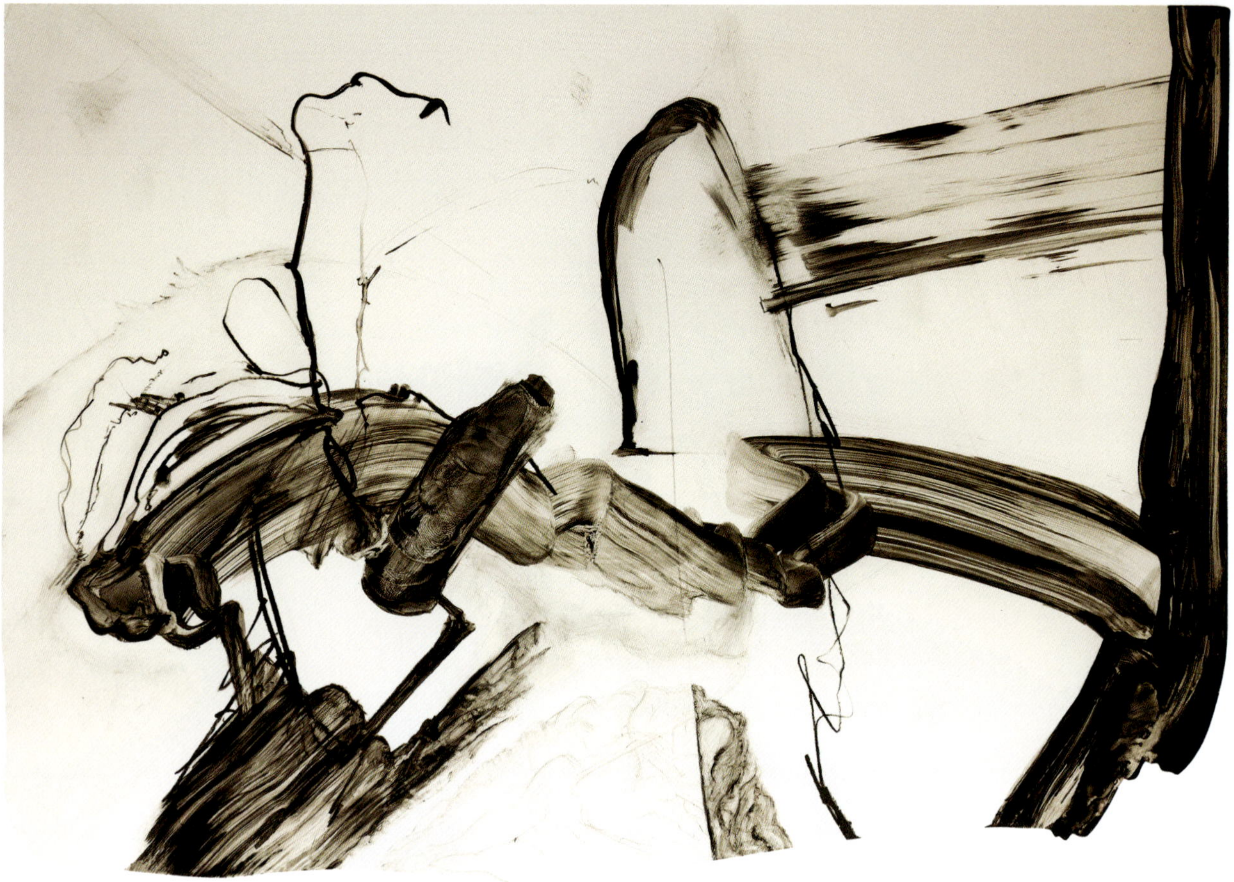

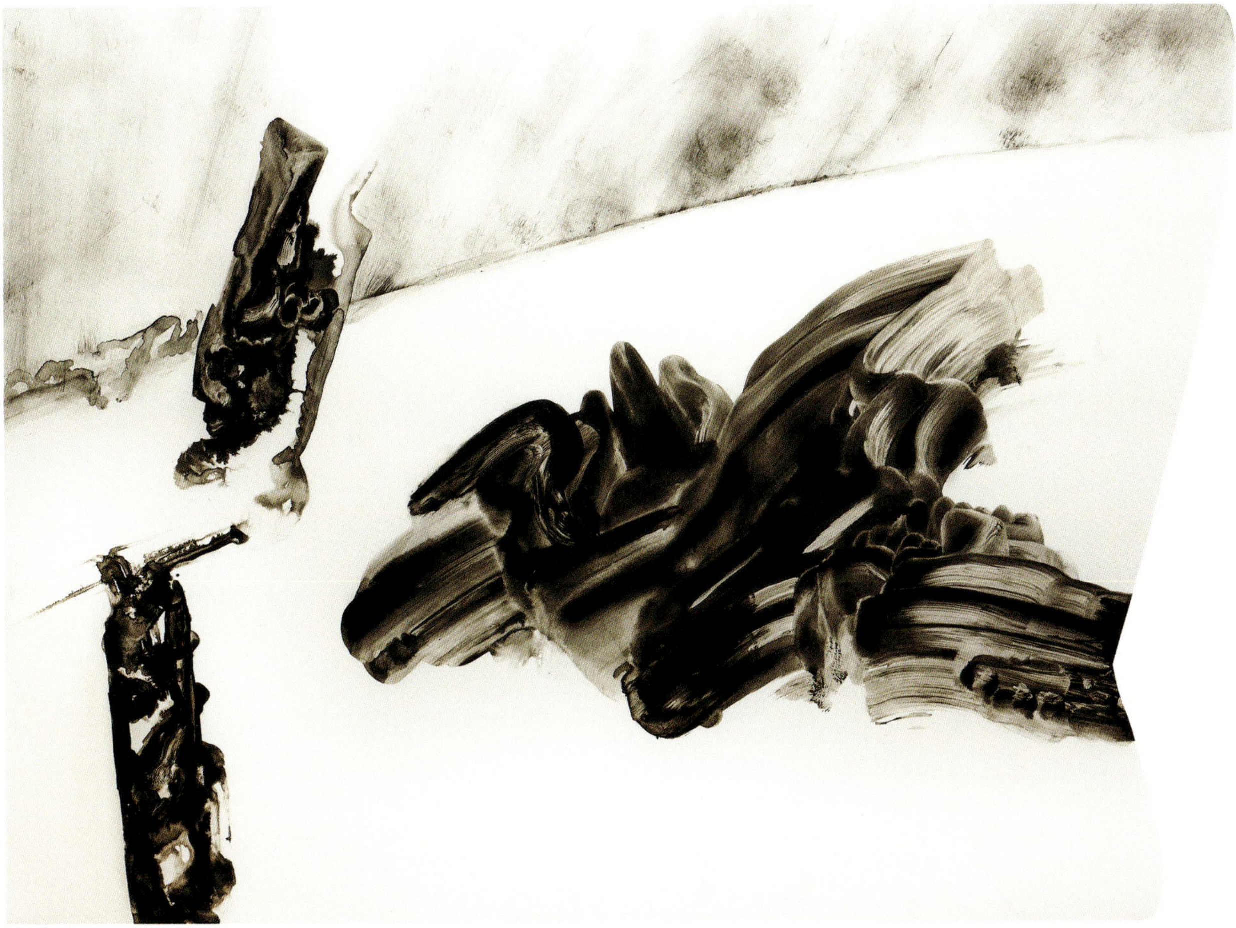

Appendix

Biografische Auswahl / Selected Biography

1977
geboren in / born in Jena, DE

1997
studierte Biologie / studied biology, Friedrich-Schiller-Universität, Jena, DE

1998–2004
Diplom in Mediengestaltung / Diploma in media design, Bauhaus-Universität, Weimar, DE

lebt und arbeitet in / lives and works in Berlin, DE

STIPENDIEN UND PREISE / GRANTS AND AWARDS

2015
Artist-in-Residence, Lunchmeat Festival, National Gallery, Prague, CZ

Artist-in-Residence, Epicenter Projects, Coachella Valley, USA

2014
Stipendium der Thüringer Staatskanzlei / State Chancellery of Thuringia Grant, Erfurt, DE

2012
Artist-in-Residence, quartier21 / MuseumsQuartier, Vienna, AT

2011
Jürgen-Ponto-Stipendium / Jürgen Ponto Grant, Frankfurt am Main, DE

2008
Walter-Dexel-Stipendium / Walter Dexel Grant, Jena, DE

Best Film Award, Digital Graffiti Festival, Alys, USA

2007
Stipendium der DEFA-Stiftung / DEFA Foundation Grant, Berlin, DE

Best Clip Award, Backup Festival, Weimar, DE

2006/2008
Stipendium der Kulturstiftung Thüringen / Cultural Foundation of Thuringia Grant, Erfurt, DE

2005
Best Experimental Film Award, Ottawa International Film Festival, Ottawa, CA

Film Music Award, Filmfest Braunschweig, Braunschweig, DE

Audience Award, Fluxus Festival, Belo Horizonte, BR

2004
Honorary Award, KunstFilm-Biennale, Filmforum Museum Ludwig, Cologne, DE

2001
Honorary Mention, Prix Ars Electronica, Linz, AT

EINZELAUSSTELLUNGEN UND -WERKE / SOLO EXHIBITIONS AND WORKS

2015
LUX AETERNA, Kunstverein Gera & Museum für Angewandte Kunst, Gera, DE

magnitude, Epicenter Projects, Coachella Valley, USA

stains, Baroque Refectory, Musée Beaux-Arts, Lyon, FR

suturae, Image Movement, Berlin, DE

2013
SHIFT (with Rafaël Rozendaal), Seoul Square Media Canvas, Seoul, KR

grapheme, Museum Wiesbaden, Wiesbaden, DE

tearing shadows, 401contemporary, Berlin, DE

2012
chiral, ASIFAkeil, MuseumsQuartier, Vienna, AT

vitreous, Target City Lights, Minneapolis, USA

2011
black mirror, Young Projects, Los Angeles, USA

Robert Seidel – Vyner Session, Vyner Studio Gallery, London, UK

2009
Blurring the Boundaries, Art Center Nabi, Seoul, KR

2008
processes: living paintings, Phyletisches Museum, Jena, DE

GRUPPENAUSSTELLUNGEN / GROUP EXHIBITIONS

2015
Lumen Prize, Jin Space Gallery, Shanghai, CN

Reflective/Perspectives, Filmmuseum, Frankfurt, DE

Light Year 4, Dumbo, Manhattan Bridge, New York, USA

RESET- Abstract Painting in a Digital World, Clemens-Sels-Museum, Neuss, DE

2014
Initiations, Festival of Lights, New York, USA

CAFKA.14 Biennial, Kitchener/Waterloo, CA

Abstraktion + Metapher, Forum Konkrete Kunst, Peterskirche, Erfurt, DE

Stop. Look. Listen., La Gaîté Lyrique, Paris, FR

2013
Lichtsicht-Biennale, Bad Rothenfelde, DE

Wilderness of Mirrors. The Wrong - Digital Art Biennale

Berlin.Status(2), Künstlerhaus Bethanien, Berlin, DE

Form and Substance, Gowanus Ballroom Brooklyn, New York, USA

2012
FOCUS I, Kunsthaus, Erfurt, DE

Expanded Abstraction, Stark Bar, Los Angeles County Museum of Art, Los Angeles, USA

RESET – Abstract Painting in a Digital World, Arti et Amicitiae, Amsterdam, NL

Kollisionen, marke.6, Neues Museum, Weimar, DE

2011
Fokus Junge Kunst, Lindenau-Museum, Altenburg, DE

German Media Art, Seoul Square / GanaArt Center, Seoul, KR

Abstract Confusion, b-05, Montabaur / Kunstverein, Ulm, DE

2010
Tripolar – 3 Positions in German Video Art, Museum of Contemporary Art, Taipei, TW

Rojo Nova, Museum of Image and Sound / SESC Pompeia, São Paulo, BR

Kinetikus Kép, 2B Galéria, Budapest, HU

2009
Come Join Us, Mr. Orwell!, Tomorrow City Open Theatre, Incheon, KR

In nachbarlicher Nähe – Bauhaus in Jena, Kunstsammlung, Jena, DE

Video Visions (TV), Edith-Russ-Haus für Medienkunst, Oldenburg, DE

2008
Projections OnLake, Pasadena, USA

Visions in the Nunnery, Nunnery Gallery, London, UK

2007
art_clips.ch.at.de, Zentrum für Kunst und Medientechnologie, Karlsruhe, DE

Sleek Art Wall, Berlin, DE

2006
Abstract Art Now - Floating Forms, Wilhelm-Hack-Museum, Ludwigshafen, DE

GORGE(L) – Oppression and Relief in Art, Royal Museum of Fine Arts, Antwerp, BE

2005
denkbilder, Internationaler SWR Medienkunstpreis, Zentrum für Kunst und Medientechnologie, Karlsruhe, DE

FILMPROGRAMME / SCREENINGS

2016
Melbourne International Animation Festival, Melbourne, AU

SundanceTV Lounge, Sundance Film Festival, Utah, USA

2015
BEYOND Festival, Karlsruhe, DE

Punto y Raya Academy, La Casa Encendida, Madrid, ES

The Third Image, International Short Film Festival, Oberhausen, DE

2014
Dream:ON, Goethe-Institute, London, UK

Deep Space Theatre, Ars Electronica, Linz, AT

Film Cologne, Film Lounge at Art Cologne, courtesy 401contemporary, Cologne, DE

2013
Exploring Visual Music, Symposium, University of California, Santa Barbara, USA

Game Art Festival, Hammer Museum, Los Angeles, USA

ARTE Creative, TV/Online Platform, FR/DE

Expanded Digital Animation, Ars Electronica, Linz, AT

2012
Intersections, Ottawa International Animation Festival, Ottawa, CA

Vimeo Awards, New York, USA

donaufestival, Krems, AT

2011
onedotzero, British Film Institute, London, UK

Concept Los Angeles, ACE Gallery, Los Angeles, USA

International Innovators, Denver Digerati, Denver, USA

2010
Alpha-ville: Visionary Cities, Whitechapel Gallery, London, UK

Videominuto, Pecci Contemporary Art Center, Prato, IT

Decode Lab, Victoria & Albert Museum, London, UK

2009
Bild-Kunst Förderpreis, Kunst-Werke, Berlin, DE/ Centre Pompidou, Paris, FR/ Museum Reina Sofia, Madrid, ES

Lichtspiel: Contemporary Abstract Animation, CalArts Theater, Los Angeles, USA

100 Years of German Animation, Stuttgart Festival of Animated Film, Stuttgart, DE

Festival Re-*, Akademie der Künste, Berlin, DE

Young Bauhaus – 90th Anniversary of Bauhaus, Bauhaus Film-Institut, Weimar, DE

International Symposium on Electronic Art, Belfast, UK

2008
International Film Festival, Rotterdam, NL

The Garden and Its Delights, Art Institution Intermediae, Madrid, ES

2007
Multimedia Literacy, University of Southern California, Los Angeles, USA

New York Digital Salon: Abstract Visual Music, New York, USA

2006
Lumen Eclipse, Cambridge, USA

Electrotecture: Architecture in Motion, Millennium Galleries, Sheffield, UK

2005
Fluxus, Belo Horizonte, BR

Art Cologne, courtesy DAM Gallery, Cologne, DE

2004
DOTMOV, Sapporo, JP

Austin Museum of Digital Art, Austin, USA

2003
YorkArts Media Lounge, York, USA

Ars Electronica Theatre, OK Center for Contemporary Art, Linz, AT

2002
Internationale Kurzfilmtage, Oberhausen, DE

Videoformes, Clermont-Ferrand, FR

PERFORMANCES

2015
glimmer, music by Andy Stott, Lunchmeat Festival, National Gallery, Prague, CZ

advection (performance version), music by Ritornell, Electric Spring, Museums-Quartier, Vienna, AT

2012
erratic, music by Richard Eigner, Vienna Independent Shorts, Gartenbaukino, Vienna, AT

2010
meander, music by Heiko Tippelt, Rojo Nova, Museum of Image and Sound, São Paulo, BR

KURATORISCHE ARBEIT / CURATORIAL WORK

2015
Afterimages, Kunstsammlung, Jena, DE

Crystallized Skins, Pavilion for The Wrong - Digital Art Biennale

Phantom Horizons, Window Display at Künstlerhaus Bethanien, Berlin, DE

2014
Penetrating Surfaces, Austrian Filmmuseum, Vienna, AT

2010
Dreaming with Open Eyes, Württembergischer Kunstverein, Stuttgart, DE

2009
Dreaming with Open Eyes, Image Forum, Tokyo, JP

VERÖFFENTLICHUNGEN / PUBLICATIONS

2015
Robert Seidel, *Afterimages – Nachhall der Schwarzen Romantik in der Film- und Videokunst / Dark Romanticism's Reverberation in Film and Video Art,* Ausstellungskatalog / Exhibition Catalogue Kunstsammlung Jena.

Jonathan Openshaw, *Robert Seidel,* in: Postdigital Artisans, Amsterdam, 140-143.

Zsuzsanna Kiràly and Daniel Ebner, *An Interview with David OReilly and Robert Seidel (Part 2),* in: ASIFA, Vol. 26, No. 2, 21-27.

2014
Cindy Keefer (Hg.), *Robert Seidel: Projections, Installations and Films,* DVD, Center for Visual Music Los Angeles.

Robert Seidel, *Penetrating Surfaces,* in: filmmuseum, Zeitschrift des Österreichischen Filmmuseums / Magazine of the Austrian Filmmuseum Vienna, May / June 2014, 32-35.

Michael Stoeber, *Blick zurück nach vorn. Abstrakte Malerei zwischen Tradition und Innovation,* in: RESET-Abstract Painting in a Digital World, Ausstellungskatalog / Exhibition Catalogue Kunstmuseum Celle / Kunsthalle Recklinghausen / Kunstmuseum Heidenheim / Clemens-Sels-Museum Neuss, 9-15.

Zsuzsanna Kiràly and Daniel Ebner, A*n Interview with David OReilly and Robert Seidel (Part 1),* in: ASIFA, Vol. 26, No. 1, 22-27.

Robert Seidel, *_grau (10 Years after _grau: Confronting Experimental Film with Reality),* in: Ars Electronica 2014 – what it takes to change, Ausstellungskatalog / Exhibition Catalogue Graz, 170-171.

2013
Zsuzsanna Kiràly and Daniel Ebner: *Interview mit David OReilly und Robert Seidel,* in: Revolver. Zeitschrift für Film, Vol. 29, 46-71.

Manfred Schneckenburger, *Robert Seidel / advection,* in: lichtsicht 4 – Projektionsbiennale, Ausstellungskatalog / Exhibition Catalogue Bad Rothenfelde, 96-105.

Sven Drühl, *Robert Seidel,* in: Berlin.Status(2), Ausstellungskatalog / Exhibition Catalogue Künstlerhaus Bethanien Berlin, 158-161.

Robert Seidel, *Aftershock into Today,* in: Oskar Fischinger 1900–1967: Experiments in Cinematic Abstraction, Ausstellungskatalog / Exhibition Catalogue Eye Film Museum Rotterdam / Center for Visual Music Los Angeles, 223-224.

2012
Robert Seidel, *Inside the Hedge Fund Manager's Head, Interview with Julian Rosefeldt,* in: World-Making, Ausstellungskatalog / Exhibition Catalogue Taipei Fine Arts Museum, 42-48.

2011
Ulrike Pennewitz, *Hinter dem Vorhang der Dinge / Behind the Curtain of Things,* in: Folds, Ausstellungskatalog / Exhibition Catalogue Lindenau-Museum Altenburg / Jürgen-Ponto-Stiftung Frankfurt am Main, 10-17.

Peter Frank, *Haiku Reviews,* in: Huffington Post, August 26th 2011.

Anne Martens, *Robert Seidel at Young Projects,* in: Flash Art (International Edition), Vol. 279, July/September 2011, 109.

Katharina Pilz, *Abstraktion und Film,* in: Kunstforum International, Vol. 206: Neue Abstraktion, 122-139.

Leah Ollman, *A fluid stream of consciousness,* in: Los Angeles Times, April 29th 2011, 16.

Christian Malycha, *Two or three things one knows about the abstract,* in: Abstract Confusion, Ausstellungskatalog / Exhibition Catalogue b-05 Kunst und Kulturzentrum Montabaur / Kunstverein Ulm / Neue Galerie Gladbeck / Kunsthalle Erfurt, 8-13, 138-143.

2010
Yvonne Spielmann, *Hybridkultur,* Frankfurt am Main, 143-177.

2009
Ulrich Wegenast, *Zeitgenossen / Contemporary,* in: Geschichte des deutschen Animationsfilms / History of German Animation, DVD, Vol. 5, Absolut Medien Berlin.

2008
Shin Akiyama, *Image, Contour, Moving State: Robert Seidel,* in: Information Bionomy: Media to be alive, Site Zero / Zero Site Tokyo, 272-281.

Randy Jones, *New Eyes for the Mind,* in: The Cinematic Experience, Amsterdam, 119-134.

2007
Robert Seidel: *_grau - an organic experimental film,* in: Animation. An Interdisciplinary Journal, Vol. 2, No. 1, March 2007, 77-84.

2006
Gerhard Johann Lischka, *90 Kurzvideos aus der Schweiz, Österreich und Deutschland,* in: art_clips.ch.at.de, DVD, Zentrum für Kunst und Medientechnologie Karlsruhe.

Robert Seidel, *_grau,* in: Abstract Art Now - Floating Forms, Ausstellungskatalog / Exhibition Catalogue Wilhelm-Hack-Museum Ludwigshafen, 76-79.

Sofie van Loo, *Insight/turning-point/borderlinking,* in: GORGE(L) – Oppression and Relief in Art, Ausstellungskatalog / Exhibition Catalogue Royal Museum of Fine Arts Antwerp / Mer. Paper Kunsthalle Gent, 52-55.

Arbeiten /
Body of work
2002–2015

FILME UND
INSTALLATIONEN

E3
Experimentalfilm
3:00 min
Musik: Michael Engelhardt
2002

_grau
Experimentalfilm
10:01 min
Musik: Heiko Tippelt &
Philipp Hirsch
2004

winzerla woods
Experimentalfilm
1:30 min
Musik: Robert Seidel
2005

futures
Experimentalfilm
3:58 min
Musik: Zero 7 & José González
2006

appearing disappearance
Experimentalfilm
Musik: Simon Pyke
2007

dive painting #1
LED-Fassade
50 × 4 m, 0:41 min
Sleek Art Wall, Berlin, DE
2007

processes: living paintings
Fassadenprojektion
35 × 16 m, 4:58 min
Musik: Gabor Schablitzki
Phyletisches Museum, Jena, DE
2008

vellum
Experimentalfilm
2:32 min
Musik: Robert Seidel
2009

vellum
Mehrkanal-Installation
56,6 × 1 m; 35 × 1,2 m
Art Center Nabi
SKT-Tower
Seoul, KR
2009

vellum
5 LED-Screens
3,6 × 1,2 m
Museum of
Contemporary Art
Taipeh, TW
2010

chiral
Projektionsskulptur
5,1 × 2,6 × 3,7 m; 2,5 × 2 m
Museum of
Contemporary Art
Taipeh, TW
2010

meander
Video-Performance
Musik: Heiko Tippelt
Rojo Nova
Museum of
Image and Sound
São Paulo, BR
2010

scrape
LED-Fassade
99 × 79 m
GanaArt Center
Seoul Square
Seoul, KR
2011

vellum
Projektion
12 × 6,8 m; 6,8 × 3,8 m;
6,8 × 3,8 m
SESC Pompeia
São Paulo, BR
2011

chiral
Projektionsskulptur
1,3 × 1,1 × 0,6 m;
6,5 × 3 × 1,2 m
Young Projects
Los Angeles, USA
2011

black mirror
Projektionsskulptur
1,6 × 1,2 × 0,8 m;
2,1 × 0,8 × 0,9 m
Young Projects
Los Angeles, USA
2011

folds
Video-Projektion
7,2 × 1,9 × 2,4 m
Musik: Heiko Tippelt
Lindenau-Museum
Altenburg, DE
2011

vitreous
Experimentalfilm
3:24 min
Musik: Nikolai von Sallwitz
2012–2015

vitreous
LED-Fassade
80 × 24 × 14 m
Target City Lights
Minneapolis, USA
2012

erratic
Video-Performance
Musik: Richard Eigner
Vienna Independent Shorts
Gartenbaukino
Wien, AT
2012

tearing shadows
Projektionsskulptur
7,9 × 4,6 × 4,2 m
Musik: Robert Seidel
401contemporary
Berlin, DE
2013

advection
Wasserfontänenprojektion
Lichtsicht-Biennale
Musik: David Kamp
Bad Rothenfelde, DE
2013

grapheme
Projektionsskulptur
4,8 × 2,9 × 8,3 m
Musik: Heiko Tippelt
Dauerinstallation
Museum Wiesbaden
Wiesbaden, DE
2013

ligature
Fassadenprojektion
56 × 25 m
Musik: Heiko Tippelt
Manhattan Bridge
New York, USA
2014

advection
Wasserfontänenprojektion
CAFKA Biennial
Kitchener/Waterloo, CA
2014

advection
Wasserfontänenprojektion
Electric Spring
MuseumsQuartier
Wien, AT
2014

stains
Video-Projektion
Musik: Richard Eigner
Barockes Refektorium
Musée Beaux-Arts
Lyon, FR
2015

recoil
Fassadenprojektion
Musik: David Kamp
Ehemaliges Innungs-
schlachthaus, Jena, DE
2015

magnitude
Laser-Performance
Epicenter Projects
Coachella Valley, USA
2015

glimmer
Laser-Performance
45 min
Musik: Andy Stott
Lunchmeat Festival
Nationalgalerie
Prag, CZ
2015

vitreous
Vertikale Projektion
4 × 14 m
Filmmuseum, Frankfurt, DE
2015

vellum
1-Kanal-Projektion
3 × 1,7 m
Museum für Angewandte
Kunst, Gera, DE
2015

chiral
Projektionsskulptur
6,6 × 3,5 × 1,2 m
Museum für Angewandte
Kunst, Gera, DE
2015

scrape
1-Kanal-Projektion
3 × 1,7 m
Museum für Angewandte
Kunst, Gera, DE
2015

lux aeterna
TV-Installation
3 × 2 × 0,6 m
Kunstverein, Gera, DE
2015

mold
Licht-Raum-Zeichnung
6,6 × 6,3 × 2,2 m
Museum für Angewandte
Kunst, Gera, DE
2015

suturae #2
Laserinstallation
80 × 50 × 55 cm
Museum für Angewandte
Kunst, Gera, DE
2015

vitreous
Kinetische Projektion
7,3 × 3,2 × 3,7 m
Kunstverein, Gera, DE
2015

ZEICHNUNGEN UND EINZELBILDER

_grau
Rendering und Skizze aus
dem gleichnamigen Film
43 × 60 cm
2004

vellum #1–3
Studien für den Film
Filzmarkerzeichnung
auf Papier
21 × 30 cm
2009

passion pit #1–2
Digitale Zeichnung
Alu-Dibond
60 × 40 cm
2010

fold #1
Digitale Zeichnung
Alu-Dibond
60 × 80 cm
2011

vitreous #1–3
Studien für den Film
Neonmarkerzeichnung
auf Papier
42 × 30 cm
2012

vitreous #2
Studie für den Film
Alu-Dibond
60 × 40 cm
2012

sputter #1–5
Rasterelektronen-
mikroskop-Aufnahmen
Digitalprint
30 × 30 cm
2014

glimmer #1–3
Entwurf für ein Bühnenbild in
der Prager Nationalgalerie
Graphitzeichnung und Tusche
auf Papier
42 × 30 cm
2015

phosphor
Postermotiv der Ausstellung
im Museum für Angewandte
Kunst und Kunstverein Gera
2015

fulcrum #1–4
Studien für einen Film
Graphitzeichnung auf
Kunststoff
48 × 34 cm
2015

Authoren

PETER FORSTER

studierte Kunstgeschichte, Christliche Archäologie, Byzantinische Kunstgeschichte und Klassische Archäologie in Mainz und Frankfurt am Main. 2006 promovierte er über die Porträts des Künstlers Vollrad Kutscher. Seitdem begleitet er zahlreiche Lehr- und Forschungsaufträge, beispielsweise an der Johannes Gutenberg-Universität Mainz und dem Städel Museum Frankfurt. Seit 2010 ist Forster Kustos für Alte Meister und Leiter der Provenienzforschung im Museum Wiesbaden, wo er diverse Ausstellungen kuratierte, unter anderem *Rheinromantik – Kunst und Natur* (2013), *Nanna – Anselm Feuerbachs Elixier einer Leidenschaft* (2013), *Aus dem Neunzehnten – Von Schadow bis Schuch* (2015) und *Caravaggios Erben – Barock in Neapel* (2016).

JOOST REKVELD

ist Künstler und Experimentalfilmer. Seit 1990 realisiert er abstrakte Animationsfilme, Installationen und kooperiert mit Komponisten und Theaterproduzenten. Rekveld ist außerdem als Kurator tätig, seine Schwerpunkte liegen in der Lichtkunst und Visuellen Musik. Er blickt auf eine lange Karriere in der Vermittlung interdisziplinärer Projekte an der Schnittstelle zwischen Kunst, Wissenschaft und Technologie zurück; so war er beispielsweise von 2008 bis 2014 Leiter des interdisziplinären Instituts *ArtScience* am Konservatorium und an der Königlichen Kunstakademie in Den Haag. Darüber hinaus ist Rekveld Vorstandsmitglied von Sonic Acts (Amsterdam) und dem Center for Visual Music (Los Angeles).

CLAUDIA TITTEL

studierte Kunstgeschichte, Kulturwissenschaft und Architektur in Berlin sowie Paris und promovierte an der Humboldt-Universität zu Berlin. Von 2009 bis 2011 war sie künstlerisch-wissenschaftliche Mitarbeiterin für Medienkunst an der Hochschule für Grafik und Buchkunst in Leipzig, von 2011 bis 2015 wissenschaftliche Assistentin am Lehrstuhl für Geschichte und Ästhetik der Medien am Kunsthistorischen Seminar der Friedrich-Schiller-Universität Jena und ist seit 2015 wissenschaftliche Assistentin an der Professur Geschichte und Theorie der Kulturtechniken an der Bauhaus-Universität Weimar. Sie erhielt zahlreiche Lehraufträge unter anderem an der Universität der Künste Berlin, der Universität Potsdam und der Hochschule für Musik und Theater Hamburg. Die Liste ihrer kuratorischen Tätigkeiten umfasst beispielsweise das Festival Re-*. *Recycling_Sampling_Jamming. Künstlerische Strategien der Gegenwart* (Akademie der Künste Berlin, 2009) und die Ausstellungen *Editing Spaces. Reconsidering the Public* (Kunstakademie Vilnius, 2011), *Imaginary Landscape. Hommage an John Cage* (Kunstverein Gera, 2012), *Serielle Materialität. Imi Knoebel und Peter Roehr* (Kunstverein Gera, 2013) sowie *Tilde. Die Anwesenheit der Abwesenheit* (Klinger-Forum Leipzig, 2013).

Authors

PETER FORSTER

studied art history, biblical archeology, Byzantine art history, and classical archeology in Mainz and Frankfurt am Main. In 2006 he received his PhD, with a dissertation that focused on the artist Vollrad Kutscher's portraits. He has since held numerous teaching and research positions at institutions such as the Johannes Gutenberg University in Mainz and the Städel Museum in Frankfurt. Since 2010, Forster has served as Curator of Old Masters and Head of Provenance Research at the Museum of Wiesbaden, where he has curated a diverse body of exhibitions, including *Rheinromantik – Kunst und Natur* (2013), *Nanna – Anselm Feuerbachs Elixier einer Leidenschaft* (2013), *Aus dem Neunzehnten – Von Schadow bis Schuch* (2015) and *Caravaggios Erben – Barock in Neapel* (2016).

JOOST REKVELD

is an artist and experimental filmmaker. He has created abstract animation films and installations as well as worked with composers and theater producers since 1990. Rekveld is also active as a curator, with a focus on light art and visual music. He has had a long career in facilitating interdisciplinary projects on the cutting edge of art, science, and technology, serving, for example, as Head of the interdisciplinary *ArtScience* Institute at the Royal Conservatory and the Royal Academy of Art in The Hague. In addition, Rekveld is a board member at Sonic Arts (Amsterdam) and the Center for Visual Music (Los Angeles).

CLAUDIA TITTEL

studied art history, cultural studies, and architecture in Berlin as well as Paris. She received her PhD from the Humboldt University in Berlin. From 2009 to 2011, she was Assistant Professor at the department of Media Art at the Academy of Visual Arts in Leipzig, from 2011 to 2015 of the chair of Media History and Aesthetics at the department Art History at the Friedrich Schiller University in Jena. Since 2015, she works as Assistant Professor for the chair of History and Theory of Cultural Techniques at the Bauhaus University in Weimar. She has held numerous teaching positions at institutions including the Berlin University of the Arts, the University of Potsdam, and the University of Music and Theater in Hamburg. Her curatorial projects include, amongst others, the festival Re-*. *Recycling_Sampling_Jamming. Künstlerische Strategien der Gegenwart* (Academy of Arts, Berlin, 2009) and the exhibitions *Editing Spaces. Reconsidering the Public* (Academy of Visual Arts, Vilnius, 2011), *Imaginary Landscape. Hommage an John Cage* (Kunstverein Gera, 2012), *Serielle Materialität. Imi Knoebel und Peter Roehr* (Kunstverein Gera, 2013), and *Tilde. Die Anwesenheit der Abwesenheit* (Klinger-Forum Leipzig, 2013).

Colophon

Diese Publikation erscheint anlässlich der Ausstellung/This catalogue is published on the occasion of the exhibition

LUX AETERNA
Videoinstallationen, Filme und Zeichnungen von Robert Seidel
04.12.2015 bis 28.02.2016
Kunstverein Gera e.V. und/and
Museum für Angewandte Kunst Gera

HERAUSGEBERIN/EDITOR
Claudia Tittel
für den Kunstverein Gera e.V.

AUTOREN/AUTHORS
Peter Forster, Joost Rekveld, Claudia Tittel

KATALOGGESTALTUNG/
CATALOGUE DESIGN
Manuel Birnbacher

LITHOGRAFIE/IMAGE PROCESSING
Vladimir Milasinoviç

LEKTORAT/COPY EDITING
Howard Atkinson, Manuela Dix, Ulrike Pennewitz, Claudia Tittel

ÜBERSETZUNG/TRANSLATION
Ross Etherton, Ehren Fordyce, Tim Othold

FOTOGRAFIE/PHOTOGRAPHY
Gilles Alonso
144–145

Christoph Beer
28–31, 104–105, 155, 157, 159, 164–165

Cristopher Chichoki
8–9, 107, 151–153

Stefan Diller
24–25, 171–173

Bryan Dodson
26–27, 139

Severin Dostal
14–15

Jacob Kohl
130–131

Remy Ogez
143

Jürgen M. Pietsch
120–121

Christian Seeling
16–19, 97, 147–149

BILDRECHTE/IMAGE RIGHTS
Robert Seidel, VG Bild-Kunst, Bonn
www.robertseidel.com

DRUCK UND BINDUNG/
PRINT AND BINDING
Druckhaus Gera

VERLAG/PUBLISHER
Artefakt, Jena

ISBN 3-937364-57-9

Die deutsche Nationalbibliothek verzeichnet diese Publikation in der Deutschen Nationalbibliografie; detaillierte bibliografische Daten sind im Internet unter http://dnb.de-nb.de abrufbar.

Deutsche Nationalbibliothek lists this publication in the Deutsche Nationalbibliografie; detailed bibliographic data are available on the internet at http://dnb.de-nb.de.

AUSSTELLUNG / EXHIBITION

AUSSTELLUNGSORTE/
EXHIBITION LOCATIONS
Kunstverein Gera e.V.
Am Markt 8/9
07545 Gera
www.kunstverein-gera.de

und/and

Museum für Angewandte Kunst
Greizer Str. 37
07545 Gera

KURATORIN DER AUSSTELLUNG/
EXHIBITION CURATOR
Claudia Tittel

PROJEKTASSISTENZ/
PROJECT ASSISTANT
Anastasiia Larchenko

AUSSTELLUNGSAUFBAU/
EXHIBITION SET-UP
Volker Milker, Heiko Reimann, Alexander Neugebauer, Robert Hagmeister, Ricky Korf, Kay Marquardt, Florian Füger, Nils Lauterbach, Elke Nolde, Christina Bitzke, Joachim B. Schulze

SPEZIELLEN DANK AN/
SPECIAL THANKS TO
Familie Seidel sowie 401contemporary, Mirko Albrecht, Uwe Ahlgrimm, AG Kurzfilm, Corinna Backhaus, Bauhaus Film-Institut, Bauhaus-Universität, Beate Baum, Thomas Bender, Berufsakademie Gera, Robert Berneis, Christina Bitzke, Iris Bohlmann, Daniel Böhm, Center for Visual Music, Manuela Dix, André Eckardt, Daniel Ebner, Jeffers Egan, Richard Eigner, Epicenter Projects, Dominic Etzold, Martin Fischer, Juliane Fuchs, German Films, Robert Hagmeister, Ralf Hänsel, Steve Häselbarth, Max Hattler, Rudi Hellmuth, Philipp Hirsch, Sarah Jahn, JenaKultur, David Kamp, Helge Kiehl, Zsuzsanna Kiràly, Uta Kopp, Ricky Korf, Sina Kühn, Kunstsammlung Jena, Anastasiia Larchenko, Florian Licht, Astrid Lindinger, Dietmar Lübcke, Sabrina Lüderitz, Rolf Luhn, Jakob Mann, Kay Marquardt, Henrik Mauler, Volker Milker, Falk Müller, Sigrid Müller, Alexander Neugebauer, Elke Nolde, Ulrike Pennewitz, Uli Pfeiffer, Franziska Pucher, Astrid und Volker Regel, Wolfgang Reichert, Frank Rühling, Nikolai von Sallwitz, Holger Peter Saupe, SBBS Gera, Regina Scheler, Hans-Jürgen Schindler, Burkhard Schlothauer, Tino Schmidt, Joachim B. Schulze, Ulrich und Angelika Schütt, Sebastian Schwartze, Christina Schwarz, Christian Seeling, Erik Stephan, Rita Stielau, Familie Szabó, Heiko Tippelt, Vienna Independent Shorts, Karoline Weber und Young Projects

MIT FREUNDLICHER
UNTER-STÜTZUNG DURCH/
WITH GENEROUS SUPPORT BY
Fonds Neue Länder der Kulturstiftung des Bundes, Kulturstiftung Thüringen, der Thüringer Staatskanzlei, ART-regio Kunstförderung c/o SV SparkassenVersicherung Holding AG, Sparkasse Gera-Greiz, Regina Scheler/Praxis für Zytodiagnostik, Stadt Gera, Verein der Freunde des Ferberschen Hauses, GUD/Recyclinghof Gera sowie den Förderern des Kunstvereins: Starke Möbeltransporte, Citykurier, TAG Wohnen.

gefördert durch den
Fonds Neue Länder der

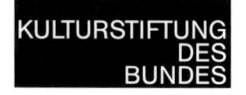

KULTURSTIFTUNG DES BUNDES